THERAPY FOR ADULTS MOLESTED AS CHILDREN
BEYOND SURVIVAL

Therapy for Adults Molested as Children
Beyond Survival

John Briere, Ph.D.

SPRINGER PUBLISHING COMPANY

New York

Springer Publishing Company, Inc.
536 Broadway
New York, NY 10012

89 90 91 92 93 / 5 4 3 2 1

Library of Congress Cataloging-in-Publication Data

Briere, John.
  Therapy for adults molested as children : beyond survival / by
John Briere.
    p. cm.
  Bibliography: p.
  Includes index.
  ISBN 0-8261-5640-1
  1. Adult child sexual abuse victims—Mental health.
2. Psychotherapy. I. Title.
RC569.5.A28B75   1989
616.865′83—dc19   89-4288
                                                         CIP

Printed in the United States of America

Contents

Foreword   ix
Preface   xi
Acknowledgments   xv

Introduction   1

CHAPTER 1: **Post-Sexual-Abuse Trauma**   4
Posttraumatic Stress   5
Cognitive Effects   11
Emotional Effects   15
Interpersonal Effects   18
Summary   28

CHAPTER 2: **"Hysteria," "Borderline Personality
Disorder" and the Core Effects of Severe Abuse**   30
Hysteria   30
Borderline Personality Disorder   35
Core Effects of Severe Abuse   39
Summary   49

CHAPTER 3: **Philosophy of Treatment**   51
The Abuse Perspective   51
The Question of Truth   52
The Question of Responsibility   54
The Phenomenologic Perspective   56
Egalitarianism   58
Growth and Strength as Operating Assumptions   60

The Context of a Victimizing Culture   61
Summary   63

CHAPTER 4: **Vagaries of the Therapeutic
Relationship: Transference and
Countertransference**   65
Transference   65
Countertransference   73
On Boundaries and Limits   77
Conclusions   80

CHAPTER 5: **Specific Therapy Principles and
Techniques**   82
Normalization   82
Facilitating Emotional Discharge   85
Disrupting the Abuse Dichotomy   88
Role-Playing   90
Desensitization   95
Tape Recognition   96
Therapeutic Restimulation   100
Reframing Intrusive Symptomatology   101
Self-Control Techniques   103
Working with the Inner Child   107
Final Comments   110

CHAPTER 6: **The Specific Problem of Client
Dissociation During Therapy**   111
Disengagement   112
Detachment/Numbing   113
Observation   114
Postsession Amnesia   114
"As If"   115
Shutdown   116
Total Repression   117
Dynamic Tension Between Dissociation and Psychotherapy 118
Intervention   119

CHAPTER 7: **Teasing the Dragon: The Fruits of
Confronting Severe Abuse**   123
Abuse Characteristics and Related "Deterioration"   124
Impact on the Psychotherapeutic Process   128
Treatment Implications   134

CHAPTER 8: **Family and Group Therapies**   137
Issues Involved in Abuse-Focused Family Therapy   137
Group Therapy   143

CHAPTER 9: **Client Gender Issues**   152
Sexuality and Aggression   153
Reaction to Abuse-Related Emotional Trauma   155
Implications for Response to Therapy   156
Summary   165

CHAPTER 10: **Therapist Issues**   167
Isolation   167
Impact of the Material   169
Remedies   171
Summary   177

APPENDIX 1: **Psychological Testing and
the Sexual Abuse Survivor**   179
The MMPI   179
The Rorschach   180

APPENDIX 2: **The Trauma Symptom Checklist
(TSC-33)**   183
Method Used To Develop the TSC-33   184
Results of Study   185
Data from Other Studies   185
Discussion   187
TSC-33   190

References   193

Index   209

Foreword

The maturity of a field of practice may be judged by many factors: the number of generations of practitioners who have worked within it; the complexity of the questions that form the unknowns which make practice in the area unsure; or the sophistication of the research which informs its practice.

The rediscovery of adult sexual abuse of children in modern times is only slightly more than a decade old. In that time we as professionals and as a society have accomplished many things. We have begun to listen to victims and believe what they tell us. We have dramatically increased public and professional awareness about the existence of sexual abuse of children, and about many of the medical, legal, and social service aspects of this problem. For example, we have trained law enforcement and health professionals to be more sensitive interviewers of young victims. We have begun making it more possible for victims to participate in the legal system; something that is among the core rights of citizens in a democratic state. We have done many things which have encouraged child victims and adults victimized as children to come out of the darkness and pain, to break the silence that made it possible for an older person to abuse them, and that has kept them alone with the consequences of such abuse.

Only recently, however, have we begun to devote serious attention to the mental health needs of victims. As in any new field, much of our thinking has been borrowed from what we learned in other mental health problem areas. Because of our newness to the problem of child sexual abuse, some of our thinking and our practice has been simplistic, despite our need to ask more complex questions and treat more complex problems.

With this book, John Briere signals a new stage of development in the field of child sexual abuse. In a literature where far too many address only the obvious question or treatment problem, Professor Briere has given us a *new* work. His formulations about the effects of childhood sexual abuse are new. The use of many of the treatment techniques and the approach to therapy with survivors is innovative. This book is a major development in the child abuse field.

Well known for his research on various aspects of interpersonal violence, Briere writes with an uncommon insight into the plight, feelings, and experiences of the abused child and the adult survivor of childhood sexual abuse. Because the book reflects this perspective, it teaches the reader not only at the conceptual level, but at emotional and experiential levels as well. Readers are likely to go away from this book with new ideas about sexual abuse and sexual abuse treatment and a greater appreciation for what sexual abuse is for the victim.

This is not an easy book to read. I found myself putting it down after a few pages to think and react to what Briere had written. In some places I carried on imaginary debates with him. In most places I wanted to reach out and ask him to tell me more, or to help me apply some idea to one of my own cases. This book is an experience as much as it is an educational exercise.

Clinical practice and clinical research in child sexual abuse will be affected by this book. I believe we are enriched by *Beyond Survival*. I believe it establishes a new expectation for all of us as we search for more effective and more powerful mental health interventions for the survivors of childhood sexual abuse. To borrow from Winston Churchill as he commented on the end of the air battle over England, this book is not the end. It may not even be the beginning of the end. But it is the end of the beginning. As a field we are well on our way to improving our capacity to help heal the wounds of childhood sexual abuse. Thank you, John, for moving us a long way in this direction.

JON R. CONTE, PH.D.
Chicago, Illinois
December, 1988

Preface

During the past decade, the shelves in my office have become filled with books written about the sexual abuse of children. One large section contains first-person accounts of victimization. They are moving and riveting in their immediacy, and speak clearly of the experience of violation. Most of the rest of the books attempt to create meaning of that experience but, unfortunately, many of the authors don't seem to have been listening.

The avalanche of disclosures by women and men about their experiences of childhood sexual abuse has formed the foundation upon which researchers and clinicians have explored the harrowing statistics, the emotional ravages, and the ongoing disruptions in adult life. However, societal denial of the extent and implications of sexual victimization has resulted in a therapeutic language of pathology, of symptoms requiring treatment, of an illness needing to be cured. With the exception of feminist scholars and clinicians, the dogged, tenacious, and creative endurance survivors developed in the face of a hostile and dangerous family environment has rarely been honored. Treatment of adult survivors continues to emphasize individual deficits and family dysfunction. The messenger is again blamed and punished for her message.

John Briere has listened carefully to the voices of survivor/clients, and has understood both the cost of the telling and the life that preceeded the tentative words. He has faithfully translated this often disguised language into complex research and clinical interventions that honor his regard for and response to adults who have been sexually abused.

In *Beyond Survival*, Dr. Briere takes us into the internal landscape of adult survivors and maps out the terrain with appreciation and caring.

Previously impenetrable, held accountable, labeled, and stigmatized by their adaptive responses, survivors are, as a result of this important treatment manual, seen through another angle of vision; one that is theoretically well-argued, clinically sophisticated, and deeply human.

Understanding that what is called *deviance* is often simply human pain, Briere dismantles the disrespectful and distancing language of children's presumed "allegations," "seductive" adolescents, "manipulative" clients, "hysterical" women, and "borderline" victims. What is often seen as pathology through a traditional lens is instead viewed through the more compassionate and sophisticated eyes of a clinician with a politically based analysis, who envisions healing as strategies for developing and maintaining a coherent life in an annihilating environment.

Healing begins with language. New forms emerge when we begin to recast the experiences of and response to child sexual abuse into interventions grounded in confirmation and respect. For many survivors, the healing process is a battle of reclamation, of redirecting growth from the deeply gnarled roots of childhood. In my own work with survivors, I call this the "celebration of scar tissue." While there is often deep scarring, the survivor is much more than a collection of wounds. She is also resilient and resourceful. The scar tissue is what remains of the ways in which she protected herself, distanced or withdrew if needed, denied, forgot, minimized, sealed off. The scars are what allowed the survivor to reach our office or agency so that we might join her as she continues to heal.

With the publication of *Beyond Survival*, both clinicians and survivors now have an important conceptual beginning that others can expand upon to illuminate the specific class, cultural, and racial issues that are relevant to adults who were sexually abused. The chapter addressing transference and counter-transference issues, wherein Dr. Briere identifies gender-specific socialized responses of survivors, their inevitable impact on the therapeutic relationship, and the unique dynamics of therapy by female and male clinicians, is an example of the politics of psychotherapy at its best.

The author's definition of the place beyond survival is that of integration and self-affirmation. I would agree that that is both an achievable and a necessary beginning. But surviving—however self-affirming and intact survivors become in a world so sexist, violent, and racist—is not nearly enough. Individual healing is the first step toward understanding that we are responsible for those who come after us: those children still trapped, silent, disbelieved, frightened; understanding that what is done to one of us is done to all of us. Only then we can join to build alliances and coalitions to challenge the origins of childhood sexual abuse. We can advocate for political and institutional change to create a safe and nourishing environment where women and children can grow and flourish. We can join with other survivors, friends, neighbors, and colleagues in ever widening spirals. One by one we change our lives. Then, together, we change the world.

John Briere has moved us toward that goal with this book, and I am grateful to him.

SANDRA BUTLER

Acknowledgments

This book is the product of several years of writing and rewriting. Before the writing began, however, there were far more years spent working with clients, learning from teachers, and talking with colleagues, trainees, and friends. I would like to take this opportunity to thank these people for their contributions to my understanding and for their support of my involvement in the abuse field.

One of the most pleasant aspects of being part of the "abuse community" has been the chance to meet and know the people most identified with this field. Almost without exception, these have been extraordinary beings: available, caring, amusing, and often brilliant. Especially valuable to me has been my association with Chris Courtois, Bill Friedrich, Vernon Quinsey, Diana Russell (most recently regarding her thoughtful and detailed feedback on the first two chapters of this book), Mindy Rosenberg, Ben Saunders, Roland Summit, and Gail Wyatt. Lucy Berliner and Jon Conte have become deeply loved and respected friends—the only thing better than either one of them is both of them together. Sandy Butler has similarly been a longstanding source of support, validation, and perspective. I would also like to thank David Finkelhor, who inspired and supported my first attempts in this field, and who continues to influence my work with his gentle and challenging opinions.

Equally important contributions to this book were made by those clinicians, researchers, and trainees who specifically worked with me in the study and/or treatment of sexual abuse effects, and those teachers who made the greatest impact on my psychological understanding in general. These people include Julie Brickman, Annette Brodsky, Josephine Buck, Laurie Chesley, Deena Chochinov, Tina

Crowe, Dano Demaré, Lisa Dveris, Evelyn Edelmuth, Diane Evans, Richard Gatley, Ed Greenberg, Ross Hartsough, Barbara Halcrow, Diane Henschel, Judy Hill, Adeena Lungen, Neil Malamuth, Maidena McLerran, Jane McCord, Ann McNeer, Bonnie McRae, Vicki Pollock, John Schallow, Brenda Sinclair, Burt Sommers, Rick Stordeur, Carmen Stukas, Shirley Tervo, Timothy Wall, and Cornelia Wicki. Several of these people are (or were) staff therapists at Klinic Inc. Community Health Centre in Winnipeg, Canada, where I first began to specialize in abuse trauma. I am very grateful to this center for the support and training it provided.

Special thanks to Lisa Zaidi, co-researcher on several projects, for her support and technical assistance with parts of this book, and to Rod Shaner for, among other things, help with the title.

I owe a major debt to Sharon Sawatzky, former coordinator of Klinic's Sexual Assault Program, for her friendship, wisdom, and patience. Many of the ideas presented in this book were first considered and expressed in conversations with Sharon.

Marsha Runtz, whose name appears throughout this volume has been a valued research collaborator, clinical colleague, and close friend since my early Klinic days. She has had a major impact on my thinking, despite the geographical distance now between us. This book clearly reflects her work as well as mine.

Richard Stille, one of the most caring and authentic people I've ever known, supported this book through his consistent support of me over the last 10 years—seemingly despite my best efforts at times. Karen Brummel-Smith has been a long-cherished friend and confidant, embodying (and modeling for me) the qualities of sensitivity, warmth, and loving attention which define the most special of people.

Barbara Watkins, vice president and senior editor of Springer Publishing Company, is living proof that one's editor can be helpful without being intrusive, and constructive without being negative. Her patience with the many delays involved in producing this book was a pleasant surprise. Thanks are also due, in this regard, to Daniel Sonkin, for his advice to publish with Springer, and for his feedback on an earlier version of this book.

It is my impression that very few scientists or clinicians thank their mothers these days. Mother-thanking is relatively unfashionable in the 1980s. Nevertheless, I would like to thank mine, Adelle O'Neale-Briere, for her lifelong love and support, and for the opportunity she offered me to grow up with optimism. I know more and more, as the years go by, the value of the gifts she gave me.

Lastly, and certainly not least, I wish to thank Cheryl B. Lanktree: my best friend, partner, and wife. Not only did she help us survive the

2+ years involved in writing this book, she also managed to believe in the project, read and reread the manuscript, and offer important suggestions in areas I had completely overlooked—all while simultaneously meeting the demands of her own professional life. Her information and feedback regarding child psychology and family therapy were especially helpful. Most of all, of course, she was there when no one else would do.

J.B.

Introduction

This book was written for psychotherapists who work, or wish to work, with adults molested as children. The need for more information on sexual abuse survivors (adults and adolescents who were sexually abused in childhood) is becoming increasingly clear. Current studies indicate that about one-third of women and one-tenth of men in North America are sexually victimized before their mid-teens (Finkelhor, 1984; Peters, Wyatt, & Finkelhor, 1988; Russell, 1983b). Other studies report that over half of teenage and adult prostitutes have histories of childhood sexual abuse and that more than 60% of one group of adolescent mothers were sexually abused as children. Even more relevant to mental health workers are the results of two recent studies (Briere & Runtz, 1987; Briere & Zaidi, 1988), which indicate nearly half of those women requesting counseling at an outpatient crisis intervention service and over two-thirds of a psychiatric emergency room sample were sexually abused during childhood. As will be shown in Chapter 1, most studies in this area indicate that such victimization is associated with serious long-term psychological harm, including poor self-esteem, depression, substance abuse, interpersonal difficulties, and self-destructiveness.

More specifically, certain adult psychological problems or "disorders" appear to arise, in part, from unresolved childhood sexual victimization. Unfortunately, most mental health professionals have had little or no training in recognizing or treating post-sexual-abuse trauma. In fact, due in part to the still powerful influences of Freud and other early writers, many workers have been trained to overlook—or actively misinterpret—evidence of prior sexual victimization in their adult clients.

The present book was written in response to this gap in mental health practice. It is intended to serve as a compendium of information on the assessment and treatment of post-sexual-abuse trauma. Chapter 1 summarizes existing studies on the long-term effects of sexual victimization. Chapter 2 presents a general theory of postabuse symptom development and suggests that certain well-known forms of adult "psychopathology," such as "hysteria" and "borderline personality disorder," may represent archaic responses to severe childhood abuse, including molestation, that persist into later life. Subsequent chapters delineate an overall philosophy of treatment and outline specific therapeutic strategies and techniques for intervening in post-sexual-abuse trauma. Finally, the impact of this sort of work on the therapist is discussed, and potential remedies for burnout are presented.

During the course of this book the reader will encounter descriptions or interventions that are relevant to individuals who were not sexually abused as children, but who nevertheless experienced other types of abusive childhood experiences, such as physical or psychological maltreatment or emotional neglect. This is not surprising, since the child's experience of any form of victimization is bound to include common feelings of confusion, fear, helplessness, and betrayal. The general focus of this book is not, therefore, to the exclusion of other ways in which children can be hurt in our society. As common as is sexual abuse, physical and emotional cruelty may be even more frequent, and are probably equally damaging (Briere & Runtz, 1988b).

In fact, in some cases sexual abuse (especially incest) can serve as a marker or indicator for other forms of grievous childhood trauma as well. We can assume, for example, that a father willing to orally rape his 7-year-old son is someone who is hurtful in many ways and who is likely to also engage in nonsexual victimization, such as severe emotional and physical abuse. It is also likely in such families that other people are being maltreated as well, including other caretakers (e.g., the mother) and siblings—all of whose subsequent difficulties impact on the child through absence, displaced aggression, scapegoating, and other trauma-inducing behaviors. Thus, the term "sexual abuse" in this book refers not only to the mechanics of the act (i.e., who did what to whom) but also to the matrix of other injurious events that coexist with or follow from sexual victimization.

A brief note should be made about the format of this book. Although a number of studies can be found that describe the long-term effects of sexual abuse, there are far fewer sources that present systematic treatment interventions for adult sexual abuse survivors. For this reason there is a noticeable—and intentional—difference between the first two chapters and the remainder of this book. Chapters 1 and 2 were written not only to describe the long-term effects of sexual victimization in adults, but also to provide specific references to the sexual abuse literature for the interested reader. Later chapters, however, function more as a treatment manual offering techniques, strategies, and philosophies that other clinicians and the author have found useful in treating post-sexual-abuse trauma. Such information is less likely to have been published in journals or books, and thus often will not be cited as such. It is hoped that by providing a "sourcebook" of therapeutic approaches to adult abuse trauma, this book not only will aid therapists who work with sexual abuse survivors, but will also stimulate clinicians and others to conduct further research to enhance the efficacy of treatment methods in this vital area.

All "cases" and client quotations presented in this book have been well disguised and cannot be traced back to any one individual. Among other alterations, the sex of the various clients described in this book has been randomly altered when possible. Most victims of sexual assault in our culture are female, whereas most perpetrators are male; therefore, I have tended to assign gender on that basis. We are becoming increasingly aware, however, of the vast number of boys who are sexually abused in North America, and thus I have included a number of male victims as well.

Finally, I would like to thank these many clients for sharing with me their hard-fought insights and knowledge. Perhaps most important, they taught me that recovery from victimization is ultimately an act of growth as much as a "fixing" of problems. In this regard, the goals of abuse-focused therapy extend beyond survival—ultimately to integration and self-affirmation.

CHAPTER 1

Post-Sexual-Abuse Trauma

"I dreamed I was in a war, like my brother was. I was trying to escape and people were shooting at me. I get away to a safe place, on a hill or something. And I start crying because I'm safe. I can't believe I got away without being shot. And then I look down, and I'm bleeding. I thought I was safe, but I was shot. And I didn't even know it. I got away, but here I am, still bleeding." (male sexual abuse survivor)

To almost anyone who has experienced sexual abuse, or has listened without bias to someone who has, there is little doubt that such experiences are hurtful. In therapy offices, crisis centers, and sharing between friends, the story unfolds. One is initially struck with the bizarreness of child molestation. Could anyone really do that to a little kid? How must it feel to know that your father or mother or teacher did such a thing? And what would it be like to live with that? With them? As therapists, we hear of violation and betrayal; we listen to the rage, the sorrow, the paradoxical self-hatred. The damage seems immense, perhaps beyond our abilities to help. We may be surprised to discover, then, that there is controversy among some authorities as to whether sexual abuse produces negative effects. A noted psychiatrist, for example, writes that "research is inconclusive as to the psychological harmfulness of incestuous behavior" (Henderson, 1983, p. 34).

This book, obviously, takes a position that is at odds with such statements. As will be shown in this chapter, most published studies indicate that sexual abuse is commonly associated with serious psychological pain and suffering—trauma that may persist over the years unless specifically resolved.

Studies on the effects of sexual victimization have proliferated in the last decade. In perhaps the most extensive review of this literature thus far, for example, Browne and Finkelhor (1986a, 1986b) describe the findings of 52 studies on the impact of childhood sexual abuse, most of which were published since 1980. They conclude that "empirical studies with adults confirm many of the long-term effects of sexual abuse mentioned in the clinical literature," and note that "the risk of initial and long-term mental health impairment for victims of child sexual abuse should be taken very seriously" (1986a, p. 72).

The purpose of this chapter is twofold: first, to acquaint the reader with those types of psychological distress commonly associated with post-sexual-abuse trauma; second, to alert the clinician to the possibility that certain relatively common adult "syndromes" or types of psychological symptoms may be related to previously undisclosed abuse experiences. Because of the large number of problems reported in the abuse literature, the known results of sexual victimization will be divided here into four primary kinds of psychological effects. These categories, which often coexist in the sexual abuse survivor, are referred to as (a) posttraumatic stress, (b) cognitive effects, (c) emotional effects, and (d) interpersonal effects. Each category is described in detail below, and relevant research is cited.

Posttraumatic Stress

"Posttraumatic stress disorder" (PTSD) is a common term in modern mental health parlance. Typically used to describe the experiences of war veterans, survivors of major earthquakes, rape victims, and other survivors of severe trauma, PTSD refers to those characteristic psychological reactions that frequently follow disaster or extreme psychological stress. According to the American Psychiatric Association's *Diagnostic and Statistical Manual of Mental Disorders*, 3rd Edition, Revised (DSM III-R), a combination of the following criteria must be met for a diagnosis of PTSD:

1. The existence of a "psychologically distressing event" that would evoke significant disturbance in almost anyone.
2. Later reexperiencing of the trauma in one's mind; for example, through recurrent dreams of the stressor, or "flashbacks" (intrusive sensory memories) to the original traumatic situation.
3. "Numbing of general responsiveness" to, or avoidance of, the external world; for example, dissociation, withdrawal, restricted affect, or loss of interest in daily events.
4. A wide variety of other reactions or symptoms such as sleep distur-

bance, difficulty concentrating, memory problems, irrational guilt, extreme alertness to danger in the environment, and an intensification of symptoms upon exposure to situations that resemble the original traumatic event.

A number of writers have suggested that sexual abuse during childhood, perhaps especially within the family, may produce either chronic or delayed PTSD in later life (e.g., Blake-White & Kline, 1985; Briere & Runtz, 1987; Donaldson & Gardner, 1985; Gelinas, 1981, 1983; Goodwin, 1984; Lindberg & Distad, 1985a; van der Kolk, 1987). Lindberg and Distad (1985a), for example, found that each of the 11 incest victims they studied described symptomatology that satisfied DSM III-R criteria for PTSD. A brief review of the sexual abuse literature emphasizes the appropriateness of viewing severe post-sexual-abuse trauma as, among other things, a specific form of PTSD. As is shown below, each of the criteria for PTSD has been described in the literature as a long-term effect of childhood sexual abuse.

A Psychologically Distressing Event

Sexual abuse, as defined in this book, refers to sexual contact between a child and an adult. Although most research definitions require that the child be under 14 or 15 years of age and that the abuser be 5 or more years older, the vast majority of cases appear to involve children under the age of 12 and men in their mid-20s or older (e.g., Briere, 1988; Briere & Runtz, 1988a; Finkelhor, 1979a; Russell, 1986). In one random clinical example of 133 female sexual abuse victims (Briere, 1988), 43% reported sexual contact from a parent or stepparent, 77% had been penetrated orally, anally, or vaginally, and 56% were also physically abused. Of this sample, 17% reported especially bizarre abuse, involving ritualistic sexual activities, multiple simultaneous perpetrators, sexual involvement with animals, insertion of foreign objects, and/or intentional torture. Similarly, of the 60% of adolescent mothers who reported childhood sexual abuse in an Illinois study (Ounce of Prevention Fund, 1987), 33% reported having been raped by one or more abusers, and 25% reported attempted rape. Over 25% of these women had been abused on 10 or more occasions by the same person.

Although early writers (especially those with a psychoanalytic bent) often sought to downplay the aversive quality and impact of such abuse, the majority of modern researchers acknowledge that sexual victimization is a frightening, painful, and psychologically overwhelming experience for most children. David Finkelhor (1979a), for example, found that of 530 university women, 58% of those sexually abused as children described reacting to victimization with fear, and 26% stated they experienced "shock." In a community sample of 930 women, Diana Russell (1986) found that 80% of those who had been abused were "somewhat" to "extremely" upset, and that 78% reported long-term negative effects of the abuse experience. Later analysis indicated that long-term psychological trauma was especially likely when incest victims had experienced severe victimization, for example, oral/anal/vaginal penetration, abuse occurring over an extended period of time, or especially violent abuse (Herman, Russell, & Trocki, 1986). The presence of such data in *nonclinical* groups (i.e., in individuals not requesting help for psychological problems) underlines the "traumagenic" (trauma-producing) qualities of sexual abuse.

Reexperiencing of the Trauma

Many survivors of childhood sexual victimization describe intrusive memories of or flashbacks to the abuse, as well as recurring nightmares (e.g., Briere & Runtz, 1987; Gelinas, 1983; Lindberg & Distad, 1985a, 1985b). These sudden "reexperiences" represent, in part, classically conditioned associations to the original abuse event(s) which are triggered by stimuli in the survivor's current environment (a more phenomenologic interpretation of this phenomenon will also be presented in Chapter 5). Such flashbacks can involve all of the senses, so that the survivor may experience sudden visual, auditory, olfactory, gustatory, or tactile memories of the assault, manifesting, for example, as briefly "feeling" someone's hands on one's leg, or "seeing" the perpetrator's angry face. These periods of reliving the abuse may be, in some instances, so sudden and so compelling as to produce a temporary break with the current environment, resulting in what may appear to be hallucinations or psychosis (Gelinas, 1983). In the words of one survivor, "Sometimes the memories are so powerful that the real world doesn't have a chance."

The nightmares of adolescents and adults who were victimized as children may involve a variety of events and images, although a few themes are especially common. Probably the most frequent abuse-related nightmares are dreams that replay actual scenes from the molestation. These may be graphically realistic or may be elaborations or variations on the original experience. Other nightmares are more symbolic in nature, involving shadowy, threatening figures by one's bed, attacks by coiling snakes or snarling monsters, frightening pursuits down dark halls or alleys, and gory mutilation or disfigurement. Typi-

cal in these scenes, regardless of manifest content, are extreme feelings
of fear and helplessness—often presented as the dreamer being paralyzed or in some way unable to find help. In light of the power of these
"posttraumatic nightmares" (Hartmann, 1984), it is not surprising that,
as will be mentioned later, many sexual abuse survivors experience
chronic sleep disturbance.

Numbing of General Responsiveness

This component of PTSD refers to a psychological withdrawal from the
outside world, wherein the individual experiences a loss of reactivity,
detachment from others, and/or constricted (limited) emotionality. A
number of clinicians have noted the prevalence of these problems
among sexual abuse survivors (see, e.g., Butler, 1978; Gelinas, 1983; and
Herman, 1981), as have researchers of sexual abuse effects. The sexual
abuse survivor's tendency to close down emotions and/or sensory inputs may best be understood as a form of psychological escape from
painful experiences and feelings. This coping strategy probably first
develops during the victimization process, when any means of avoiding
acute pain, fear, and humiliation would be reinforced. This "going
away" defense may then generalize to other aversive and anxiety-
provoking experiences later in life, eventually becoming a relatively
autonomous and pervasive "symptom" (Briere & Runtz, 1987, 1988c).

Alice B.

Alice, a 19-year-old woman, is brought to the emergency room by
her roommate, who states that she has been "zoned out" for nearly
24 hours: not eating, not responding to conversation, "just looking
at the wall." During her interview, Alice's eyes are fixed and staring,
and her face is blank. She responds to questions in a monosyllabic,
distracted manner, denying hallucinations or recent drug use.
When told that she might be admitted to the hospital, she states to
the psychologist, without perceptible emotion, "If you're going to
hurt me, I don't want to know about it, OK?" This will be Alice's
third hospitalization, the first of which followed a suicide attempt
at age 12, prompted by her father's imprisonment for molesting
Alice, her sister, and a friend.

Perhaps one of the most dramatic and important aspects of reduced
responsiveness is that of dissociation. Several studies of sexual abuse

survivors (e.g., Briere & Runtz, 1987, 1988a; Briere, Evans, Runtz, & Wall, 1988; Lindberg & Distad, 1985a; Runtz, 1987) report a constellation of symptoms such as cognitive disengagement from the environment into a seemingly neutral state ("spacing out"), derealization (the experience that things around one are false or unreal), depersonalization (the sense that one is different from one's usual self), out-of-body experiences (often involving the sensation of floating outside of one's body and travelling elsewhere), and circumscribed blanks in otherwise continuous memory. Dissociation is defined in DSM III-R as

> a disturbance or alteration in the normally integrative functions of identity, memory, or consciousness. The disturbance or alteration may be sudden or gradual, and transient or chronic. If it occurs primarily in identity, the person's customary identity is temporarily forgotten, and a new identity may be assumed or imposed . . . , or the customary feelings of one's own reality is lost and is replaced by a feeling of unreality . . . If the disturbance occurs primarily in memory, important personal events cannot be recalled . . . (p. 289)

The frequency of such experiences in the sexual abuse survivor suggests that dissociation may represent a powerful defense against memories or events that contain abusive elements. Whether such symptoms occur as components of PTSD, or exist in relative isolation as a "dissociative disorder" (DSM III-R), they appear to function as a way for the victim to state that "this isn't actually happening" (derealization), "it isn't happening to me" (depersonalization), or "it never happened to me" (amnesia). Perhaps the most dramatic example of this dissociation from abusive event(s) is that of "multiple personalities" ("it happened to somebody else"), recently linked by researchers to (among other factors) sexual abuse trauma (e.g., Bliss, 1984; Coons & Milstein, 1986; Putnam, Post, Guroff, et al., 1983). Because of its special relevance to post-sexual-abuse trauma and its frequent impact on therapy, dissociation is addressed at considerable length in Chapters 2 and 6.

Other Symptoms

As mentioned earlier, PTSD often involves a variety of other symptoms, including sleep disturbance, difficulties in maintaining concentration, memory problems, irrational guilt, hyperalertness, and an intensification of symptoms when the victim is exposed to situations or stimuli that resemble the original traumatic event. Just as many of these symptoms are found in rape victims (Burgess & Holmstrom,

1974), sexual abuse survivors are likely to experience similar difficulties at some point in their lives. With the exception of irrational guilt, which will be described in a later section, these symptoms are briefly presented below. Because of the importance of these problems in the lives of sexual abuse survivors, most will be discussed further in later chapters.

Sleep problems. As many clinicians will attest, sleep disturbance (involving insomnia, restless sleep, nightmares, and middle of the night or early morning awakenings) is a common result of psychological trauma. Researchers such as Sedney and Brooks (1984) and Briere and Runtz (1987) report that sexual abuse survivors are approximately twice as likely as nonabused individuals to have sleep problems of some sort. Browne and Finkelhor (1986a) relate sleeping difficulties to the chronic anxiety and tension often found in former victims of sexual abuse. Chronic tension can delay the onset of sleep and cause sleep to become more shallow, resulting in restlessness and proneness to awakening. More psychodynamically, it is clear that sleep is experienced by the survivor as a time of maximal vulnerability, when vigilance and defenses are at their lowest and when frightening dreams are likely. This sense of helplessness is compounded by the likelihood that the abuse (especially if it was incest) occurred in darkness and/or in the bedroom. We may understand, then, when sexual abuse survivors in therapy report that "nighttime is the worst time."

Concentration problems. The anxiety felt by many sexual abuse survivors (presented in the "Emotional Effects" portion of this chapter) is likely to produce other signs of high autonomic arousal, such as extreme alertness to the possibility of danger. This hypervigilance and tension may, paradoxically, coexist with an inability to concentrate for extended periods of time, producing an individual who is constantly scanning the environment but who may have problems focusing her or his attention when needed. Although only scantily documented in the sexual abuse literature, it is the author's experience that such chronic fearfulness is even more common in sexual abuse victims who have also been physically maltreated in childhood.

Impaired memory. Memory disturbance in some former sexual abuse victims has been established by clinicians in the area (e.g., Gelinas, 1983; Herman, 1985; Herman & Schatzow, 1987; Maltz, 1988), primarily involving complete or partial amnesia for the original abuse experience. As noted by Blake-White and Kline (1985), "the adult victim of incest wants to avoid the anxiety of remembering; she wishes to forget the trauma and push it into the past" (p. 396). As we will see in Chapters 2 and 6, such motivated forgetting or "repression" of childhood events is a powerful dissociative defense against reexperiencing the trauma and pain of victimization—sometimes producing complete lack of memory for extended periods of childhood.

Unfortunately for the survivor, defenses as primitive as "not remembering" the abuse are rarely totally successful. Instead, he may experience the sudden, intense, and intrusive images of previously repressed events referred to earlier as flashbacks or may present to the clinician with vague complaints such as "Something isn't right about me and my past, but I don't know what it is" or "They say that I was molested as a child. Could that be why I hate sex?"

Intensification. The last PTSD phenomenon relevant to sexual abuse survivors is the restimulation of early abuse memories and emotions by immediate events and interactions, resulting in an intensification of posttraumatic symptoms. Similar to flashbacks but more complex, restimulation may produce what appear to be setbacks during therapy (see Chapter 7) or "bizarre" or "regressive" behavior during everyday living. Common triggers of restimulation are developmental milestones during adolescence (Gelinas, 1983), sexual interactions (e.g., Jehu & Gazan, 1983), exploitation by a more powerful person or persons (Briere, 1986), physical violation or assault, and in some cases, first disclosures of having been sexually abused as a child (Zingaro, 1985). As described by Gelinas (1983), these experiences may be intense enough to warrant, in extreme cases, psychiatric hospitalization. In most instances, however, the immediate result is a dissociative episode or a period of depression or withdrawal.

Cognitive Effects

In addition to PTSD effects, it is clear that child abuse, including molestation, can produce negative changes in the way in which the victim perceives and understands herself, others, and the future (Jehu, Klassen, & Gazan, 1985–86; McCann, Pearlman, Sackheim, & Abrahamson, 1988; McCord, 1985). Such altered beliefs and perceptions, often long-standing in nature, are typically referred to as "cognitive effects," since they relate to thinking as opposed to feeling. Cognitive theorists have shown, however, that these "distortions" are often the basis of severe affective (mood) changes such as clinical depression and the anxiety disorders (Beck, 1967; Beck, Emory, & Greenberg, 1985). The most common abuse-related cognitive changes appear to be (a) negative self-evaluation and guilt, (b) perceived helplessness and hopelessness, and (c) distrust of others.

Negative Self-Evaluation and Guilt

"Negative self-evaluation" refers to the tendency of many sexual abuse survivors to see themselves as "bad," "evil," unintelligent, unattractive, and the like, as well as generally responsible for their unhappiness and pain. As Herman (1981) noted of her group of adults sexually abused as children, "with depressing regularity, these women referred to themselves as bitches, witches, and whores. The incest secret formed the core of their identity" (p. 97). In an examination of the cognitive distortions found in former sexual abuse victims, Jehu, Gazan, and Klassen (1984–85) found that over 50% of their female sample endorsed statements such as "I am worthless and bad," "No man could care for me without a sexual relationship," "I am inferior to others because I did not have normal experiences," and "I must have been seductive and provocative when I was young." In agreement with the findings of Jehu et al., several clinicians report that over half of the sexual abuse survivors they studied demonstrated clinically significant levels of impaired self-esteem (e.g., Courtois, 1979a, 1979b; Herman, 1981).

Roger M.

Roger is a blind, 28-year-old man, who originally came to his local community mental health center requesting help with relationships. Over time, he reveals involvement in "sadomasochistic" sexual practices, wherein he inevitably acts in the passive role. When asked if this is what he wants, Roger admits that "I really don't care for the sex that much." He appears unconcerned, however, about the dangers that he faces as a blind person who is habitually tied up, beaten, and violated, stating "I don't care what happens to me." He later describes feelings of self-hatred and self-disgust, and reports a sense of calm when he is being "punished." Roger's childhood includes extensive sexual torture from age 6 to 13 at the hands of at least two older brothers.

There are several reasons for the negative self-evaluation of sexual abuse survivors. First, as noted by Symonds (1975), there is often a "marked reluctance and resistance [of society] to accept the innocence or accidental nature of victim behavior" (p. 19)—a perspective that is frequently communicated to the survivor. Society's tendency to blame the victim impacts on him or her in a variety of ways, as will be discussed below.

Equally disturbing, however, is the victim's tendency to blame herself/himself for having been injured or hurt regardless of the circumstance (Janoff-Bulman & Frieze, 1983; Miller & Porter, 1983). This phenomenon appears to involve what some theorists refer to as "just world" beliefs. Lerner (1980), for example, notes that "people want to and have to believe [that] they live in a just world so they can go about their daily lives with a sense of trust, hope, and confidence in their future" (p. 14). This perspective invests the victim in believing that "I got what I deserved" as opposed to the potentially more frightening notion that violence is random (unjust) and that one cannot do things to avoid being victimized. Thus, in addition to its negative effects, self-blame may serve as a defense against feelings of total powerlessness (Lamb, 1986; Wortman, 1976).

Although the mechanisms cited above produce an element of self-blame (and subsequent self-derogation) in victims of many forms of violence, there appear to be specific aspects of childhood sexual abuse that yield especially negative self-perceptions. As noted by Sandra Butler (1978), there is often a "conspiracy of silence" surrounding sexual abuse, invoked both by the abuser in the interests of self-protection and by the reactions of society to abuse disclosures. Such secrecy often conveys to the abuse victim the notion that she or he was involved in a shameful act and was, in fact, a guilty coconspirator. This process, which David Finkelhor (Finkelhor & Associates, 1986) calls "stigmatization," includes

> the negative connotations—for example, badness, shame, and guilt—that are communicated to the child about the [abuse] experiences and then become incorporated into the child's self-image. . . . They can come directly from the abuser, who may blame the victim for the activity, denigrate the victim, or, simply through his furtiveness, convey a sense of shame about the behavior. . . . (p. 184)

As Finkelhor notes, it is therefore not surprising that many sexual abuse survivors report guilt and shame related to their victimization (e.g., DeFrancis, 1969; de Young, 1982; Jehu et al., 1984–85; Russell, 1986).

The sum total of these negative esteem effects on the sexual abuse victim tend to generalize and elaborate over time, producing in many

cases chronic self-hatred and self-destructiveness (McCann et al.,
1988). Several studies indicate, for example, that sexual abuse survivors
have up to twice the likelihood of engaging in (or seriously considering)
suicidal behavior as compared to nonabused individuals (Bagley &
Ramsay, 1985, February; Briere & Runtz, 1986; Briere & Zaidi, 1988,
August; Harrison et al., 1984, August; Herman, 1981; Sedney & Brooks,
1984).

Helplessness and Hopelessness

Because of the violation and "temporary loss of all personal choice"
(Terr, 1985, p. 821) which accompanies child abuse, sexual abuse survivors often experience pervasive feelings of helplessness and hopelessness, as noted above in terms of "just world" beliefs. Many aspects of
sexual victimization are antithetic to feelings of personal power or self-
efficacy. As noted by Finkelhor (Finkelhor & Associates, 1986), these
include (a) the child's experience of invasion of her or his body by a
hurtful (or at least coercive) person, (b) the often repetitive nature of
incest and other types of sexual victimization, resulting in chronic
feelings of vulnerability and inability to protect oneself from danger,
and (c) the experience of many victims that their abuse disclosures are
not believed by others, despite their best efforts. Together, these abuse
dynamics suggest to the survivor that she is relatively powerless in the
face of adversity or negative events. This "learned helplessness" (Seligman, 1975) may be at the root of a number of behaviors and reactions
found in many sexually abused individuals, including susceptibility to
later victimization by others, passivity, and basic perception of self as
"victim" (Peterson & Seligman, 1983). As will be described later, such
feelings of helplessness and hopelessness, in combination with low
self-esteem, may also produce negative mood states—perhaps most
notably clinical depression.

Distrust of Others

Having discovered at an early age that safety is not guaranteed and that
betrayal can occur at any moment, many sexual abuse victims become
preoccupied with what might be described as "the reality of danger." As
Terr (1985) notes in a more general context: "Traumatized children so
sharply fear many directly trauma-related and mundane items that they
demonstrate massive interferences with optimism and trust" (p. 820).
Although this dynamic clearly relates to pervasive feelings of anxiety

and fear, as described below, there are also interpersonal impacts of betrayal and experienced lack of safety (McCann et al., 1988; Perloff, 1983). As Finkelhor (1987, April) notes: "[Abused] children discover that someone on whom they were vitally dependent has caused them or wishes to cause them harm" (p. 15), a lesson that can easily generalize to later distrust of others (Briere & Runtz, 1987; Courtois, 1979a; Gelinas, 1983; Herman, 1981; Tsai & Wagner, 1978), expectations of injustice, and pervasive anger—especially toward individuals of the same gender as their abuser (Briere, 1984; Courtois, 1979a; Peters, 1976; Russell, 1986). As we will consider in the treatment sections of this book, this lack of trust and sometimes inexhaustible depot of rage have real implications for psychotherapy with sexual abuse survivors, as well as for the optimal gender of the psychotherapist.

Emotional Effects

Anxiety

Anxiety is described in one psychiatric dictionary (Hinsie & Campbell, 1973) as "an affect that differs from other affects in its specific unpleasurable characteristics. Anxiety consists of a somatic, physiological side (disturbed breathing, increased heart activity, . . . trembling or paralysis, increased sweating, etc.) and of a psychological side." The authors then cite Piotrowsky's (1957) psychological characteristics of anxiety, which include (a) awareness of being powerless to do anything about a potentially dangerous situation, (b) a feeling of impending doom or catastrophe, (c) tension and hyperalertness, and (d) a preoccupation with personal fears and worries that interferes with effective daily functioning. This definition also suggests that "anxiety is to be differentiated from fear . . . [which is] a reaction to a real or threatened danger, while anxiety is more typically a reaction to an unreal or imagined danger" (Hinsie & Campbell, 1973, p. 49).

The reader will note that these psychological symptoms of anxiety are highly congruent with the sexual abuse survivor's early experiences. In fact, in this context we might question the "unreal or imagined" qualities of such reactions, since they were at one time entirely justified. Thus we introduce at this time a concept that will be repeated throughout this book: Many long-term effects of sexual victimization were entirely reasonable, and often adaptive, responses at the time the child was victimized—only becoming "inappropriate" in the later, postabuse environment.

The somatic aspects of anxiety, as described above, are also common in sexual abuse victims. Gelinas (1983) notes that "when patients describe what the incestuous contact was like for them, the predominant reported affect is fear; many describe feeling paralyzed. Several have said that they felt their minds had 'short-circuited' and they became cognitively incapacitated" (p. 315). A number of studies document anxiety attacks, phobias, hypervigilance, the various somatic effects of heightened autonomic arousal (e.g., stomach problems, sleep disturbance, anorexia), and the earlier described symptoms of PTSD in both sexually abused children (e.g., Burgess & Holmstrom, 1978; Conte & Berliner, 1987; Conte & Schuerman, 1987; DeFrancis, 1969; Friedrich, Beilke, & Urquiza, 1987; Justice & Justice, 1979; Summit & Kryso, 1978; Tufts, 1984) and in adults who were abused as children (e.g., Bagley & Ramsay, 1986; Briere & Runtz, 1987, 1988; Murphy et al., 1988; Runtz, 1987, June; Sedney & Brooks, 1984).

Notable among women who were molested as children is their tendency to report multiple bodily complaints. This "somatization" process, which Derogatis and his associates define as "distress arising from perceptions of bodily dysfunction" and as reflecting "the somatic equivalents of anxiety" (Derogatis, Lipman, Rickels, Ulenhuth, & Covi, 1974, p. 4), has been associated with post-sexual-abuse trauma in women (Briere & Runtz, 1988; Pearce, Cunningham, Pearce, & Conte, 1988, April; Runtz, 1987) and is thought to partially underlie the specific reports of chronic pelvic pain in some female abuse survivors (Haber & Roos, 1985; Gross, Doerr, Caldirola, Guzinski, & Ripley, 1980–81; Walker, Katon, Harrop-Griffiths, Holm, Russo, & Hickok, 1988).

As indicated in the "Cognitive Effects" section, these various manifestations of anxiety arise, to some degree, from the physical trauma and powerlessness that accompany childhood sexual, as well as physical, abuse. In addition, however, it is likely that the child's early awareness of the "reality of danger" precludes the formation of a belief in a safe, just world—eventually leading to an adolescent or adult who understands the world to be a dangerous place where constant vigilance and a defensive stance are imperative for continued survival.

Although it has yet to be established empirically, it is the author's clinical impression that, as a result of these factors, certain DSM III-R Anxiety Disorders (e.g., "agoraphobia" and "generalized anxiety disorder") are overrepresented among adult sexual abuse survivors (as well as victims of other forms of child abuse), above and beyond those who satisfy criteria for PTSD. More clearly documented, however, are the abuse-related effects of anxiety on sexuality, which arise when fear and pain are associated with sexual stimuli during victimization. Meiselman (1978), for example, found that 87% of her clinical sample of sexual abuse survivors had "serious" sexual problems, as compared to 20% of those not sexually abused in childhood. Similarly, Maltz and Holman (1987) report that 60% of their group of incest survivors experienced pain during intercourse and 46% were anorgasmic. The large number of other studies finding increased sexual dysfunction among abuse survivors (e.g., Becker, Skinner, Abel, & Treacy, 1982; Briere & Runtz, 1987; Courtois, 1979a; Finkelhor, 1979a; Herman, 1981; Langmade, 1983; McCord, 1985; Tsai, Felman-Summers, & Edgar, 1979) suggests that sexual problems may be a primary symptom in this area (Jehu & Gazan, 1983; Maltz, 1988).

Depression

DSM III-R describes depression as dysphoric mood "or loss of interest or pleasure in all or almost all activities" (p. 218) and lists the following symptoms as common: poor appetite, sleep disturbance, psychomotor retardation or agitation, loss of interest or pleasure in usual activities, decreased sex drive, loss of energy, feelings of worthlessness, self-reproach, excessive or inappropriate guilt, impaired concentration, re-current thoughts about death, suicidal ideation, wishes to be dead, and suicide attempts. It further discriminates between "major depressive disorder" which involves a relatively intense and circumscribed period where these symptoms are present, and "dysthymic disorder," a milder form which typically has a longer course (i.e., lasting for many months or years).

Theories of the etiology of depression stress a variety of factors, most of which are directly relevant to the experience of sexual abuse victims. These include early loss and abandonment (e.g., Bowlby, 1973); rejecting, punitive, and uncaring parent-child relationships (e.g., Blatt, Wein, Chev-ron, & Quinlan, 1979); chronic negative, self-blaming cognitions devel-oped during childhood (e.g., Beck, 1967); and "learned helplessness" aris-ing from chronic experiences of having no control over painful or aversive events (e.g., Seligman, 1975). Given the importance of these factors, and the frequency of such experiences in the lives of sexual abuse victims (Peters, 1984), we might reasonably predict that "in the clinical literature, depression is the symptom most commonly reported among adults molested as children" (Browne & Finkelhor, 1986a, p. 152).

The research literature highlights the frequency of depressive epi-sodes among sexual abuse survivors as well. Bagley and Ramsay (1986), for example, found that in a community sample of 387 women, those with a history of childhood sexual abuse were approximately twice as likely to be clinically depressed as were women with no history of sexual abuse. Similarly, Peters (1984) found that women who had expe-

rienced sexually abusive contact as a child had an average of two times
more depressive episodes in their lives than nonabused women, and
were more likely to have been hospitalized for depression. Other
studies that have examined the relationship between childhood sexual
abuse and depressive symptoms have typically found it (e.g., Briere &
Runtz, 1987, 1988; Jehu, Gazan, & Klassen, 1984–85; McCord, 1985;
Runtz, 1987; Sedney & Brooks, 1984). This tendency toward depression
may also partially explain the higher incidence of suicidal ideation and
suicide attempts in sexual abuse survivors. As noted earlier, a number
of studies have found that suicide attempts are over two times more
likely among those with sexual abuse histories (Briere & Runtz, 1986;
Herman, 1981; Sedney & Brooks, 1984).

In her discussion of the clinical presentation of sexual abuse survivors, Gelinas (1981) states that

> most incest victims will not request treatment for incest, but for
> symptoms relating to longstanding depressions. The criteria for
> Dysthymic Disorders in the (DSM III) provides a good characteriza-
> tion of this type of depression. However, incest victims show atypi-
> cal depression with strong dissociative and impulsive elements.
> (p. 488)

Gelinas specifically refers to a sort of "needy depressiveness," which
includes a mixture of anxious, depressive, and interpersonal symptomatology. In a similar vein, Briere and Runtz (1987) suggest that the
clinical picture presented by the symptomatic sexual abuse survivor is
often an amalgam of many types of "psychopathology" such that a
variety of DSM III-R labels, including Major Depression or Dysthymic
Disorder, are often applied.

Interpersonal Effects

Because child abuse occurs, by definition, within the context of some
sort of relationship, however brief or destructive, sexual abuse survivors often experience problems in the interpersonal domain. As noted
by Berliner and Wheeler (1987): "From their abuse children learn certain patterns of behavior that are harmful to themselves or others, or
that restrict their development and prevent them from attaining adequate functioning" (p. 420). Such effects are often very painful to the
survivor, since they are associated with feelings of alienation, believing
oneself to be incapable of having a "normal" (i.e., satisfying and rela-

tively conflict-free) relationship and a sometimes chronic and dysphoric "neediness." In addition, the survivor's childhood experience may produce generalized feelings of anger and rage, mixed with fearfulness as noted above—emotions easily evoked in later interactions with others. Despite these negative affects, the interpersonal sequelae of sexual abuse may be understood as, in part, necessary accommodations that the child is forced to make in order to survive the abuse process (Summit, 1983).

Recently clinicians have reported a variety of sexual-abuse-related "symptoms" in this area, most of which have been further documented in the empirical literature. These may best be understood in terms of three general and overlapping groups of problems: (a) disturbed relatedness, (b) "acting out" and "acting in," and (c) withdrawal.

Disturbed Relatedness

Sexual abuse may be relatively unique among forms of interpersonal aggression in that it combines exploitation and invasion with, in some instances, what might otherwise be evidence of love or caring (e.g., physical contact, cuddling, praise, perhaps some positive physical sensations). As Sandra Butler notes: "Such activity is not always traumatic and frightening at the time it occurs if the father is not physically abusive, because he is able to count on his daughter's inability to understand the inappropriateness of his behavior and the warmth and sensual feelings his fondling generates in her" (1978, p. 32). To some extent this mixture may even be found in sexual abuse where "loving" was not present (e.g., where the abuse was more obviously rape), since in a general context of physical or emotional maltreatment or neglect, any attention or validation (if only for one's sexual value) may be perceived as positive. Further, as noted by Jill Blake-White and Christine Kline (1985): "The fact that the perpetrator is a trusted adult makes her ambivalent and confused by her own feelings, and she may even doubt her own reality. She wonders if she had experienced a punishment or if she had elicited the incest by her own sexuality" (p. 396). Given this concatenation of stimuli, many sexual abuse survivors are highly ambivalent about intimate relationships—especially ones where sexual or romantic themes predominate.

Idealization and disappointment. Such ambivalence may express itself as mixed and sometimes contradictory motivations for relating to others. Thus survivors may feel distrust or fear of others in combination with a paradoxical tendency to idolize individuals they perceive or want to perceive as "good." Herman (1981), for example, found in her sample of female abuse victims that "the majority of the incest victims, in fact, tended to overvalue and idealize men" (p. 103). As will be discussed in upcoming chapters on psychotherapy and "borderline dynamics," such idealization often leads to disappointment and anger, both because of the survivor's underlying distrust and rage, which may stimulate less than ideal responses from others, and the tendency for the idolized to inevitably emerge as human at some point. Thus an unfortunate effect of the idealization process may be frequent, intense, but highly unstable attachments to others which end in anger and further loss.

Peggy P.

Peggy is a 34-year-old woman, living alone in her apartment with her two cats. She seeks therapy "to become more of a woman." Although a bit of a loner at work, she frequents singles bars at night in search of "male companionship." At the end of these forays Peggy frequently brings a man home with her, but rarely hears from him again after that night. She describes most of these men quite positively, and she bitterly speculates about what it is about her that they just "do their number and leave." Further exploration reveals that she has been raped by two of these men, and beaten by two others; events for which Peggy blames herself, citing her many negative qualities and shortcomings. She reports, upon questioning, sexual abuse by an uncle and a "friend of the family" during most of her adolescence.

Another result of the idealization dynamic may be described as "revictimization." This term refers to the findings of several studies (Briere & Runtz, 1987; Fromuth, 1985; McCord, 1985; Miller et al., 1978; Runtz, 1987, 1987, June; Runtz & Briere, 1988, April; Russell, 1986) that female sexual abuse survivors are several times more likely to be victimized again later in life (e.g., via rape or battering) than are women with no history of childhood sexual abuse. Although a number of explanations have been offered for this phenomenon, one possibility is that in their drive to see men in a positive light, some survivors overlook cues or behaviors that nonabused women would see as danger signs, such as aggressiveness or extreme sexism. Further, when confronted with abusive behavior, the survivor may be more prone to "forgive and forget"; both because she learned long ago to expell such painful events from memory and in the hope that her current abuser will redeem himself in ways that her original perpetrator(s) did not.

Given the complexity of this phenomenon and the potential for such behavior to be erroneously labelled as masochistic (Runtz & Briere, 1988, April) or for the victim to be seen as deserving her abuse (in the words of one psychiatrist-in-training: "Once, maybe. Three times? You have to wonder what she does that so many people agree on the same solution"), further research is clearly indicated in this area. Additional reasons for revictimization may include the possibilities that (a) the survivor's low self-esteem and self-punitiveness may attract her to abusive individuals, (b) the learned helplessness arising from sexual abuse may create victims who become passive in the face of impending victimization (McCord, 1985), and (c) abusive men may learn to identify women who have been previously abused and thus are easy prey.

Drama. Although never examined in the empirical sexual abuse literature per se, the tendency for some survivors of severe sexual molestation to exaggerate their concerns and to present themselves dramatically is well known to clinicians. In many cases this behavioral style is seen as evidence of a "histrionic" personality disorder, as noted in Chapter 2. At a more phenomenological level, we may understand dramatic and emotionally intense survivor communication to be a reflection of negative self-evaluation.

Specifically, the tendency for such individuals to make their predicaments appear even worse than they are is an outgrowth of the survivor's belief that she does not deserve attention for "ordinary" problems. Thus she must exaggerate her difficulties before others will see them as worthy of response. For example, a client who feels isolated and empty may believe that she must engage in a "hysterical emotional outburst" (Shapiro, 1985), outlining how lonely, desperate, abandoned, and interpersonally destitute she is, to elicit compassionate responses from her therapist. This same low self-esteem may underlie some survivors' positive exaggerations (e.g., how wonderful her friend is, how brilliantly he plays the piano), since they imply that only extreme content can garner attention or credibility given the low value of the speaker.

"Compulsive" sexuality. A dynamic similar to that of idealization is sometimes present in the abuse survivor's sexual relationships. On the one hand, she has seen for herself the potential for sex to include exploitation and trauma and thus appropriately fears the vulnerability and intimacy inherent in sexual relationships. This fear may lead not only to sexual dysfunction (Jehu & Gazan, 1983) and powerful dissociative states during sexual contact, but also to a general distrust of sex partners and men in general (e.g., Briere & Runtz, 1987; Courtois, 1979a, 1979b; Jehu, Gazan, & Klassen, 1984–85; Maltz, 1988; Meiselman, 1978). Yet, as described by Herman (1981): "At the same time that these women had little hope of attaining a rewarding relationship with anyone, they desperately longed for the nurturance and care which they had not received in childhood" (p. 100).

Having learned at an early age that one of their most powerful assets in gaining some sort of contact with or control over others was their sexual availability, many sexual abuse survivors report periods of "promiscuity" or compulsive sexual behavior (Courtois, 1979a; de Young, 1982; Herman, 1981; Maltz, 1988; Meiselman, 1978). The frequent yet short-lived nature of these sexual encounters can thus be understood as the competing needs to seek nurturance, love, power, and self-affirmation in the only way thought possible, in combination with historically valid fears of exploitation, and only partially repressed rage at having been so deeply hurt by "similar" individuals. This complex dynamic may become, in some instances, a vicious cycle, wherein the survivor (a) behaves in a flirtatious or "seductive" manner with men from whom she seeks approval or wishes to control, which (b) places her at risk from predatory males who frequently exploit and victimize her, motivating (c) her increasing belief that "all men are alike" and "just want one thing," resulting in (d) further verification to the survivor that her only value with regard to males is her sex.

Adversariality. Although the sexual abuse survivor may experience ambivalence with regard to her contacts with others, she is often more clear, as noted above, about how to engage in such interactions. Specifically, many survivors of extended sexual victimization learn during childhood that things are gained only through exchange of other things—never inherently deserved and thus never freely given. This adversarial perspective assumes that love, caring, physical goods, or attention are available only to the survivor if she trades sex for them, or tricks someone into providing them. The former, which we shall refer to as "sexual adversariality," is commonly seen in adolescent "street kids" and teenage prostitutes (Zingaro, 1985), whose cynicism about their ultimate value to others may be startling.

Prostitution, in fact, is described by some survivors as one of the most representative of human interactions, since it involves the exchange of sex for money, just as the (forced) exchange in childhood was for attention, momentary contact, or escape from injury. As Sandra Butler describes in her book *Conspiracy of Silence*:

> Even before puberty a girl often learns to use her sexuality to please her father. After several years she may see prostitution as a logical extension of selling sex at home. Many abused women decide that if they have to have sex with a man, they might as well get paid for it. (1978, p. 41)

Studies in this area highlight the association between sexual abuse and subsequent teenage prostitution, noting that 60 to 73% of three groups of adolescent prostitutes were sexually abused as children (Bagley & Young, 1987; James & Meyerding, 1977; Silbert & Pines, 1981).

Such adversariality is not limited to overtly sexual actions, however. The survivor may also service her therapist with compliments, flirtations, superficial agreement, and "good client" behaviors in order to ensure continuing therapeutic contact and support or, as described below, may tolerate abusive behavior from a spouse, partner, or employer in order to ensure continued security or to forestall abandonment.

Finally, this adversarial perspective often manifests as a chronic tendency to view interpersonal interactions as battles, which the former child abuse victim seeks to win (or lose) in order to survive. Given her childhood experience of injustice (i.e., the unfairness of being hurt but not rescued, and of the abuser being "bad" but not punished), she may decide early in life that "all bets are off" with regard to honesty or fairness. In the vacuum that this perception creates, the survivor may learn to utilize almost any options she has available to her in order to prevail in her interactions with others. This survival pattern can specifically motivate behavior that is often attributed by clinicians to "personality disorders"—that of manipulation.

Manipulation. As typically understood, "manipulation" refers to those behaviors engaged in by an individual in order to receive goods or services from others who would not otherwise bestow them. As is noted in an upcoming section, this behavior is especially worrisome to psychotherapists, who may fear that they are being taken advantage of or exploited in some way. From the victim's perspective, however, manipulativeness can be seen as a historically appropriate survival behavior, in some ways similar to drama. Such actions appear to be based on several underlying dynamics: (a) low self-esteem, (b) the survivor's belief that nothing good is freely given, and (c) her previously developed skills at extracting needed resources from a hostile environment (i.e., "survival" per se). To paraphrase a former sexual abuse victim during psychotherapy: "Even though I needed it, I knew I didn't deserve it, and I knew you wouldn't just give it to me, so I tricked you."

Although, from the former sexual abuse victim's perspective, the intent of adversarial behaviors is survival, a major result may be social isolation and rejection—especially when the ambivalent dynamics of rage, neediness, and distrust are present. These problems of relatedness, in combination with the other sequelae of sexual victimization, may drive the former abuse victim to engage in a variety of extreme behaviors, including aggression and self-destructiveness, in order to "win" attention or contact.

Acting-Out and Acting-In

A number of writers have noted that adolescents and adults who were severely abused as children are prone to a variety of socially problematic behaviors. Such behavior is often referred to as "acting out," a term commonly used to describe acts that are self-destructive or harmful to others and that are thought to arise from internal conflict. In the case of sexual abuse, such behaviors include truancy and other school problems (e.g., DeFrancis, 1969; Reich & Gutierres, 1979; Runtz & Briere, 1986), running away from home (e.g., McCormack, Janus, & Burgess, 1986), aggression (e.g., Bagley, 1984; Reich & Gutierres, 1979), drug and alcohol abuse (e.g., Bagley, 1984; Briere & Runtz, 1987; Briere & Zaidi, 1988, August; Herman, 1981; Miller, Downs, Gondoli, & Keil, 1987), self-mutilation (Briere, 1988; Briere & Zaidi, 1988, August; de Young, 1982; Goodwin, Simms, & Bergman, 1979; Lindberg & Distad, 1985b), delinquency or criminality (e.g., Ross, 1980; Reich & Guttierres, 1979; Runtz & Briere, 1986), and those behaviors described in earlier sections—prostitution, suicidality and "promiscuity."

A casual review of these behaviors reveals their heterogeneity, with the only obvious common quality being their tendency to be seen as trouble by others—perhaps especially by caregivers and law enforcers. Such behaviors arise from a variety of motivations or underlying psychological processes, as opposed to some hypothetical unitary quality reflecting "adjustment problems" or "badness." At minimum, we may understand these different behaviors to be "instrumental" (involving activities that were adaptive during the abuse experience) or "self-destructive" (reflecting abuse-related self-hatred, desire for punishment, or suicidality). As noted below, even this dichotomy may be an oversimplification, since certain behaviors (e.g., self-mutilation) may reflect both instrumental and self-destructive intentions.

Abuse-related instrumental behaviors are those activities that were adaptive during the period in which sexual abuse took place which are less relevant to the postabuse environment. These behaviors are continued after the abuse experience because, as described in the "Cognitive Effects" section, sexual victimization (especially incest and chronic abuse) frequently distorts subsequent perceptions of self and the world. These cognitive distortions may then produce behaviors that are situationally, but not historically, inappropriate. As noted earlier, the survivor's view of herself as "bad," unworthy, and unlovable, in combination with a perception of others as untrustworthy and the world as dangerous, may support what appears to be needless attention-getting ("Help me," "Pay attention to me," "Care for me"), manipulativeness ("I need it," "I don't deserve it," "I'll trick you into giving it to me") or delinquency ("You already hate me, so what do I care?" "I hate you," "Can't you see that there is something wrong?").

Even certain forms of self-injurious acting out, most notably drug and alcohol abuse, self-mutilation, and parasuicidality (intentionally sublethal suicide attempts) may have significant instrumental components. As noted by writers such as Reich and Gutierres (1979) and Lindberg and Distad (1985b), for example, such behaviors may ensure social avoidance and reduce stress (at least temporarily) and may serve to decrease feelings of helplessness through direct action.

Alice B.

As described earlier, Alice was brought to the emergency room of a local hospital during a severe dissociative episode. After being admitted to a psychiatric unit, numerous old and recent scars were found on her abdomen, thighs, arms, and wrists during a routine physical examination. Alice admits that these healed and healing wounds are due to intentional self-injury: primarily involving lacerations with razor blades, but also including what appear to be cigarette burns. Records from a previous hospitalization indicate that, on one occasion, Alice cut an 8-inch opening in her inner thigh, which extended nearly to the bone. She appeared somewhat proud of this, describing a 4-hour "operation" wherein she progressively cut deeper and deeper, efficiently dealing with increased bleeding through the use of paper towels and pressure. In an intellectualized manner, Alice states: "The pain's the hard part, at least at first. You have to get past the pain, but you can."

Self-mutilation is an especially good example of the mixture of adaptive and self-punitive qualities of certain survivor behaviors. Intentional yet nonsuicidal self-injury (e.g., cutting or carving on one's arms or legs, burning oneself with matches or cigarettes, biting one's fingers, tearing out one's hair, cutting one's genitalia) is sometimes described by survivors as an effective way to (a) terminate dissociative episodes (an extreme version of the proverbial pinch to end a bad dream), (b) distract themselves from painful memories or flashbacks (what one survivor calls "using new pain to hide old pain"), (c) reassure themselves that they are alive and "in reality," and even (d) increase their sense of autonomy (as one male survivor put it: "I can do whatever I want to my body. When I hurt myself, it is me doing it and me feeling it." A teenage girl stated, somewhat cynically: "It's my hobby. What's yours?").

In a similar vein, nonlethal suicidal behavior may represent a cry for help in individuals who believe themselves to have no other effective way to communicate psychological pain. Thus suicidal behaviors in some abuse survivors may reflect the belief that extraordinary measures are required to gain the caring attention of others, given their perceived lack of power and undeservingness in more conventional contexts (Briere & Runtz, 1986).

Finally, drug and alcohol abuse may serve as a form of "chemically induced dissociation," allowing the survivor to escape from abuse-related memories or painful mood states. The frequency of this latter defense is suggested by the findings of one study that psychotherapy clients with a history of sexual abuse are over 2 times more likely to have a history of alcoholism and 10 times more likely to report having been addicted to drugs in the past than a control group of nonabused clients (Briere & Runtz, 1987). This numbing effect of drugs and alcohol is so substantial that psychotherapy may be considerably less effective when the survivor is addicted to—or regularly using—such substances.

In addition to instrumental behaviors, a number of abuse-related "symptoms" reflect self-hatred and a desire for self-punishment. Some therapists refer to such activity as "acting in," suggesting that the survivor turns his or her conflict inward, thus punishing self rather than others for abuse-related pain. As noted earlier, Finkelhor and Browne (1985) trace such behavior to the low self-esteem and frequent self-hatred in the sexual abuse survivor, who may blame herself for the abuse and perceive herself as evil, unattractive, and dirty. Survivors who self-mutilate, for example, often describe a period of escalating guilt, self-criticism, and increasing disgust with self just prior to self-injury, leading to an overwhelming desire for punishment. After self-injury these negative cognitions usually abate and a period of calm and almost palpable relief may ensue. Unfortunately for some chronic self-mutilators, this pattern is likely to recur in the near future with the onset of "new" guilt or self-derogating cognitions.

In contrast to the seemingly compulsive quality of repetitive self-mutilation, survivors with suicidal ideation may report an ongoing preoccupation with dying and death, usually as a result of feelings of helplessness, hopelessness, and a combination of anger at self (for being so weak/disgusting/stupid/etc.) and others (for not caring/loving/supporting/etc.). In the words of one sexual abuse survivor, "it's not a question of whether or how, only when." These suicidal thoughts and impulses are often quite chronic, dating back to the time of the first incident of sexual abuse. Briere and Runtz (1986), for example, found that of 14 women who had made a suicide attempt before age 13, 13 (93%) had been sexually victimized. As will be described in Chapter 7, suicidality is a frequent problem in the treatment of sexual abuse survivors and thus requires continual assessment during the psychotherapeutic process.

It should be noted at this point that the ultimate motives for self-mutilation and suicide may be notably different for the former sexual abuse victim, despite the tendency for some writers and clinicians to see them as similar forms of self-destructiveness. Specifically, in many (but not all) cases, the self-mutilator is struggling to stay alive, while the suicidal survivor is considering death. As mentioned earlier, self-mutilation is often an attempt to block or interrupt negative cognitions or feelings (e.g., dissociation, rage, extreme dysphoria, overwhelming guilt, etc.) and thus may be an attempt to *survive* incapacitating symptoms rather than ending life. In the words of one survivor: "I came to school with cigarette burns all over my left arm. I had done it because I was feeling scared that I was beginning not to feel anything. I needed to see if I was still real, if I could still hurt" (Butler, 1978, p. 45). Even in cases where self-mutilation serves as self-punishment, in fact it is often described by sexual abuse survivors as a substitute for more lethal behaviors. Thus self-mutilation can—in some instances—be a sign of continuing struggle for symptom relief and survival and therefore may be dealt with differently from intentionally self-lethal behaviors. It is important to note, however, that some intensely suicidal individuals (who may or may not be abuse survivors) also self-mutilate, sometimes describing the superficial slashing of wrists or the throat as "dry runs" before "the real thing." For this reason, self-mutilatory behavior should be assessed carefully for its function and meaning to the survivor before diagnostic or prognostic assumptions are made.

Although drug and alcohol abuse has been discussed in terms of its adaptive or functional value (i.e., escape or "chemical dissociation"), therapists working with sexual abuse survivors often sense a self-destructive quality to such behaviors as well. Specifically, former sexual abuse victims may report a desire to "fry my brains out" or "drink myself into the gutter," as if chronic intoxication (and the degradation, pain, and losses often associated with it) serves as a deserved punishment or appropriate retribution for abuse-related sins. Indicative of this process is the tendency for survivors' drug or alcohol binges to follow events that stimulate self-hatred, such as fights with loved ones, rejection, or failure. One middle-aged male sexual abuse survivor, for example, described his alcoholism as "the bottom line that's always waiting for me when I screw up. I'm a loser and that's all I deserve to be." This sense of the suitability of substance addiction may partially explain the difficulties encountered in treating alcoholism and drug abuse among former sexual abuse victims, especially when the client's early victimization experiences have not been directly addressed.

Withdrawal

Given the various interpersonal problems of many sexual abuse survivors, it follows that a final group of "symptoms" associated with prior sexual victimization involve the survivor's experience of estrangement, isolation, and alienation from others. In addition to the stigmatization of sexual abuse, which, as discussed, may lead to feelings of being unworthy and "bad" compared to others, the sexual abuse survivor's difficulties in relating to others (e.g., ambivalence, "manipulation," expressions of underlying fear and rage, etc.) can result in a tendency to withdraw from the social milieu or to be rejected by it. Briere and Runtz (1987), for example, found that 64% of the sexual abuse survivors in their clinical sample felt isolated and alone, while 73% of the incest victims in Courtois' (1979a) community sample reported moderate to severe isolation and alienation. These feelings, often exacerbated by coexisting depression, may make it especially difficult for the survivor to reach out for help or support from others, thereby potentially increasing his or her sense of isolation. Alternatively, this alienation may produce increased emotional neediness leading to, in turn, further inappropriate interpersonal behaviors (e.g., demandingness, dependency, or "promiscuity") and subsequent greater rejection and estrangement.

Summary

Taken together, the empirical and clinical literature on the long-term effect of childhood sexual abuse provides little doubt that such victimization can be quite harmful and long lasting. As opposed to other subjects in the behavioral sciences, the relationship between abuse and effects appears quite straightforward: A sexually abusive environment usually hurts children and, in the absence of appropriate treatment, hurt children often grow to become hurt adults. The extent of this injury appears to be a function of a large number of variables, including type, duration, and frequency of abuse; interpersonal resources available to the victim; who the offender was (i.e., father, brother, teacher); when it occurred; how significant others responded to the abuse disclosure; and whether physical force was involved (see Browne & Finkelhor, 1986a, 1986b, for a review of the literature in this area). Despite the complexity of such mediating variables, very few studies performed in the last 10 years show any form of childhood sexual abuse to be benign or harmless.

Why then, we may ask, has so little of this research penetrated into the basic clinical literature? If sexual abuse has been associated with anxiety, depression, dissociation, self-injurious behavior, even multiple personalities, why do the standard clinical texts on these subjects routinely fail to mention sexual victimization and other forms of child abuse as potential etiologic factors? Although answers to such questions may include such notions as the politics of psychotherapy and society's drive to deny the extent and implications of sexual victimization (as described in Chapter 3), part of the problem appears to reside in the fact that clinicians *already have* explanations for many of these patterns without specific reference to sexual abuse. This blind spot (Briere, 1984, April; Summit, 1988) not only is due to the relative newness of our information on sexual victimization, as opposed to the many years of theorizing entailed in "modern" theories of psychopathology, but also reflects the specific tendency of traditional theorists to discount abuse reports as fantasies.

As an example of the psychiatric redefinition of post-sexual-abuse trauma, and because of their special relevance to many survivors in the traditional psychiatric care system, we will consider in the next chapter two commonly diagnosed mental disorders: Hysteria and borderline personality disorder. Finally, a list of hypothesized "core" effects of sexual abuse will be presented, representing the basic clinical phenomena thought to underlie the empirical findings described in Chapter 1.

CHAPTER 2

"Hysteria," "Borderline Personality Disorder," and the Core Effects of Severe Abuse

Hysteria

As described in one psychiatric reference (Hinsie & Campbell, 1973), "hysteria" refers to a constellation of symptoms including (a) physical problems for which no organic cause can be found (e.g., paralysis, tics, tremors), (b) alterations in sensation (e.g., loss of feeling in areas of the body, persistent tingling, or sudden blindness), (c) "visceral" symptoms (e.g., "anorexia, bulimia, vomiting, hiccoughs . . . [and] various abdominal complaints"), and (d) "mental" symptoms, including amnesia, somnambulism (sleepwalking), and "fugues, trances, dreamstates, [and] hysterical 'fits' or 'attacks'" (p. 367).

Although hysteria is no longer an acceptable diagnosis in current psychiatric nomenclature (i.e., in DSM III-R), it remains a common explanation among psychiatrists, psychologists, and other mental health workers for the behavior of (almost always) women whose physical complaints appear groundless. A related diagnosis, that of "Histrionic Personality Disorder," however, remains in DSM III-R. Hinsie and Campbell describe this disorder as including:

> any of the following: vain, egocentric, attention-seeking, dramatic descriptions of past symptoms and illnesses with a multiplicity of vaguely described complaints and overtalkativeness during the psychiatric interview; suggestibility; soft, coquettish, graceful, and sexually provocative although frigid and anxious when close to attain-

ing a sexual goal; easily disappointed, excitable, emotionally labile, and often unaware of inner feelings; dependently demanding in interpersonal situations . . . Such a manipulative adaptational pattern occurs in those with a tendency toward rigid repression of dysphoric emotion . . . Conflicts in such patients are often centered around *genital incest strivings,* [emphasis added] and/or oral disappointments." (p. 369)

To this list DSM III-R adds craving for "novelty, stimulation, and excitement," behavior that is "overly reactive and emotionally expressed," constant needs for reassurance, approval and praise, overconcern with physical attractiveness, "inappropriately sexually seductive," and "frequent complaints of poor health . . . or feelings of depersonalization" (1987, p. 349).

The reader will no doubt recognize many of these symptoms as having been linked (it is to be hoped in a less pejorative manner than Hinsie and Campbell) to childhood sexual victimization in the sexual abuse literature cited in Chapter 1. Among other symptoms, hysteria and severe post-sexual-abuse trauma appear to share (a) dissociation in its various forms, (b) somatic complaints, (c) problems with sexuality, and (d) a variety of interpersonal difficulties (e.g., ambivalence, idealization, attention-getting, sexualization, dependency, and manipulation). In fact, Briere and Runtz (1987, 1988a) specifically document similar abuse-related symptoms (dissociation, dysphoria, somatization, and interpersonal dysfunction) in both clinical and nonclinical samples of sexual abuse survivors, while Herman (1985) and Rosenfeld (1979) found similar clusters of "hysterical" symptoms in abuse survivors within two psychiatric outpatient samples. Herman notes, quite eloquently, that "the hysteric, although banished from DSM-III, is still frequently seen as a psychiatric patient, and she is still suffering, as Freud noted long ago, from memories" (p. 13).

Emilia E.

Emilia is a bright, intense 22-year-old woman who entered a therapy group for "adult children of alcoholics" at a local community center. Initially liked by most group members for her wit, charm, and "openness," she gradually becomes ostracized from the group—partially as a result of her sexual involvement with two older group members, who subsequently stop coming to meetings. It becomes clear, as well, that Emilia needs to be the center of the group's attention, and she becomes increasingly angry and depressed as the group begins to ignore her. With the passage of time, Emilia's superficially cheerful and excited facade disappears, and her underlying loneliness and poor self-esteem become obvious. During session number eight, Emilia reveals that her alcoholic father sexually molested her from ages 7 to 16, and still approaches her at family reunions. She tearfully relates times when her father would call her "my little baby" as he penetrated her sexually.

Other writers have also described specific "hysterical" symptoms in victims of sexual abuse, including several reports of "hysterical seizures" or "pseudoepilepsy" (e.g., Goodwin, Simms, & Bergman, 1979; Gross, 1979; McAnarney, 1975). A typical case history (one of four) was presented by Goodwin et al. (1979):

> A. was . . . hospitalized at age 14 following convulsions in the detention center in which she was placed after running away from home for the second time. Two weeks previously, her natural father had had intercourse with her . . . She said her father had been seductive with her before, as had a maternal uncle. The father admitted having had intercourse with her. A. was sexually active with peers and had threatened suicide. She said that she was conscious during the seizures and that they usually occurred when she was alone . . . Electroencephalogram was normal. Conversion disorder with hysterical seizures was diagnosed. Psychotherapy was begun and the seizures disappeared, but promiscuity and runaways continued as problems. (p. 699)

Although concurring with the presence of certain "hysterical" symptoms in some sexual abuse survivors, the sexual abuse literature would obviously not agree with the notion of such individuals struggling with "genital incest strivings" as described by Hinsie and Campbell (1973). The history of how trauma arising from sexual abuse could be redefined as the results of "striving" for incest may appear bizarre to those not familiar with the Freudian theory of psychosexual development. Although the basic outlines of this phenomenon will be briefly described here, the reader is referred to the essay on "the Freudian Cover-up" in Florence Rush's (1980) book *The Best Kept Secret: Sexual Abuse of Children*, as well as Hannah Lerman's (1986) *A Mote in Freud's Eye: From Psychoanalysis to the Psychology of Women*, Jeffrey Masson's (1984) analysis entitled *The Assault on Truth: Freud's Suppression of the Seduction Theory*, and Alice Miller's (1984) *Thou Shalt Not Be Aware: Society's Betrayal of the Child*.

Freud's View of Hysteria, and the "Oedipal Complex"

As Hinsie and Campbell (1973) note, Freud's initial work with his women clients led him to believe that

> the hysterical attack was a symbolic representation of a repressed sexual trauma. He believed that the patient had undergone a passive sexual experience in childhood, but that this psychical experience could not find adequate discharge because the nervous system was incapable of dealing with it at that time; the experience was forgotten, but with puberty the memory of it was reawakened ... This theory was later revised [by Freud] *when it was discovered that the sexual traumata uncovered in hysterical patients were really fictitious memories designed to mask the autoerotic activities of childhood* [emphasis added].

In Freud's own words,

> Almost all my women patients told me that they had been seduced by their fathers. I was driven to recognize in the end that these reports were untrue and so came to understand that the hysterical symptoms are derived from phantasies and not from real occurrences ... It was only later that I was able to recognize in this phantasy of being seduced by the father the expression of the typical Oedipus complex in women. (cited in Rush, 1980, p. 83)

In a similar vein, Freud concluded in *The Interpretation of Dreams* (1900) that "the theory of the psychoneurosis asserts as an indisputable and invariable fact that only sexual wishful impulses from infancy, which have undergone repression ... are able to furnish the motive force for the formation of psychoneurotic symptoms" (pp. 605–606). As Judith Herman (1981) notes in *Father-Daughter Incest*, Freud's sudden change of heart regarding the basis for his clients' incest reports "was based not on any new evidence from patients (i.e., the "discoveries" implied by Hinsie and Campbell), but rather on Freud's own growing unwillingness to believe that licentious behavior on the part of fathers could be so widespread" (p. 10).

Freud's concerns about the implications of his original theory for the frequency of incest in his culture are reproduced at length by Masson (1984), who quotes from Freud's letters to his friend and colleague Wilhelm Fleiss. Among other misgivings, Freud states that "surely such widespread perversions against children are not very probable" (p. 108).

As has been noted in the introduction of the present book, current data reveal that incest and sexual abuse are relatively common in our society and suggest that, in fact, the (especially female) caseloads of many clinicians do contain a preponderance of sexual abuse survivors—data to which Freud, in all charity, had no access.

Freud's ultimate belief, his theory of the "Oedipus complex," was that boys and girls sexually desired their opposite-sexed parent and, through a complex series of events involving male fears of "castration" and female "penis envy," ultimately developed rich fantasies of seducing said parent—fantasies that some could not differentiate from reality at later points in their lives (hence the "hysterical" reports of incest). Freud further hypothesized that it was the *mother*, in fact, who was responsible for any childhood sexual stimulation. As cited by Lerman (1986, p. 105), Freud somewhat bizarrely concluded in 1931 that

> this is because they [children] necessarily received their first, or at any rate their strongest, genital sensations when they were being cleaned and having their toilet attended to by their mothers . . . The fact that the mother thus unavoidably initiates the child into the phallic phase is, I think, the reason why in phantasies of later years, the father so regularly appears as the sexual seducer. (p. 238)

A number of modern writers (e.g., Armstrong, 1983; Herman, 1981; Lerman, 1986; Masson, 1984; Miller, 1984; Rush, 1980; Russell, 1986) seriously question both the empirical and logical basis for Freud's Oedipal theory of psychosexual development and discount his theory regarding the "fictitious" nature of his female clients' sexual abuse reports. In the words of Hannah Lerman (1986): "Freud's knowledge of female sexuality was limited, to put it most charitably. It was due to the sparse information available in his time. His theory, which is built on very scant and often erroneous evidence, nevertheless became quite expansive and authoritative" (p. 84). As psychoanalyst Shengold (1963) additionally notes, somewhat wryly: "Most patients who have an actual history of incest intensely wish that their memories were mere fantasies."

Freud's theoretical misstep has had major implications for the future of mental health practice, since it (a) introduced a probably false (but nevertheless immensely popular) set of assumptions regarding the etiology of "hysteria" and other psychological maladies and (b) set a precedent for following generations of psychotherapists to disbelieve their clients' reports of childhood sexual victimization.

As a study of modern psychoanalytic writings and scholarly articles will attest, this tendency to discount individuals who report incest or other sexual abuse continues—with some notable exceptions—as does a heavy reliance on Oedipal interpretations. Although fewer authorities are willing to denounce a client's incest report as a total falsehood, there is often the strong implication or direct statement that Oedipal strivings caused the (often hysterical) client to actively pursue her abuser, who was then unable to resist the temptation. From such a perspective, the clinician may reject the notion of the survivor as victim, or as injured. James Henderson, for example, noted in the *Comprehensive Textbook of Psychiatry—II* (perhaps the major teaching reference in that discipline) that "the daughters collude in the incestuous liaison and play an active and even initiating role in establishing the pattern . . . [she] is unlikely to report the liaison at first or to protest about it. If she eventually does, it is as much precipitated by anger at her father for something else . . . as a real objection to his incestuous behavior" (1975, p. 1356).

What makes this phenomenon all the more unfortunate is that women who display "hysterical" symptoms in therapy and who also report sexual abuse are probably the most likely to be discounted, despite the possible cause-effect relationship between such symptoms and the sexual abuse. Her "sexually provocative," "coquettish," or "easily excitable" style may instead be interpreted as evidence of her prior "collusion" with her abuser, or her abuse disclosure may be seen as fiction in the service of seducing the therapist. As is discussed in Chapters 3 and 5, successful psychotherapy with the sexual abuse survivor demands a high level of respect and support for the client's abuse disclosures and an understanding acceptance of whatever survival behaviors he or she may need to display during therapy—a treatment approach that many survivors with previous therapy experiences find novel. Alice Miller, the Swiss psychoanalyst, notes this well when she states:

> In every psychiatric and psychoanalytic diagnosis, the description of a hysterical patient is inconceivable without the use of the word "exaggerated." What is meant by this is that these patients' complaints are out of all proportion to their cause. But how can we measure the dimensions of the true cause if it is unknown or is ignored by the therapist? (pp. 31–32)

Borderline Personality Disorder

Although the history of the concept of hysteria is inextricably linked to Freud and his theory of feminine psychosexual development, the

diagnosis of "Borderline Personality Disorder" is a more recent phenomenon. It receives attention here because, in the author's experience, it is
perhaps the most common label attached to individuals who present
with severe post-sexual-abuse trauma in psychiatric settings.

DSM III-R describes borderline personality disorder, which it sees as
more common in women, as a chronic disturbance in which there is "a
pervasive pattern of instability of self-image, interpersonal relationship, and mood, beginning by early adulthood and present in a variety
of contexts" (p. 346). Among the symptoms of borderline personality
disorder, according to DSM III-R are:

> (1) "impulsiveness in at least two areas that are potentially self-
> damaging," (e.g., sex, substance use, reckless spending, shoplifting,
> overeating, etc.), (2) "a pattern of unstable and intense interpersonal
> relationships" (e.g., idealization, manipulation, and marked shifts in
> attitude), (3) "inappropriate, intense anger," (4) "marked and persis-
> tent identity disturbance" manifested by uncertainty about several
> issues related to self (e.g., self-image, gender identity, friendship
> patterns, and values), (5) "affective instability: marked shifts from
> baseline mood to depression, irritability, or anxiety," (6) "recurrent
> suicidal threats, gestures, or behavior, or self-mutilating behavior,"
> (7) "chronic feelings of emptiness or boredom," and (8) "frantic ef-
> forts to avoid real or imagined abandonment." (p. 347)

The reader will note that the above description closely approximates
the pattern of problems seen in many adolescents and adults who have
experienced severe or prolonged sexual abuse in childhood. It can be
shown, for example, that almost all of the symptoms listed in the
DSM III-R for borderline personality disorder have been independently
reported as victimization effects in the sexual abuse literature (Briere,
1984, April). Although little empirical work has been done on the
actual relationship between a borderline diagnosis and previous sexual
abuse, four preliminary studies (Briere & Zaidi, 1988, August; Gross
et al., 1980–81; Herman, 1985, Herman, Perry, & van der Kolk, 1988),
utilizing widely disparate clinical samples, suggest that women with
childhood histories of abuse may be two to five times more likely than
nonabused women to receive a diagnosis of borderline personality
disorder. In addition, several writers (e.g., Briere & Runtz, 1987; Gelinas,
1981, 1983; Herman, 1985; Herman & van der Kolk, 1987; Reiker &
Carmen, 1986) have theorized that sexual abuse—especially incest—
may predispose some individuals to behavior that satisfies borderline
diagnostic criteria. Finally, a well-designed study by Zivney, Nash and
Hulsey (1988) of female abuse victims' Rorschach responses indicates

that molestation, especially before age 9, is associated with the "disturbed cognition, damaged self, and preoccupation with [primitive] themes" (p. 104) often found among borderline clients.

Alan P.

Alan is a 34-year-old man who presents for an intake session at a Student Counseling Center. He has recently returned to his first year of Junior College after a series of unsuccessful jobs, most of which lasted for less than a month. He blames his occupational difficulties on being "too smart for my bosses," at the same time tearfully describing never being liked by peers or managers in work settings. During his interview, Alan describes having seen five previous therapists in the previous year and a half, "but they all turned out to be assholes or idiots." Past history includes four suicide attempts and periods of self-mutilation, beginning at age 12 when his sexually abusive uncle died. There is also a history of substantial cocaine abuse. He reports a pervasive sense of emptiness and isolation, although he hastens to add that he has "more friends than I know what to do with." He is currently on probation for driving under the influence of alcohol. Initially Alan is highly complimentary of the current therapist, stating "I wish I had someone as good as you when all this started," but soon becomes tearful and angry, accusing the therapist of "jacking me around." He demands to see a "real doctor" (the therapist is a clinical social worker), and threatens to report the clinician to the college dean for incompetence. He does not return to the center.

As will be described shortly, established psychiatry does not explain borderline psychopathology in terms of its possible relation to sexual abuse (Herman & van der Kolk, 1987). Instead, this disturbance is typically seen as resulting from "early object loss" and "difficulties in the separation–individuation period of childhood" (Davis & Akiskal, 1986, p. 689). Interestingly, there has been considerable controversy in psychiatry over the specific symptoms of borderline personality disorder (see Gunderson & Singer, 1975, and Perry & Klerman, 1978, for reviews of the various features attributed to this syndrome). Despite this variability and given the steadying influence of concrete DSM III and III-R criteria, the diagnosis of borderline personality disorder has become increasingly frequent in inpatient and outpatient psychiatric settings.

Most current theories of borderline development (e.g., Kernberg, 1975, and Masterson, 1978)—perhaps predictably given their psychoan-

alytic roots—trace the genesis of this disorder to inadequate or dysfunctional maternal nurturance (what Winnicott and others refer to as
insufficient "good enough mothering") in the first year or two of the
child's life. As a result of aversive mother-child interactions, the soon-
to-be-borderline child is thought to be arrested at a "pre-Oedipal" level,
such that she or he is unable to form the capacity for healthy "object
relations." Groves (1975) summarizes this failure as follows: "Whereas
in normal development the child learns to separate from important
objects [e.g., mother] with sadness and anger rather than with despair
and rage, the borderline cannot tolerate negative affects asociated with
separation and continues into adulthood the pre-Oedipal child's cling-
ing, as if others were desperately-needed parts rather than separate
persons" (p. 338). Donald Rinsley (1980) summarizes this process as
follows:

> We have postulated that the mother of the future borderline child
> and adult, herself borderline, rewards (provides libidinal supplies
> and gratification to) her infant when he [sic] behaves in a depen-
> dent, clinging manner towards her, but threatens to reject or aban-
> don . . . him when he makes efforts toward being independent of
> her, that is, toward separation-individuation. Thus, the infant (later
> the borderline individual) comes to perceive that independence,
> growth, and autonomy lead only to abandonment, while remaining
> symbiotically dependent guarantees the flow and acquisition of
> necessary support and supplies, albeit at the ultimate and disaster-
> ous expense of healthy independence and autonomy. Thus, the
> borderline individual's double bind; to remain infantile is to retain
> the mother and her love, to grow is to lose them (the ultimate
> meaning of the term *loser*). (p. 290)

Much of this discussion regarding "borderline dynamics" would be
irrelevant to this book were it not for the relative commonness of this
diagnosis among survivors of severe sexual abuse. We are, of course,
immediately at odds with current psychodynamic perspectives on the
development of "borderline symptomatology," given our information
that much disturbance is often associated with sexual child abuse.
Among other points of disagreement are the gender of the most traumagenic parent (the vast majority of sexual abusers are male), age at the
critical trauma (the average survivor is first sexually abused between
ages 6 and 12, although in cases of severe abuse victimization may
occur considerably earlier), and the prognosis associated with the problem (borderline personality disorder is often considered to be relatively
unresponsive to therapy). Such differences are critical to an understanding of abuse-related "borderline" symptoms and their treatment.

An interesting attempt to reconcile these two perspectives in favor of analytic theory was recently offered by Henderson (1983) who, while admitting the possibility that borderline individuals may have histories of childhood sexual abuse, suggested that "an equally plausible conclusion" was that these women developed borderline characteristics in early childhood and then later *sought out* incest as a result of their character pathology (p. 37).

In contrast to writers such as Henderson, Kernberg, or Masterson, the perspective offered in this book is that a significant proportion of cases (although undoubtably not all) of borderline personality disorder arise from early and extended childhood sexual victimization, usually with concurrent and extreme emotional maltreatment. The psychic injuries that arise from a sexually victimizing environment are well established and do not rest on complex and (to some) improbable theories of mother-child interactions in the first one or two years of life. Instead of positing contingent "libidinal supplies and gratification" by the inevitably disordered mother (see Caplan & Hall-McCorquodale, 1985, for a discussion of "mother-blaming" in psychiatric theory), a survivor-oriented perspective suggests that the cognitive, affective and interpersonal effects of severe child abuse are sufficient to account for many cases of what is referred to as "borderline" behavior.

Core Effects of Severe Abuse

As opposed to the enumeration of individual abuse effects found in Chapter 1, and the traditional psychiatric interpretation of such symptoms as outlined above, the remainder of this chapter will present a broader analysis of the impacts of sexual victimization and will link these general effects to "borderline" (and, to a lesser extent, "histrionic") symptom development. This more phenomenological perspective will refer to "core effects": those impacts of sexual victimization thought to underlie the clinical problems or "symptoms" of abuse survivors, especially in terms of what is often referred to as "personality disorder" or "character pathology." Although these expressions of trauma appear to be especially relevant to early onset, chronic sexual abuse, the reader may recognize aspects of these impacts in victims of severe physical and emotional abuse as well.

Clinical experience, in combination with the abuse literature cited in Chapter 1, suggests that the core impacts of severe or extended sexual victimization in childhood may be divided into a number of overlapping areas that underlie the survivor's clinical presentation.

Each of these meta-effects is thought to be the direct result of traumatic interruptions of normal childhood development, such that the child's early personality is shaped by adaptation to victimization rather than in response to the usual environmental demands. These early responses are thought to elaborate and generalize over time, eventually resulting in painful and maladaptive patterns of perception and behavior in adulthood.

Other-Directedness

The early life experiences of the severe abuse survivor—especially in the case of intrafamilial victimization—are often characterized by invasion, exploitation, sudden and unpredictable dangers, and shifting demands. Faced with what may be a tyrannical abuser and few personal resources, the survivor may literally exist in what Louise Armstrong (1983) calls "the family war zone." Such victimization may deprive the child of any real sense of control and autonomy and often involves frequent threats or actual instances of physical violence. Briere and Runtz (1987) found, for example, that of 133 psychotherapy clients who reported childhood histories of sexual abuse, 77% had experienced oral, anal, or vaginal penetration as a child, and 56% reported concomitant physical violence. In her important book *The Secret Trauma: Incest in the Lives of Girls and Women*, sociologist Diana Russell (1986) quotes one woman's story:

> He got me out of bed and put me in his bed with him. He said if I hollered he would smother me with his pillow. He was kissing me and I started to fight him off, but he was a big strong man. He started feeling all over me, my breasts and my genitals. He took his fingers and forced them into my vagina. Then he started to force his penis into me. He got part of the way in when I remembered that my mother kept a hammer under the bed. I reached down, got it, and hit him on the head with it. (p. 239)

In such an atmosphere the victim of sexual or physical abuse quickly learns that "safety" is predicated on hypervigilance. He or she may become expert at reading the slightest nuance in the abuser, since rapid and correct assessment of the perpetrator's psychological state may allow the victim either to (a) avoid or forestall an abuse incident by escaping in some manner or (b) placate or fulfill the abuser's needs before a more aversive consequence ensues. Within the abuser's seemingly total control, the child may struggle to become "better" and "better," ultimately defining her or his own intrinsic value by the extent to which punishment or maltreatment can be avoided or the abuser can be pleased (note that since the abuse continues in most cases, the child can rarely achieve the goal of "goodness").

This conclusion that "you are only as good as powerful others see you to be" can produce a generalized sense of other-directedness, wherein the survivor comes to rely on the reactions of people outside of himself as a basis for self-esteem. This dynamic may result in later "histrionic" or "borderline" hypersensitivity to others' negative opinions and the belief that one must engage in a variety of pleasing or attention-getting behaviors in order to be valued. And, of course, if one is rejected or found wanting, one is (by definition) bad or unworthy, a perception that can result in intensely negative affects and feelings— especially in the context of relationships.

The growing child's proficiency at meeting the needs and/or avoiding the violence of the abuser exacts an additional price. The sustained and concentrated attention she or he must pay to a threatening environment inevitably pulls energy away from the developmental tasks of self-awareness and early individuation. During childhood and early adolescence, the child normally develops a growing sense of self-efficacy as she interacts with others and confronts surmountable challenges in the environment. Among other revelations, the child learns that there are significant people besides one's mother and father, that certain events and experiences are not relevant to one's parents, and that certain needs cannot be met within the family. More basically, however, the growing child becomes acquainted with self— celebrating a developing sense of autonomy and the first inklings of independence and personal power. These experiences are often missing or incomplete for the abuse victim, who must, instead, attend to the task of survival.

As noted by Reiker and Carmen (1986): "Ultimately, these children are deprived of the experience of separateness and of any sense of their own value in being separate" (p. 364), a process that may eventually present as boundary problems or lack of individuation in the adult survivor. Instead, the victim may internalize (introject) the values, beliefs, and perceptions of his or her perpetrator, developing a fierce loyalty and fealty to those who have done the most harm. This traumatic bonding, in combination with the victim's desire to be a "good" boy or girl, may result in what has been called "identification with the aggressor." Such an introjection of abuser values and attitudes may result in (for boys) the creation of future sexual abusers or (for girls) a tendency to see oneself (and perhaps other women) as deserving or, in very extreme cases, enjoying exploitation, domination, or pain.

Thus the net effects of the radical other-directedness of many abuse survivors may include (a) an absence of a true sense of self (as separate from others), with resultant identity confusion, sense of emptiness, and inability "to soothe and comfort oneself" (McCann et al., 1988, p. 84), (b) hypersensitivity and extreme emotional reactivity to others (e.g., affective instability, overreaction to "minor" interpersonal events), especially in the face of rejection or abandonment, (c) gullibility and suggestibility when confronted with the expectations or demands of peers or authority figures, in light of the survivor's poor self-reference, (d) complaints of isolation and neediness, in the absence of self-support, and (e) boundary problems, arising from a relative inability to conceive of self without reference to others, and the reverse.

Chronic Perception of Danger

Given the salience of maltreatment and invasion in the survivor's early environment, the abuse victim's understanding of life must necessarily include such themes. Specifically, the child developing in an abusive context often makes important attributions or assumptions regarding the dangerousness of others, the likelihood of further injury or victimization, and the justness of the world. As noted earlier, these assumptions have been referred to as "cognitive distortions" since, from our perspective, they are not grounded in accurate perceptions of current reality. Briefly stated, the severe abuse victim tends to perceive the world as dangerous and unjust and his continued existence as tenuous. From this perspective, the child grows to view survival as the ultimate goal of life.

This understanding of danger as a constant and survival as a daily task produces a specific sense of isolation in the abuse victim. Because she has found that the world is not necessarily or typically fair and that betrayal is possible, the survivor learns to "look out for Number One" in any way possible—in behaviors ranging from prostitution to violence or manipulativeness to serving as a "doormat" for powerful others. This understanding of human relationships as an adversarial process (as described in Chapter 1) can produce a somewhat paradoxical dynamic: The survivor becomes highly invested in control as a result of chronic feelings of helplessness (Cockreil, 1987, December). She is, in some ways, strongly authoritarian: going "one down" when necessary, striving to be "one up" when possible, but almost always defining her actions in terms of control or power. Thus, for example, "seductiveness" becomes a way to influence dangerous, powerful others (i.e., men), and passivity serves to reassure such beings that their rule will not be challenged. Contact with survivors who especially embody the qualities described in this section (e.g., "street kids" or manipulative patients) may suggest a sense of hardness or undue cynicism; qualities that may be perceived by others as evidence of "badness" or incorrigibility. It is important that the clinician instead understands these behaviors as not freely chosen but rather as the logical extension of the survivor's view of herself and the world.

Self-Hatred

At various points in this book we have described the "low self-esteem" or "poor self-concept" of the sexual abuse survivor. As noted by Roland Summit (personal communication, 1987, April), however, such a relatively mild term does not embody the true extent of self-derogation experienced by some severely abused individuals. A more appropriate term may be "self-hatred," for two reasons. First, it more accurately describes the extent of self-disgust and loathing seen in many survivors of severe sexual victimization. Some former sexual abuse victims, for example, turn the mirrors in their homes to the wall so that, as one woman put it, "I won't have to be reminded of who or what I am." Others describe elaborate self-mutilatory rituals that serve as "punishment" for what they believe to be a basic badness (what one male psychotherapy client refers to as "my original sin").

A second reason for the use of the term "self-hatred" with reference to abuse survivors is its implication of introjection. To hate oneself is somewhat paradoxical: Hatred is most often thought of as an affect directed toward others. To hate oneself, therefore, implies a split of some sort: the one who is hateful, and the one doing the hating. In the case of the sexual abuse survivor (as well as victims of other types of abuse), the "hating" part no doubt arises from the abuse process, where the victim incorporates from others the notion that she or he is essentially bad. Also implicit in hatred, however, is anger. Those we hate we often desire to harm. These combined qualities of self-dislike and desiring to harm/punish self may arise from a variety of abuse-related processes, as described below.

"Stigmatization," as described earlier, refers to the message the child directly receives from her/his abuser during or after victimization (e.g., "you are a whore," "you deserved every minute of it," "you asked for it") or roughly equivalent communications when the abuse is discovered and/or dealt with by others (e.g., the victim-blaming often engaged in by parents, the police, or the courts). These direct sources of disconfirmation, involving verbal statements or labels, are often internalized ("introjected") by the child, ultimately becoming part of his or her self-image.

In contrast to such direct inputs, the victim also comes to devalue herself during the *process* of abuse. Based on the disclosures of many clinically depressed survivors, we may hypothesize that self-blame also arises from early attempts by the child to make sense of her or his victimization (Silver, Boon, & Stones, 1983). Specifically, the child who is faced with painful and/or intrusive events at the hands of an adult is, to some extent, forced to accept one of two possibilities: either (a) "this grown-up/daddy/teacher is hurting me because he/she is bad," or (b) "I am being hurt because I am bad." This "abuse dichotomy" is likely to be resolved in the favor of the child's own badness, given the many social (and abuser-delivered) messages that (a) adults know best, (b) sometimes unpleasant things are done for your own good, and (c) adults sometimes rightfully hurt kids as punishment for things children have done wrong. In addition, from the child's perspective, the notion that one's own parents or caretakers are bad or dangerous may be sufficiently frightening for any such thoughts to be denied or repressed.

"Negative Specialness"

Despite the self-hatred of many sexual abuse survivors, they may experience a paradoxical, almost magical sense of power—the ability to do harm. This arises, in part, from the early injunction to the child "not to tell," that disclosure of the abuse may result in the break-up of the family, the arrest of the perpetrator, or other painful outcomes. The perpetrator may also blame the abuse on the victim, telling her that some quality about her (e.g., her sexuality, "seductiveness," or attractiveness) rendered him incapable of restraining himself. In this way the growing survivor may develop a belief in her own specialness with regard to (typically) males and/or individuals in power. This specialness, however, is usually confined to sexual or sexualized interactions and is often seen by the survivor as further confirmation of the "badness" in herself and in the object of her "power." As expressed with considerable disgust by a former teenage prostitute who was trying to succeed in the "straight" world: "When it's the worst, I always remind myself: This guy isn't any different from any other guy—you can screw him, they all want to screw you. They're all pigs who want what you've got."

Angela G.

Angela is a 27-year-old office worker, who was brought to the attention of her Employee Assistance Program by her manager. She willingly starts counseling with a social worker after demanding (and receiving) a male therapist. She reports in her second session that she was forced to "make love" with her father, beginning at age 8, and her two brothers at age 14. She still "goes out" (has sex) with her oldest brother (now age 32) on occasion, usually when he arrives at her apartment intoxicated. Angela frankly informs her therapist, "I'm not really good at much besides sex," and later asks if he "likes" her. She states, in a challenging way, that she has a "strange power over men," and that "I always get what I want." Her demeanor during therapy is what many clinicians would call "seductive," although the therapist in this instance correctly discerned an underlying anger and brittle desperation. Angela appears paradoxically reassured when the social worker states that sex has no place in the client–therapist relationship, although she comments "Since when?" [Upon questioning, she refuses to identify any therapist with whom she had sexual contact.] She is eventually transferred to a woman therapist experienced in the treatment of sexual abuse victims, to whom she confides that "sex isn't an experience, it's a tool."

This sense of power to control others through sex (and, therefore, shared "badness") may cause some survivor behavior to be seen as narcissistic by psychotherapists, especially when the former victim is able to mask his or her self-hatred. The facade of cynicism and streetwise arrogance may be quite important to the survivor, who needs to feel control over at least some portion of her or his interactions with others, if only those related to further exploitation. More deeply, this "power to do bad" is a projection of self-hatred that may increase over time as a self-fulfilling prophesy: I do bad because I am bad, and I am bad because of what I do.

Conditional Reality

The tendency to view self and the world through assumptions developed during childhood maltreatment has been noted by a number of writers, although typically without reference to abuse per se (e.g., Beck, 1967). Most commonly, this distortion of perspective is understood as an inability to perceive "reality" as it truly exists. There are perhaps two major components to what may be described as the poor reality testing of survivors of severe abuse: dissociative phenomena and impaired self-reference. The first refers to a notion described earlier, that is, that the world of the survivor is frequently dissociated from "real" experience. Individuals whose abuse has produced a significant posttraumatic stress syndrome, for example, may experience flashbacks to the abusive experience(s), periods where they and/or the environment appear unreal, or even episodes of detachment so severe that the survivor has to struggle to "come back" to consensual reality. Given such alterations in awareness, the survivor may even, on rare occasions, appear catatonic or psychotic to the psychiatric observer.

More basically, however, the sexual abuse victim (as well as the survivor of severe physical or emotional abuse) has often been deprived of the experience of self-knowledge. As noted earlier, through the necessity of viewing "other" as critically important in order to avoid greater pain or danger and "self" as irrelevant (i.e., "What difference does it make what *I* feel?"—in fact, "I'm better off not knowing what I feel"), the survivor may fail to develop a personal "map" of reality that is stable across different interpersonal situations.

This paucity of reliable internal landmarks means that the survivor may view reality as a nebulous abstraction that is ultimately conditional, as opposed to concrete. From this perspective, what one perceives may not be true (e.g., the perpetrator's statements that "I'm doing this because I love you," "You made me do this," "That never happened," etc.); it can be verified or defined only by others. The flip side of this process may manifest as "pathological" lying, given the survivor's understanding that reality is not, in fact, "real" but rather a construct that can be molded or altered according to external events. Lies become, then, both a survival technique (as the child learns that misrepresenting "truth" can sometimes forestall abusive or punitive behaviors from others) and a problem (as the survivor becomes increasingly unclear about where the lies end and reality begins). In most cases the personal contingencies for such misrepresentations include the need to escape pain, to be liked or respected by a given individual, or to be someone "better" than who one "really" is.

Fernando C.

Fernando is an 13-year-old male who was referred to a school psychologist for "chronic lying." Reports from his teachers as well as his behavior during a diagnostic interview indicate that this young man makes up elaborate stories on a regular basis without obvious provocation. These stories are often self-contradictory or clearly false, yet it often appears that Fernando believes his fabrications as he relates them (although he rarely remembers them later). Most of these "lies" are self-aggrandizing or self-justifying, although occasionally they are about unrelated events or people. Overall, there is a sad, ingratiating quality about this boy that causes people to pity him at the same time that they castigate him for his lack of truthfulness. School records indicate that Fernando lives in a group home, where he was placed after his father was arrested for involving him in child prostitution and pornography. It appears, however, that the crimes for which his father was incarcerated were only the "tip of the iceberg" compared to the years of extreme emotional, physical, and sexual abuse that Fernando experienced from this man.

The understanding of reality as externally determined also places survivors at significant risk from those who would exploit them or, ironically, treat them. Here, the psychotherapist must understand that what she or he presents as truth (e.g., through depth interpretations or advice) may have greater immediate salience for the former abuse victim than for other clients, since the survivor has a less complete internal model of reality from which to evaluate therapist statements. As many of those who work with sexual abuse survivors will attest, this absence of self-reference is especially problematic when the sexually abused client is seen by a traditionally oriented clinician, who may convince the survivor that he fantasized or (at best) sought out childhood victimization as a result of "Oedipal strivings." As one former sexual abuse victim noted: "It is crazy-making to believe something you're also pretty sure isn't true."

Although the weakness of reality for many survivors of severe sexual abuse may underlie a variety of symptoms and behaviors, including pathological lying, poor boundaries, split-off ego states, and idealization of the therapist, most basically the problem is a disturbance of self, perhaps best described by a male adolescent who exclaimed in frustration during a juvenile hall interview, "Don't you understand? There's nobody inside here to hear what you say. I'm just empty. I just do what happens."

Heightened Ability To Avoid, Deny, and Repress

Withdrawal from stressful or aversion stimuli is a normal, adaptive human behavior. Clearly, it is not helpful, nor healthy, for anyone to dwell upon or constantly confront every painful aspect of life—such activity would not only produce chronic dysphoria, but would also interfere with successful daily functioning. Thus, most people have developed ways to circumvent or ignore some things they otherwise might find distressing. The last core effect presented here refers to the overdevelopment of these coping strategies in the former sexual abuse victim, who has had to become an expert in these areas in order to survive his or her history, but for whom such proficiency ultimately becomes maladaptive.

Avoidance refers to conscious, intentional behavior designed to reduce contact with stressful phenomena. Originally used by the survivor to minimize interactions with abusive individuals (e.g., staying away from home, feigning sickness, or avoiding certain activities in the presence of the perpetrator), such behaviors may later interfere with normal functioning or access to helpers. For example, the survivor who has learned to procrastinate, make excuses, or "disappear" when confronted with an abusive situation may use these same strategies to miss psychotherapy sessions, avoid AA meetings, or keep from attending classes or work.

Somewhat similar to avoidance, denial involves a less conscious attempt to underestimate, not think about, or block complete awareness of threatening events. Some survivors are prone to using such coping behaviors, due in part to their reinforcement in the past (e.g., the relief felt by the child victim when she was able to not completely acknowledge the reality and horror of her abuse situation). Survivor denial can lead to increased gullibility and susceptibility to injurious activities or revictimization, since the individual may "overlook" warning signals that might lead others to avoid specific persons and/or situations. Denial may additionally allow survivors to underestimate the extent of their victimization and its long-term effects, thereby supporting avoidance of psychotherapy or other help-focused interventions.

Thus, although abuse-related denial may temporarily reduce dysphoria, the down side of this defense for the survivor is that attenuating anxiety can disarm early warning systems which might otherwise alert her or him to danger. Herein lies what seems to be a contradiction: How can the survivor be hypervigilant to danger, and yet be unaware of it due to overdeveloped denial mechanisms? This inconsistency is more apparent than real, however, since (a) most survivors predominate in one mode or the other—some tend toward fearful apprehension, whereas others are prone to denial (see Byrne, 1961, for a well-known personality theory which divides most people into "sensitizers" and "repressers"), and (b) even in those survivors for whom denial is a major defense, there is often an underlying tension or "brittleness," which appears to reflect only partially inhibited fearful awareness. This impression of fragility may be accompanied by a facade of extreme positivity (e.g., "I feel wonderful. Everything's great" or "I had a perfect child-hood"), as is often described for "histrionic" clients.

Repression, as the term is used in this book, refers to an unconscious dissociation or splitting off of memories from awareness, in order to avoid the painful affects which would otherwise accompany such recol-lections. This response is not, of course, specific to sexual abuse survi-vors; probably all humans are capable of "forgetting" things that we would rather not confront. What merits the inclusion of this response here is its extreme development in many severely abused individuals (Berliner & Wheeler, 1987; Herman & Schatzow, 1987). As it applies to sexual abuse trauma, and as originally posited by Freud, repression refers to some survivors' ability to banish from memory the most painful aspects of early childhood victimization. Such behavior may be understood as learned, cognitive "solutions" to the extreme anxiety associated with memories of severe childhood trauma (Wachtel, 1973). In its most typical presentation, this avoidance learning results in patchy or incomplete memories of the abuse, so that the survivor may not recall "exactly what happened," while nevertheless having a negative emotional reaction to it. This absence of "hard facts" may be used by the survivor—as well as others in her life—to discount the importance or truthfulness of her abuse. Such repression may also interfere with therapy, since the former abuse victim may not immediately understand the need to address some-thing he cannot clearly recall. As one client put it, "Like they always say, it must not be too important if I can't remember it."

Even more problematic than such partial repression is a phenomenon only recently appreciated by abuse-oriented therapists: complete loss of childhood sexual abuse memories (e.g., Agosta & Loring, 1988). Clients who are completely amnestic regarding their abuse may present with a variety of psychological complaints and issues, such as abnormal reac-tions to sex, repeated involvement in destructive relationships, or inex-plicable anger or distrust of males. Many therapists in the abuse area describe such clients, in whom they see multiple signs of a sexual abuse history despite the client's protestations of a "happy" childhood. Fortu-nately, as described in Chapter 6, many of these individuals recover their abuse memories during therapy—especially if the therapist remains open to the possibility that abuse has occurred.

Summary

These first two chapters have described, in some detail, the potential long-term effects of childhood sexual victimization. We have specifi-

cally referred to "severe and continuous" abuse, even though all sexual
abuse is severe in the sense of "significant." It is important, nevertheless, to recognize the entreaties of workers like Finkelhor (1987, April)
that not all sexual abuse automatically confers major long-term psychological problems. There are many survivors in the general population who appear to have "gotten past" their victimization and who
report few (if any) long-term consequences. Additionally, because most
adults molested as children did not receive appropriate therapy at the
time, the sexual abuse literature is primarily concerned with the effects
of untreated victimization. Thus individuals who have received therapy for abuse may be less likely to present with post-sexual-abuse
trauma in adulthood.

Nevertheless, as has been presented, there are many women and men
whose childhood experiences were so destructive that they continue to
suffer as adults. These experiences are described as severe in light of
their power to overwhelm the victim's immediate resources and/or
equilibrium. Thus abuse severity is a relative notion in the sense that
different victims may have greater or lesser abilities to resist injury—
what may be severe abuse for one person may be less destructive for
another. As noted in Chapter 7, however, certain aspects of sexual
abuse are especially likely to increase its impact, such as early onset,
especially violent or intrusive acts, incest, or extended periods of victimization. People who have experienced these more extreme events
are often among those who come to psychotherapists for help—help
that is not always forthcoming. The rest of this book is concerned with
describing a treatment philosophy and a variety of therapeutic techniques and approaches that may be helpful for such people.

CHAPTER 3

Philosophy of Treatment

Having considered the major long-term effects of childhood sexual victimization, the remainder of this book is devoted to treatment of the abuse survivor. A presentation of abuse effects and treatment techniques alone, however, does not necessarily result in therapeutic effectiveness—even in accomplished psychotherapists. Perhaps even more important than these technical aspects is the therapist's general orientation toward working with sexual victimization. For this reason this chapter outlines a general philosophy of treatment—one that may be relevant to any work with abused or victimized individuals, which is, nevertheless, specifically presented here in terms of the treatment of sexual abuse effects.

The Abuse Perspective

The primary axiom in work with former abuse victims is, we should hope, intuitively obvious at this point: As opposed to other approaches, survivor-oriented therapy specifically focuses on the original abuse context as one of the key issues in treatment, relating this early trauma to later and current experiences and behavior. While other aspects of the survivor's childhood are likely to have been destructive as well (e.g., dysfunctional family dynamics, inconsistent and/or uncaring parenting, psychological or physical abuse by other family members), those symptoms most distressing for the survivor, such as flashbacks, sexual dysfunction, extreme dissociation, certain interpersonal problems, or self-mutilation, are often the direct result of severe childhood molestation experiences and must be approached as such.

Although this analysis may seem obvious to some when the client describes sexual abuse as the presenting problem, it is often harder to convince therapists to focus on abuse issues when (as is usually the case) the client complains of more "garden variety" problems such as chronic self-destructiveness, sexual dysfunction, or being "a woman who loves too much." In such cases subsequent abuse disclosures are likely to be treated as irrelevant to the problems at hand or as remote factors too distant to address. A survivor-oriented perspective, on the other hand, suggests that childhood molestation may be relevant to a variety of adolescent and adult mental health problems, and that therapeutic attention to such "ancient" events may nevertheless have a significant impact on current psychological functioning.

The therapist is counseled to (a) accurately assess the client's current difficulties, (b) determine whether there was sexual abuse in childhood, and then (c) drawing on the relevant literature and clinical experience, consider the possibility that the client's presenting problems arise from his or her molestation history. In the event that an abuse-symptom relationship is likely (obviously not all problems of abuse survivors are due to victimization), the clinician is then advised to approach the problem from an "abuse perspective," as outlined in subsequent chapters. Failure to do so (e.g., ignoring chronic incest in a borderline client) may doom the therapist's best efforts to relative failure, since the etiologic roots of the problem will not have been adequately addressed.

The Question of Truth

Although in many cases, the well-meaning therapist may be willing to accept the relevance of abuse experiences to certain later psychological problems, there are often instances when the client's disclosure of molestation is disbelieved. This tendency to deny that sexual abuse took place often occurs when the client presents as "histrionic" or "borderline" (e.g., dramatic, sexualizing, or manipulative) or appears to be out of touch with reality. In such instances the therapist may assume that the abuse disclosure serves a secondary gain, intended primarily to accomplish increased credibility or greater attention, or that it reflects fantasy material or "primary process thinking" in a highly disturbed individual. As was described in Chapter 2, however, it is exactly this sort of clinical presentation that has been empirically and clinically associated with a history of childhood victimization.

Given this conundrum, the clinician may be left with the question "How do I know what happened, and what didn't?"

Some therapists have dealt with this ambiguity by constructing an internal list of what they believe to be truisms regarding abuse, and then comparing the client's presentation to this list. Among these "truths" are the notions that (a) abuse disclosures should be accompanied by intense negative affect—the client should cry or show some other evidence of obvious psychological pain, (b) the story should be consistent—there should be no major gaps in the recounting, and the major points should be consistent from disclosure to disclosure, and (c) the client should appear authentic—there should be no hidden agendas.

Unfortunately, as noted in Chapters 1 and 2, these litmus tests for abuse are quite likely to be invalid. Molestation disclosures often occur during dissociation, when the client is unconsciously detaching herself from the feelings that accompany replaying an abuse memory. This coping technique may result in either little visible emotional response (affective blunting) or "inappropriate" responses such as laughter, inordinate casualness, or intellectualization. Secondly, the survivor's unconscious attempts to deal with the painful affect surrounding victimization experiences may have generated periods of amnesia or confusion regarding the specifics of the abuse and may be associated with conflicting memories and perceptions (including mixed flashbacks to more than one victimization episode). The client's continuing attempt to "not know" about the abuse (and thus render it nonexistent) may unfortunately be all too successful in the short term, producing questions in the therapist's mind regarding the truth of the disclosure. Finally, sexual abuse often results in disturbed interpersonal functioning, and thus the client's behavior in therapy (an intensely interpersonal process) is likely to include some "gamesy," adversarial, or dysfunctional components.

More basically, the therapist must question herself as to why the "real facts" are so important in treating adults who report childhood molestation. In other areas of psychotherapy, it is often benignly assumed that clients' reports of past events—although frequently distorted by defenses and previous experiences—are essentially true, and the client is rarely cross-examined as to the detailed aspects of her historical account. Nevertheless, some therapists appear to be significantly invested in determining absolute truth or falsehood when the client issue is sexual victimization. It is in this regard that the clinician must examine his or her assumptions: Do I especially question the honesty of this disclosure in part because I have been trained (socially and professionally) to doubt reports of sexual victimization? To the extent that this answer is affirmative, resolution of the veracity question may ultimately become a therapist's (as opposed to client's) issue.

Even if one overlooks the potential bias in helpers' clinical judgments of sexual abuse survivors, there remains a second reason for not unduly confronting "questionable" abuse disclosures—something that statisticians call the "expected value" of a decision. This concept refers to the expected losses associated with a given decison, as opposed to the expected benefits. In the case of sexual abuse, we may restate this problem as follows: What are the negative results of incorrectly believing an abuse disclosure, as opposed to the benefits of correctly rejecting it as false?

In the first instance, one may have been "tricked"—a possibility that many therapists find unacceptable, believing that such gullibility reflects badly on them as clinicians. It is likely, however, that we are often misled, to some extent, by our clients—a state of affairs that may not prove overwhelmingly destructive. On the other hand, "catching the client in the act of lying" may not be especially therapeutic, especially to the extent that the therapist recapitulates, by her behavior, aspects of the original abuse experience (e.g., punitiveness, intrusiveness). Additionally, as described by Summit (1983), such recantations of abuse reports do not necessarily mean that abuse did not occur, perhaps only that the victim was unable to withstand the pressures of doubting interrogation.

As thorny an issue as the above may be, most specialists in the area of sexual abuse agree that only a very small proportion of people who describe sexual abuse experiences "make them up." As has been presented in Chapters 1 and 2, far more likely is the reverse scenario: A therapist is told of a client's sexual abuse experiences and, for a variety of personal and social reasons, disbelieves them. This is the critical part of the "expected value" equation: Although little harm may come from accepting a distorted or technically false disclosure, much damage can be done by a trusted therapist who disagrees with a client about injurious experiences that have actually transpired.

The Question of Responsibility

Just as the issue of truthfulness may come up for therapists working with sexual abuse survivors, another frequent question is in the area of responsibility. As described earlier, it is a common practice in our society to blame the victim, even when he or she is a child. Therapists are no more immune to this bias than any other group, although they may be in a position to do more harm as a result of it. This tendency to assign responsibility for abuse to the victim frequently manifests in psychotherapy as questions such as "What was your part in all this?" or "Didn't you get something out of it, though, for it to have gone on for so long" or even "Deep down, didn't you want it to happen/like it?"

These questions, or their more honest incarnation as direct statements ("interpretations"), often reflect the Oedipal notion that children wish for sexual contact from adults and thus to some extent are responsible for any sexual interactions that subsequently transpire. We need only recall psychoanalyst Henderson's statement that "the daughters *collude* in the incestuous *liaison* and play an active and even *initiating* role in establishing the pattern" (1975, p. 1356; emphasis added) to understand the extent to which the sexual abuse survivor may be blamed in mainstream mental health philosophy. Words such as "collude" suggest a conspiracy between two equals, "initiating" goes further to place primary responsibility on the victim, and "liaison" implies that the abuse experience was an enjoyable, romantic affair rather than an act of exploitation and, possibly, violence.

As opposed to this perspective, abuse-oriented therapy assumes what to many is intuitively obvious: Children have less power than adults, are dependent upon them, and are intellectually incapable of free and informed consent to sex with them (Finkelhor, 1979b). This position must be nonnegotiable for the therapist; as Herman (1987) notes, "a 'neutral' or non-commital stance has no place in the treatment of crime victims" (p. 2). Further, we would argue that it is a misinterpretation to assume that children inherently desire *sexual* contact in the first place—as opposed to needs for nurturance, love, cuddling, and other affectionate expressions. Finally, even in the rare instance where a child behaves in a truly "seductive" manner, as occasionally may happen when she or he has already been sexualized by previous molestation experiences, the adult's moral obligation to resist such approaches is transcendent. As noted by Gelinas (1983):

> It is the adult who has the initiative, the knowledge, the control, and usually the child's loyalty and trust. At times children seek attention and affection in ways that can be construed as sexy; but it is the adult who has the knowledge *and* the responsibility to differentiate between affection and actual sexual contact. (p. 328)

What does this issue mean for work with adult survivors? Most obviously, the victim of an assault or crime is more likely to feel rapport and support from a therapist who sees her as an injured party, as opposed to a guilty coconspirator. As indicated in previous chapters, the survivor is often plagued by feelings of guilt and responsibility—reactions that should be ameliorated, not reinforced. Additionally, certain healing processes in abuse-oriented therapy, such as the healthy expression of rage and other aspects of working through the trauma, require that the survivor understand the extent of her injury at the time and the coping strategies she necessarily marshalled in order to survive (psychologically or otherwise). Obviously, such therapeutic processes are unlikely in an atmosphere where the client is "helped to understand" that either the abuse never happened or, if it did, that it was her responsibility.

The Phenomenologic Perspective

A phenomenologic perspective emphasizes the notions of reaction and accommodation in the development of later abuse-related problems, as described in Chapters 1 and 2. It views many of the symptoms of post-abuse trauma as either logical, adaptive responses to victimization that become inappropriate in the postabuse environment or as conditioned reactions to abuse-related stimuli that persist into later life. This approach denies the need for convoluted concepts in the analysis of abuse-related psychological dysfunction, instead understanding such adult "pathology" as the psychological extension of early reactions and solutions to aversive childhood events. This perspective may be communicated to the client by statements such as: "The things you describe helped you to survive what was a horrible experience. They aren't bad things—they just aren't necessary any more, and they are causing their own problems now," or "I don't see what else you could have done. You're an adult now, but you didn't have adult options or adult power back then."

As well as helping the therapist to understand the child's experience of abuse, a phenomenological analysis points to the need to "stay with the client's experience" in adulthood. Among other constraints, this perspective discourages the use of abstract interpretations or intellectualizations—even when such statements are technically true, let alone when they are based on experientially remote (e.g., Oedipal) concepts. Thus for example, although statements like "It sounds as if you feel out of control of your life, like when you lived with your father" may be appropriate, the interpretation "I wonder if you aren't acting this way so I'll stop you from getting into trouble, and thereby prove I care in ways that your father never seemed to" is not. The latter statement, for example, assumes (a) that the client's behavior is "for" the therapist (although to some extent a possibility, nevertheless a relatively therapist-centered and client-negating comment), (b) that the client is "in control" of behaviors that, in fact, he may experience as compulsive or otherwise "out" of his control, (c) that the client may be symbolically or otherwise covertly requesting that the therapist assume control (something that may more accurately reflect the clinician's needs than the client's), and (d) that the client would ultimately construe such control behaviors as caring.

This injunction to "stay with the client," rather than with a theory that may (or may not) fit her, applies not only to the content of therapist interventions but also to the process of treatment. Most important, the therapeutic process must fit the client's (as opposed to therapist's) current psychological and emotional state, so that the content and process of therapy are congruent with the client's immediate experience and her ability to process new information or feelings. When therapist statements are "out of sync" with the client's present experience, they will be seen either as a disconfirmation of the client's reality (e.g., statements that "It's OK to feel angry" when the client is, in actuality, in a state of mourning—a mismatch that may cause the survivor to believe she *should* feel differently), or as evidence that the clinician, like many others, does not understand her. Although both of these concerns are relevant to work with most clients, the sexual abuse survivor, as described earlier, is especially vulnerable to feelings of "wrong"ness ("I'm not feeling/thinking the right things") or social isolation ("She doesn't understand, either").

Finally, the survivor's internal state must be continually assessed with regard to the pace of therapy. A common danger in this regard is the clinician's tendency to move faster than the survivor is able to follow. This dissynchrony may be due to the fact that while the therapist is "hot on the trail" of meaningful connections and insights, the client is having to confront and integrate frightening memories, images, and affects—a process for which she may feel unprepared. Faced with what appears to the therapist as a sudden unwillingness to deal with certain abuse issues, the clinician may assume that "resistance" has set in and interpret this conclusion to the client. Although the concept of resistance has validity in work with abuse survivors, the primary contribution of a phenomenologic perspective to this issue is a philosophical one; that is, that resistance may be the client's appropriate attempts to "titrate" (adjust the emotional intensity of) the therapeutic process. Such adjustments allow the survivor to digest new ideas or discoveries at her own rate, as well as ensuring her continued control over the psychotherapy session.

At its lower levels, this titration may involve periods of silence, dissociation, not "getting" certain points or concepts, or sudden changes in the direction of discussion. At more extreme levels, this attempt to slow or stop the rapid rate of painful clinician-induced affects may include "acting out," verbal attacks on the therapist, a sudden increase in adversariality, or in the worst case, abrupt termination of therapy. Such client behaviors appear to be, at their roots, further survival behaviors—invoked against currently perceived dangers, as opposed to childhood ones. Perhaps the key notion here is that the client knows best; assuming that she is invested in therapy, she will generally move as fast as her internal processes will allow. In this context, resistance is often a message to the therapist to adjust the intensity or speed of her interventions downward.

Interestingly, respect for the client's need to regulate the flow of therapy does not preclude certain forms of confrontation by the therapist—especially vis-à-vis client distortion of the therapeutic relationship, or his use of defenses so primitive that they render treatment ineffective. Although this issue will be covered in a later chapter, it is noted in passing that the experienced therapist should be able to discriminate between appropriate client reactions to process errors (feedback), as opposed to specific attempts by the client, based on an underestimation of her own strengths, to reduce anxiety by derailing effective psychotherapy (resistance).

Egalitarianism

By definition, sexual abuse occurs in a context of powerlessness, intrusion, and authoritarianism. By the last we refer to relationships where there is a "one up" person who has some form of control or authority over a "one down" person. Since therapy for sexual abuse trauma is intended to remedy the effects of such dynamics, it is important that the treatment process not recapitulate them. Experience suggests, in fact, that authoritarian, power-laden interventions are likely to result in a variety of "negative" survivor behaviors, such as manipulation, rage, or "acting out."

In his or her most obvious form, the authoritarian therapist presents as the all-knowing expert who tells the client what her problem is, how she is feeling about it, and what must be done to fix it. A more sophisticated version of this type of clinician is also common: Implying by her behaviors that she is certain of who the client is and what he needs, this therapist often projects the frustrating message "I know, but

I won't tell." In either incarnation, such therapists are often distant beings who, at best, are most comfortable interacting in the mode of the benevolent parent. Because they are the expert, any setbacks or problems that occur must be the client's fault or due to the client's pathology. Interestingly, such clinicians are often highly invested in a specific notion of "transference," whereby any negative reaction the client has to the therapist is interpreted as the client's long-standing issues with parental figures. Unfortunately, it is more likely that the survivor's reactions to such therapists are precisely because the clinician *is* acting as a harsh parent and/or abuser. In such an environment the survivor is likely to act out unresolved abuse issues, since the current therapy setting actively recapitulates them.

For an example of the potential hazards of authoritarian interventions, consider the frequent correlation between such behaviors and subsequent client "acting out." What is the client to think if (a) the therapist is an expert who, by his behavior, implies omnipotence, but (b) the client continues to feel considerable emotional pain? It must be true, then, that the therapist is *withholding* the cure from the client, since he has the power to bestow it. If so, then either (a) the therapist doesn't like the client and is intentionally hurting him (as did his abuser in times past) or (b) the therapist is insensitive and doesn't know how bad the client is feeling (as may have been true of others in the survivor's early history). In the former instance, the survivor's rage is often restimulated, and a variety of "getting back" behaviors may ensue. In the latter case, the survivor may feel that he has to show the clinician just how "bad off" he is through suicidal "gestures," increasingly disorganized behaviors, or more florid clinical presentations during the therapy session. Additionally, as a result of this perceived betrayal (typically a major issue for survivors, as noted by Finkelhor and others), the therapist may undergo the often cited transition from idealized savior to devalued villian.

As opposed to an authoritarian perspective, abuse-focused therapy is most successful when it fosters a relatively egalitarian atmosphere, whereby the client is seen as an equal partner in treatment. Although this approach does not discount the experience, training, and skills of the therapist (or the power imbalance entailed in any helper-helpee relationship), it nevertheless assumes that, ultimately, the client is the authority with regard to what postabuse trauma feels like, what seems to help, and whether therapy is progressing as it should. It further assumes that therapists are human beings who inevitably make mistakes, and who may not always be able to maintain the empathic bond that guides accurate helping behaviors. Finally, more egalitarian therapy fosters independence in the client; both specifically from the therapist and more generally in terms of his/her own individuation from powerful others.

From this perspective, "cure by the therapist" is replaced with "recovery by the survivor" with assistance from the therapist. This redefinition is not mere rhetoric. Ideally, the client is made aware early in treatment that good therapy is more an environment than an inherently curative procedure, and assuming that the clinician can provide a healing context and helpful guidance, the client is "in charge of her own recovery" (Herman, 1987, December, p. 2).

Growth and Strength as Operating Assumptions

Like a number of other therapies, the philosophy of treatment advocated here for sexual abuse survivors stresses a growth model, rather than a clinical one. The survivor is not seen as inherently "sick" but, instead, as someone who has made entirely appropriate accommodations to a toxic environment. These accommodations were "healthy" at the time of the abuse, and thus the client's current predicament is more one of updating her survival behaviors and perceptions than being cured of an illness. Unfortunately, the abuse environment may have been so insidious and so grievous that these learned responses were, to some extent, "burned in," such that new, seemingly contradictory, learning is often quite difficult. Additionally, by the time the typical abuse survivor is able to access therapy, she has already spent a number of years evolving a life view and an ingrained way of dealing with the world, the bulk of which was directly or indirectly affected by her abuse experiences.

For this reason, the updating of survivor behaviors is a long-term endeavor, both in and out of therapy. One is never "cured" of an abuse history; one can only integrate those experiences and live more fully in the present. In this regard, the client should be warned that she will never not be an abuse survivor—the past will continue to exist as memories, and it will always be a part of her life. In most cases it need not, however, continue to be an overwhelming source of adult "symptoms" and discontent.

In eschewing a pathology perspective, and stressing the adaptive basis of postabuse difficulties, abuse-centered therapy reveals itself to be less interested in client weaknesses than client strengths. In fact, the very term "abuse survivor" emphasizes the fact that the victim persevered despite her or his psychic injuries. In the words of one psychotherapist: "I keep forgetting what she's been through. I think I know what happened, but it's harder to realize that she made it through it all. I'm honestly not sure *I* could have." As will be described in later chapters, this resilience and willingness to struggle should be reinforced and relied upon by the therapist, whose task is lessened by the existence of the "strong, healthy part" in most survivors.

The Context of a Victimizing Culture

Although many clinicians see psychological difficulties as primarily "intrapsychic" events (i.e., caused by internal mental processes), studies in areas as diverse as psychological anthropology, sociology, and community psychology stress the impact of an individual's culture on his or her mental health. Perhaps nowhere is this cultural contribution more obvious than in therapy with victims of socially prevalent acts of violence (Brickman, 1984; Walker, 1978, March). As noted in the Introduction, in our culture about one-third of women and probably one-tenth of men have experienced some form of sexual molestation as children. Such numbers suggest that sexual abuse is, to some extent, a socially supported (or at least not socially prevented) phenomenon, much in the way as has been demonstrated for rape (e.g., Brownmiller, 1975; Malamuth, 1981) and wife-battering (e.g., Briere, 1987; Walker, 1979). This "extero-psychic" aspect of sexual victimization has ramifications for the survivor that should be addressed in therapy.

The cultural aspects of the survivor's victimization are, at minimum, fourfold: (a) adversarial social forces that support the devaluation and exploitation of those with lesser social power (especially women, children, and the aged—each of whom are common targets for abuse in North America), (b) cultural dynamics that seek to deny or discount the results of such victimization, by referring to abuse disclosures as lies or distortions, or by blaming the abuse on the victim, (c) social reactions to the abuse survivor's subsequent behavior, based on his or her "abnormality" and deviation from social norms regarding what is appropriate conduct, and (d) socialization of the psychotherapist, such that he or she, too, is prey to aspects (a) through (c) and thus may be less able to optimally assist the survivor in the process of recovery.

The therapeutic implications of the first three social aspects are substantial. Perhaps most important, and as noted in Chapters 1 and 2, the survivor is frequently driven to understand (construct meaning from) her abuse and thus may benefit from therapy that includes a didactic component. These information-providing functions of abuse-focused therapy ideally work to counter the former victim's socially learned assumptions regarding her victimization, such as the notion that she was responsible for what transpired, or that sexual victimization is a rare occurrence that happens only to abnormal individuals. Therapists who attempt to externalize survivors' self-blame by attributing all aspects of the abuse to the perpetrator alone run several risks. These include the client's continued sense of guilt by association (e.g., "OK, so we were *both* weird") and the likelihood that specific, idiosyncratic aspects of the abuse will be used by the survivor to explain away the abuser's culpability (e.g., "Well, he was drunk at the time" or "He was lonely").

As compared to a "perpetrator only" perspective, a social analysis of sexual victimization may facilitate certain aspects of psychotherapy. Perhaps foremost of these, externalization of the client's self-blame (and stigmatization by others) may be aided by her awareness of social factors such as pornography (Malamuth & Briere, 1986), cultural attitudes supporting the exploitation of those with lesser social power (Butler, 1978; Briere & Runtz, in press,a; Herman, 1981), and the widespread sexualization of female youth by the media (Davidson & Loken, 1987) which indirectly contributed to her abuse. The notions that "it happened because of what I did and who I am" or that "I am different (and worse) than everyone else because of what happened to me" may become less tenable when the survivor truly understands the extent of sexual exploitation and victimization of women and children in our society and, in fact, its prevalence throughout recorded history. Such insights may lead to a healthy anger at "the system"—typically a considerable improvement over equivalent anger turned inward.

Andrea Z.

Andrea is a 43-year-old woman, who works as a secretary at an architectural firm. She has been married for 17 years to the same man, and has three teenage sons. Sexually abused from ages 7 to 13 by an older brother, Andrea has experienced periods of severe depression and anxiety throughout much of her life. Until 3 years ago, her major recourse had been a heavy reliance on "supportive psychotherapy," tranquilizers, and occasional trials of antidepresssant medication, as prescribed by her psychiatrist of 11 years. Although these interventions provided some intermittent relief, they served to convince Andrea that she was "mentally ill" and that she would require medical care for the rest of her life.

When Andrea's therapist retired, she began seeing a female psychiatrist, who insisted she gradually reduce her dependence on medication and start attending a group for incest survivors. Unlike her previous psychiatrist, this therapist stressed the role of victimization in Andrea's chronic distress, suggested various books on incest and women's issues, and continually highlighted the "negative trade-offs" she had been trained to make in terms of giving to other (e.g., as a wife and mother) rather than caring for herself. Initially resistant to her therapist's "feminist" analysis, Andrea eventually became quite excited about the notion that "the problems aren't all me." In the last 2 years of treatment she has not experienced a major depressive episode, although her co-workers and family see her as generally more irritable and "harder to get along with." Andrea, herself, is quite clear about her psychological status: "I was asleep all those years, I really was. And afraid—I was afraid to rock the boat, to complain or speak out. I'm getting stronger now, and more mad than scared. And I'm still growing."

As important as its impact on the content of psychotherapy, a social analysis also highlights the potential for cultural forces to impact on the psychotherapist. If we assume that sexual abusers are, to some extent, socialized as such in our culture, then we must also consider the possibility that these same social forces influence the clinician's perceptions and behaviors as well. As described in Chapters 4 and 10 and has been touched upon in this chapter, such social training may cause the therapist to deny instances of sexual victimization when confronted with them, blame the victim for her molestation when abuse cannot be denied, and discount abuse effects when victimization has been established.

It is the author's experience that such social biases occur at many levels and in many individuals, including well-meaning experts in child abuse. Thus the issue is less one of blaming clinicians whose attitudes are destructive than of confronting the socially ingrained assumptions that reside within us all which may creep into therapy when we least want or expect them to.

Summary

This chapter has outlined some of the major philosophical issues involved in therapy with adults who were sexually molested as children. Overall, it is suggested that optimal work with sexual abuse survivors demands respect and acceptance of the client's personal experience and encourages awareness, growth, and autonomy. The following chapters will include a number of additional recommendations regarding the therapist's orientation to practice with abuse survivors. These suggestions, however, will be more directly integrated with specific techniques or discussion of specific clinical problems.

CHAPTER 4

Vagaries of the Therapeutic Relationship:
Transference and Countertransference

As important as are the specific abuse-focused treatment techniques and activities outlined in subsequent chapters, undoubtedly even more crucial is the quality of the therapeutic relationship per se. Psychotherapy is, ultimately, a highly personal interaction between two people— each of whom is unavoidably the product of a long chain of life experiences. Thus, although we may sometimes wish to see therapy as a corrective "procedure" or clinical "intervention," it is more accurately understood as a special form of human connection. As with other types of relationships, both members of the psychotherapy dyad are vulnerable to biases in perception and expectation as they seek to define and understand one another. Abuse-specific treatment may be especially difficult in this regard, since it directly accesses childhood trauma and thus increases the likelihood that current interpersonal behaviors will be affected by historical events.

When the distortions in perception and expectation occur in the client, we refer to therapeutic "transference," whereas similar effects on the clinician are frequently described as "countertransference." Because of the critical importance of these processes, especially in terms of their ability to derail effective abuse-focused psychotherapy, each is considered in some detail below.

Transference

As we will use the term in this book, "transference" most generally refers to contextually inappropriate perceptions and expectations of significant others in one's adult life—including one's therapist—based on important interpersonal learning that occurred in childhood. This definition is more inclusive than that of the psychoanalytic perspective, which more often focuses on "Oedipal" or "pre-Oedipal" dynamics per se.

The author has found it useful to divide transference, broadly defined, into three overlapping domains: (a) those chronic distortions of adult interpersonal perception tht reflect a general world view skewed by childhood experience, resulting in archaic responses to relevant interpersonal stimuli, (b) more acute, dramatic emotionality, which arises when some aspect of the survivor's current interpersonal environment restimulates childhood issues and/or traumas, and (c) sustained alterations in how a significant person is perceived in adulthood, based on certain similarities to a psychologically important person in the survivor's childhood. A final form of biased perception, not presented here, involves the effects of the survivor's sex-role training, a phenomenon important enough to warrant its own chapter (see Chapter 9).

With regard to the first type of transference, and as noted in Chapters 1 and 2, cognitive theorists suggest that many of our most basic assumptions and beliefs about ourselves, others, and the future are developed during childhood, as the growing person struggles to make sense out of the world she or he encounters. It is through such understanding (sometimes referred to as "cognitive schemata") that subsequent perceptions are filtered. For example, the chronically maltreated child may come to expect abusive responses from those with greater power such that she tends to view interactions with authority figures as basically dangerous. This type of response is more global than what is normally considered to be transference, since it refers to a variety of childhood experiences—frequently with more than one person—that alter the survivor's adult reactions in certain interpersonal contexts.

The second form of transference is more related to PTSD-like responses in that such reactions are often quite brief and are perceived as emotionally intense and psychologically intrusive. Here, the client may encounter an interpersonal stimulus (e.g., a comment or action by her therapist) that produces what is essentially a cognitive flashback to early trauma. This sudden memory, in turn, generates aversive emotional responses, such as seemingly inappropriate emotional outbursts or sudden bouts of fearfulness.

The third form of transference, in which thoughts and feelings about a person in one's childhood are projected onto a psychologically "similar" person in adulthood, is closest to that usually described by psychoanalysts. Most typically, this process involves alterations in how an authority or a love figure is viewed based on the survivor's experience with her or his abuser. As noted by Hinsie and Campbell (1973), this person "is reacted to as though he [sic] were someone from the patient's past; such reactions, while they may have been appropriate to the conditions that prevailed in the patient's previous life, are inappropriate and anachronistic when applied to [the person] in the present" (p. 781).

As the reader may imagine, transference of all three types is typically quite negative for the sexual abuse survivor, since aspects of her early interpersonal reality were characterized by exploitation, betrayal, and/or pain. The world view the victim constructs in this environment logically leads her to see future important others as dangerous and potentially abusive. Additionally, the many instances of trauma in such an environment provides a reservoir of painful memories that can be restimulated by a variety of adult interactions, especially those involving aggression, power, intimacy, or sexuality.

As indicated in Chapters 1 and 2, these various perceptual distortions may generate, in turn, a variety of painful feelings and behaviors—many of which are situationally (but not historically) inappropriate. Among those transferentially based reactions to significant others are episodes of intense fear and rage, extreme reactivity to perceived injustice or abandonment, generalized distrust, sexualization, and adversariality. These responses may occur in interactions with lovers, friends, authority figures, and, most relevant to this discussion, psychotherapists.

Psychotherapy, almost by definition, involves client interactions with a powerful, psychologically important person in an intimate context. In this environment, especially if the clinician is of the same gender as the original abuser, the survivor is easily reminded of similar scenarios early in life and thus is prone to seeing the therapist as a potential victimizer.

Herein lies the "catch" for the survivor: In order to find relief from injuries sustained in one or more abusive childhood relationships, he or she must voluntarily enter into what is, in some ways, an equally threatening one as an adult. The trust and hope that the survivor is somehow able to bring to this new relationship is, nevertheless, almost always incomplete. Also present are those painful feelings the client experienced in childhood and a tendency to utilize those behaviors he or she initially invoked to survive ongoing trauma.

Of the many client responses that appear to reflect transferential dynamics, probably the two most problematic ones for the sexual abuse survivor and/or her therapist are rage and sexualization. Although both are discussed more generally at various points in this book, each is especially prone to occur during abuse-focused psychotherapy, and each is likely to have specific impacts on the treatment process.

Rage

As described in Chapters 1 and 2, the exploitation and psychological injury entailed in most childhood sexual victimization can easily foster a growing sense of anger at one's perpetrator and, in many cases, other nonoffending individuals present at the time of the abuse. This anger may be known to the former victim or may be defended against via rationalization or denial. In the former instance, the survivor may become preoccupied with rageful thoughts, including repetitive ruminations about the wrongness of his or her abuse (e.g., "How could he have done such a horrible thing to me"), the injustice involved (e.g., "I was just a little kid . . . I trusted him and he used me"), and fantasies of retribution (e.g., "I'd like to kill her, stab her, make her hurt like I did"). Conversely, in cases where the survivor's anger is repressed or denied, these cognitions may emerge in disguised or global forms (e.g., "Sometimes I get so mad I could kill someone, but I don't know why") or may be turned inward (e.g., "When I'm around men who come on to me, sometimes I get this surge of hating myself. It makes me want to hurt myself").

The chronic presence of these and similar cognitions understandably places the survivor at risk for sudden and extreme episodes of rage in response to certain interpersonal stimuli—especially those that restimulate feelings of exploitation, injustice, or injury. The net effect of such abuse-related anger may be what appears to be highly inappropriate hostility in otherwise neutral interpersonal contexts. Of particular relevance to this chapter are those angry reactions that occur during psychotherapy as a result of perceived similarities between the therapist-client and abuser-victim relationships.

As will be noted in Chapter 6, the therapeutic relationship often mirrors aspects of the survivor's relationship with his perpetrator, hopefully sans the victimization of the latter. Among these qualities are the notion of relationship per se and the greater authority and power of the other person, as well as the likelihood that the therapist and perpetrator share the same gender and relative age status. Finally, and somewhat ironically, both the therapist and the perpetrator intentionally intrude and impact on the survivor, although their actions and goals obviously differ.

Given these similarities, the "inappropriate outbursts" of anger and the sudden, seemingly inexplicable surges of hostility that sometimes occur in psychotherapy with survivors may be understood as the logical results of restimulated abuse-related rage. Among the many triggers of such affect are implicitly benign therapist behaviors that, unknown to the clinician, nevertheless remind the former victim of her abuser. The clinician's manner of speaking, dressing, or gesturing, or even his tendency to tap his fingers or brush a hand through his hair may evoke client irritability or even verbal attack.

Other therapist activities, however, may be more clearly inappropriate or ill-advised, such as visible impatience, interrupting the survivor's discourse, or appearing to discount her concerns—behaviors that can stimulate client "overreaction" by virtue of their similarity to more extreme abuser actions. Finally, some therapist behaviors paradoxically stimulate angry transferential responses because of their *positive* nature. Caring, complimentary clinician behaviors, for example, may nevertheless trigger survivor rage if, during his childhood, such activities were originally used by his abuser for entrapment or were engaged in to ensure or reward victim compliance. In addition, therapist supportiveness may engender anxiety and subsequent anger in the survivor because he, in fact, values and longs for such attention and thus has more to lose if the therapeutic relationship degenerates or the clinician abandons him.

Sexualization

Although clients' responses to their therapists occasionally include sexually related thoughts, especially during intensive psychotherapy, this potential dynamic is intensified considerably if the client is a survivor of sexual abuse and the therapist is of the same gender as was the original perpetrator. Sexual issues may become even more salient if the survivor was originally forced to participate in her abuse (e.g., trained to stimulate the perpetrator or to behave as if abuse were desirable, as will be described in Chapter 7) or if the molestation occurred over an extended period of time in the context of an ongoing relationship.

Such sexualized interactions with the therapist may include flirtation, sexual suggestions or invitations, dressing or acting in a manner intended to be sexually interesting or arousing. These behaviors are often quite stereotyped, however, almost as if the survivor were acting the role of a seductive person in a play. A prominent characteristic of such client behavior is hypervigilance regarding its effect on the therapist. As noted by one male clinician: "It's not sexy, really, in the sense that the interaction is about sex. It's more as if the issue is a mixture of her wanting to please me and, at the same time, wanting to control me through my reactions to sexually provocative female behavior."

Contrary to common belief, sexualization is not necessarily equivalent to actual sexual interest. Instead, it is the intrusion of sexually related issues into what are not inherently sexual interactions. For example, the client may misperceive (or, unfortunately in some cases, all too accurately understand) her therapist's caring responses as sexual and may therefore respond to them with behaviors that she learned in childhood are indicated in the presence of an attracted male: a sexualized but not sexual response.

Even the more commonly assumed scenario—that of the client who behaves in an explicitly sexual manner—is often not sexually motivated per se, despite the many concerns voiced by clinicians regarding "seductive patients." Instead, the survivor may be (a) making assumptions, based on early abuse experience, about what sorts of basically dissociated and stereotyped behaviors are expected of her by this powerful, frequently male other, (b) seeking support, affiliation, and protection in the only way she knows (the "trading" cited earlier under sexual adversariality), and/or (c) attempting to turn an anxiety-arousing situation into a more familiar one (as several clients have commented: "better the devil you know"). In those relatively infrequent instances where actual sexual gratification appears to be the goal of the survivor's behavior during treatment, such desires frequently reflect the client's conditioned confusion between sexual arousal and (originally coexisting) subjugation such that the underlying motivation is unclear.

Clinical Response to Transferential Issues

Viewed from the above perspective, transference is seen not as a clinical phenomenon per se nor as a therapy-based "neurosis" but rather as the logical extension of the client's childhood experience. It additionally follows from this perspective that (a) client responses to her therapist can provide valuable information to both members of the therapeutic dyad regarding the survivor's early relationship with her abuser and her current response to important or psychologically similar others and (b) that, as relied upon by analytically oriented clinicians, transference provides an opportunity to "redo" or reconsider important childhood issues and interactions as an adult, without violence and exploitation.

It is therefore quite important that the clinician not respond to transferential behaviors as if they were really directed at him or her but, instead, view them as samples of the survivor's understanding of herself and others. The therapist who, for example, responds to rageful behaviors from her client with angry or punitive behaviors of her own is likely to recapitulate the original abuse context and thereby reinforce the survivor's belief that his victimization-based assumptions are correct.

It is not uncommon for abuse survivors to vent transferential anger at their therapists, who then respond punitively, thereby restimulating greater client rage, resulting in even more harsh clinician behaviors, and so on. This downward spiral may eventually end in a frighteningly close approximation of the client's childhood experience of psychological victimization. As noted in a paper by Waldinger (1987) on "Intensive Psychodynamic Therapy with Borderline Patients" (as usual, the reader may wish to substitute the words "survivor of severe abuse" for "borderline"):

> The therapist must be able to withstand the borderline patient's verbal assaults without either retaliating or withdrawing, so that the patient's hostility toward the therapist is not buried but examined and understood as part of a more general pattern of relating to important others. (p. 268)

The need to view transferential anger not only as input regarding the survivor's sense of self and others but also as a chance to more positively impact on what otherwise might be another abuse scenario is noted well by Summit (1987, December), who states that

> the most minor failings from the therapist can trigger torrents of misplaced fury and fledgling righteousness. The need to either apologize or to punish ignores the meaning of the primary betrayal. While the client has every right to enrage or provoke, the therapist must attenuate angry or hurt reactions into supportive, optimistic responses. (p. 2)

Obviously, it is not only angry transference that must not be reciprocated. As noted later in this chapter under "Countertransference," a minority of clinicians (apparently primarily male ones; see, e.g., Holroyd & Brodsky, 1977) are prone to sexual responses to their clients—a destructive state of affairs that may be intensified when the client has formed a sexual transference to the therapist. Not only is therapist-client sexual contact manifestly unethical, and throughout much of North America illegal, it represents the ultimate recapitulation of the survivor's molestation history. From such revictimization the client learns not only that sexual abuse is a chronic event and that she still cannot trust intimacy or relationship, but also that her sexuality is the most (or perhaps only) value that she has for others—even in the supposed sanctity of the client-therapist relationship.

The outcomes described above highlight the ambivalence of the "seductive" abuse survivor. Although manifestly striving to introduce sexuality into the therapeutic relationship, she or he almost never truly wishes it to occur. The message "Let's be sexual (please don't show me that sex is what you want, please say no)" to some extent reflects the underlying conflict for many chronically abused children: Sexual contact signals betrayal and pain but also sometimes produces temporary "love" and support.

Given the distinct possibility of sexualized client behavior, clinicians working with survivors of severe abuse (especially those with major "histrionic" or "borderline" characteristics) must be prepared to respond to such transference in ways that do not reinforce sexualization but remain supportive and helpful. Such therapist responses are typically noteworthy for the presence of three activities: nonparticipation, boundary clarification, and reframing.

"Nonparticipation" refers to the conspicuous absence of therapist involvement in sexualized interactions during psychotherapy. This may be as basic as overlooking the client's "accidentally" disarrayed skirt or not laughing at a sexually explicit joke or as complex as choosing not to encourage client presentation of a sexual issue at a specific point in time, because of one's intuition that the topic has been raised to titillate or arouse. The goal of such studied nonparticipation is the client's perception that sex, although an important issue worthy of therapeutic exploration, is not a useful "hook" or bargaining chip in his or her relationship with the clinician. It is the author's experience that those therapists most concerned about (or reportedly plagued with) "seductive clients" are often among those who unconsciously reward such behaviors with increased attention and reactivity.

There are times, of course, when clinician nonreinforcement is inadequate to deal with client sexualization. The male client, for example, who directly propositions his therapist is unlikely to stop doing so merely because she does not enter into a discussion of her sexual interests. In such instances the therapist must instead address the issue more directly: by clarifying the boundaries between client and clinician and by reframing the client's behavior in terms of its underlying motivation.

Boundary clarification involves the therapist's reiteration of the nonnegotiable limits of psychotherapy, including the absolute inappropriateness of client-therapist sexual or romantic behavior. Such proscriptions need not be presented in a harsh or punitive manner, although threatened or inexperienced clinicians can be prone to a lecturing style in this regard. Instead, the client is reminded of the importance of having a relationship that is neither exploitive nor adversarial, one whose parameters and functions are all aboveboard and therefore more trustworthy and reliable.

Finally, sexualized client behavior can often be rendered unromantic and nonproductive by being carefully analyzed as to its ultimate purpose in the session. This analysis may be positive in the sense that it affirms the survival basis of such behaviors and their logic earlier in life. Thus, for example, client "seductiveness" in a given session may be reframed by the therapist as an expression of the importance of the therapeutic alliance to the survivor, and as a way for the client to communicate her need for reassurance, approval, and even self-determination. Such reframes are perhaps most effective when they (a) directly identify the sexualized behavior (b) interpret it as a historically logical but currently inappropriate way of communicating other needs, and (c) focus attention on the underlying emotional or interpersonal issues that motivate such behavior. When done well, such therapist feedback may be received quite positively by the survivor, since it implies both deeper understanding and an unwillingness to be derailed from the process of assisting the client in her recovery.

Impact on the Therapist

Transferentially based survivor issues require considerable effort and clarity from the clinician. He or she not only must correctly respond to evocative and/or challenging behavior, but also must keep from reacting on a personal level—despite the potential for survivor dynamics to bring to the fore the therapist's own childhood issues or socially learned biases. As noted in the next section, this task is rarely completely accomplished, although, as described in Chapter 10, careful attention to one's own issues, needs, and socialization can usually forestall the potentially destructive aspects of negative countertransference.

Countertransference

As opposed to "client transference," "countertransference" is defined here as biased therapist behaviors that are based on earlier life experiences or learning. The therapist, despite her or his training and professional demeanor, is electing to enter into an intense, probably long-term relationship with someone who is interpersonally dysfunctional and whose issues may stir up or echo unresolved aspects of the clinician's early life. There are two major sources of negative therapist countertransference to abuse-focused psychotherapy: the therapist's own childhood experience of abuse, maltreatment, or neglect, and issues related to therapist gender.

Therapist's Abuse History

Based on the incidence data reported earlier in this book, we might predict that about one-third of female therapists and perhaps 10 to 15% of male therapists have sexual abuse histories, and that much larger percentages of each have been physically and/or emotionally victimized in childhood. Even disregarding the author's impression that psychotherapists are considerably more likely than others to have been maltreated as children, it is probable that child abuse issues have personal relevance for many therapists.

The impact of one's own abuse history on working with survivors varies from person to person and from one situation to the next. On the one hand, if one's abuse has been worked through in one's own therapy or in some other manner such that one's responses are integrated and relatively conscious, the experience of having "been there" can definitely be an asset in working with survivors. As a survivor herself, the therapist is likely to have a basic understanding of her client's dynamics, as well as a sense that positive outcomes are possible. On the other hand, individuals who are still at odds with their abuse, who use denial, dissociation, or splitting to deal with abuse-related dysphoria, are likely to discover that working with other people's victimization issues restimulates their own. This restimulation, in turn, usually increases the problems described in Chapter 10, such as PTSD symptoms and over- or underinvestment in the client.

Perhaps most typical of the intrusion of the therapist's abuse issues into his treatment of survivors is the problem of projection. Specifically, because his victimization experiences are still "alive and well," although often split off from consciousness, they may be activated by the client's disclosures. This process may lead the therapist to project (misperceive and misattribute) his own difficulties onto his client's. Thus, for example, the unconsciously angry therapist may interpret client behaviors as rageful when, in fact, they more accurately reflect sorrow, or may push the client to confront her abuser when her strongest desire is actually to escape him. Similarly, the fearful therapist may counsel the client to be careful, to watch out, to be constantly vigilant for danger, or to forego challenging experiences.

Another common problem in such treatment situations involves avoidance and denial. Because the repressing therapist spends considerable psychic energy keeping her abuse out of consciousness and her anxiety down to manageable levels, she may unconsciously work to prevent the client from exploring her own memories and feelings. In such instances the clinician may actually become resentful of the client for restimulating her repressed memories or affects and may present to her supervisor or consultant with statements such as "I don't know why, but that woman makes me so mad" or "His self-indulgence is really irritating. He just can't seem to put his past behind him!"

Finally, abuse victims who have become therapists in an attempt to understand or heal themselves may find that they are, instead, overwhelmed by the needs and problems of survivor clients. As a result, psychotherapy may become chaotic, and boundaries between helper and helpee may blur or in some instances dissolve. The author has consulted on cases, for example, where the client ultimately became the "strong one" in the sessions and was actively working to put the therapist back together. Less dramatically, the therapist may come to rely on the client for validation and support, such that client anger or even "failure to improve" is seen by the therapist as a personal attack or invalidation. Because the client survivor may have had many years of experience with role reversal and boundary violations, she may have little sense that such situations are inappropriate. In instances where her projected anger toward the therapist (as described earlier) evokes inappropriate therapist anger in return, she may additionally perceive the therapy environment as verification of the continuing need for adversariality in adult relationships.

Gender-Related Issues

As noted by Herman (1981), therapist reactions to survivors may also be affected by their gender, especially in response to female clients. While not strictly a countertransferential process per se, in the sense of representing the biasing effects of personal history, the lessons of a sexist or sex role stereotypic society are nevertheless learned early in life and quite commonly distort subsequent interpersonal perception and expectation. Males in our culture, for example, are socialized in adolescence by peers and role models to view most emotionally intimate relationships as potentially sexual ones (Finkelhor, 1984), resulting in a tendency to respond to certain essentially nonsexual interactions as if they were sexual in nature. Given this proclivity, male therapists must somehow unlearn this false equation early in their clinical careers (and, it is to be hoped, in their personal lives) if they wish to relate in nonpredatory ways toward women. Not all male therapists have done this, however, and thus some are prone to sexualizing female clients during psychotherapy.

This sexualization dynamic may be intensified, as noted earlier, in the presence of the female abuse survivor, whose frequent neediness and tendency to respond to male power with acquiescence or pseudosexual behaviors may make her an obvious target for various forms of revictimization during "treatment." Even those instances where such therapists do not behave in an overly sexual manner, their attention to the sexual aspects of the survivor's presentation (e.g., her attractiveness, anatomy, or disclosures regarding sexual issues) can alter the agenda from healing to adversariality and further harm. As described by Herman (1981): "The male therapist's sexual response evokes in the patient all her original feelings of shame, guilt, and disappointment, even when the therapist is careful not to act on his feelings" (p. 187).

Because of this potential for revictimization, a number of writers suggest that female abuse survivors should be seen only by female therapists. The current author agrees with this concern, as described in Chapter 8, and recommends that women see women in therapy if an effective female therapist is available or, in any event, if the client requests one. It is not his experience, however, that all male therapists demonstrably sexualize their female clients, just as not all female psychotherapists are effective in the treatment of sexual abuse trauma in females. Thus in the absence of an available, qualified female clinician, male-female therapeutic dyads may be inevitable. The issue then becomes one of determining which male therapists are appropriate for female survivors and, more globally, how the effects of male socialization can be ameliorated so that such screening is no longer necessary. The latter task is a long-term one, of course, requiring changes not only in society as a whole but also specifically in the clinical training system that produces psychotherapists.

The potential gender effects on female therapists, although more benign in terms of sexualization, can still be substantial. The most frequent impact is probably overidentification. The therapist may closely relate to her female client's experience of victimization, based on her own history of being the target of male aggression, or her fears of such aggression. For example, it is probably far different for a male therapist to hear of a rape of a 13-year-old girl than it is for a woman to do so. The man, although perhaps empathic and sensitive, can understand the act of rape only intellectually unless he was, in fact, raped or feared raped himself at some point. The woman, on the other hand, who has approximately a 44% chance in her lifetime of being a victim of rape or attempted rape (Russell, 1983), has undoubtedly feared the possibility of sexual assault since early adolescence and may additionally fear the molestation of her own children in ways that differ from those of their father.

As Herman (1981) reports:

> The female therapist generally tends to identify with the victim. Her first reaction to the incest history may be feelings of helplessness and despair. She correctly recognizes the patient's childhood feelings of betrayal and abandonment, but she may find these feelings so overwhelming that she is unable to react calmly. (p. 182)

This overidentification with one's own potential victimization may produce one of two patterns. Most commonly, such clinicians respond, as Herman notes above, with agitated concern and extreme nurturance and/or with the overinvolvement described in Chapter 10. The therapist's preoccupation with the horror of the client's experience may be additionally perceived by the client as evidence of her own deviance or of her being in some way irrevocably "broken." As one client put it: "When she got all excited like that, it made me feel like I was a head case, or at least worse off than I thought; I figured that I was a bad case to be able to do that to someone who heard problems all day long."

The second pattern is one of denial. In an attempt to keep the pain and/or fear of victimization well tucked into her unconscious, or to reassure herself of the justness of the world and therefore of her own continuing safety, the clinician may adhere to a perspective that either denies the abuse took place or doubts its negative impact. Such clinicians are typically viewed by their survivor clients as harsh and, ironically, parental. Thus a tragedy unfolds: Because of her actual extreme empathy for the abuse survivor, the therapist may be especially nonsupportive of her. The client soon learns that there are things that you shouldn't talk about in therapy—otherwise one's therapist may become upset and rejecting. The net effect is the clinician's modelling of denial and psychological avoidance, processes that may serve to drive the survivor's symptoms underground.

On Boundaries and Limits

The material presented in this chapter thus far has stressed the reactive aspects of transference and countertransference. From this perspective, therapeutic behaviors are seen as, to some extent, mutually projected, and based on restimulated childhood issues. Also relevant to the psychotherapeutic relationship, however, is the tendency for child abuse to interfere with the development of durable interpersonal boundaries, as described in Chapter 2. This developmental arrest, in turn, may lead some survivors to misunderstand the constraints of the therapeutic relationship, such that treatment is used to satisfy unmet social needs, or is avoided as manifestly unsafe.

An early experience of many psychotherapists-in-training, in this regard, is that of working with a "borderline" client who either (a) responds to an appropriate therapeutic behavior as though it were a personal invasion or, more frequently, (b) seeks to transcend the parameters of the therapeutic relationship. Such clients, as noted earlier, are frequently abuse survivors, and the extremity of their issues in this area can be understood as reflecting the blurred or nonexistent boundaries characteristic of most childhood sexual exploitation (Reiker & Carmen, 1986). Such boundary problems can arise from early learning regarding the roles and responsibilities of adults versus children and parents versus daughters/sons; however, they can also reflect the very notion of invasion of one's body and psyche by another.

Abuse survivors who "overreact" to what they believe to be invasion by their therapist are often individuals for whom hypervigilance and resistance were primary counterabuse strategies during childhood. Their complaints that the clinician is asking too many questions, "getting too close," inappropriately rejecting "I don't know" as an answer, or "spending too much time on abuse" partially reflect, as noted in this chapter, the fear that their childhood trauma will be recapitulated—symbolically or actually—in the therapy session. Because the survivor's early victimization often took place in the guise of relationship, intimacy, or authority, such clients may find similar themes in psychotherapy threatening.

More frequently, however, the survivor combines such resistance with a desire to transform the psychotherapeutic relationship into something "more," such as friendship, love or an affair. Having learned early in life that formal roles may have little to do with actual behavior, and often feeling profoundly empty and needy, the survivor may attempt to create the perfect friend/lover out of the typically idealized therapist.

This felt negotiability of relationship, along with the tendency for some survivors to sexualize or seek to control power relationships, may manifest as propositions during therapy (sometimes irrespective of therapist gender), requests to "go out for lunch," invitations to parties, extensive questioning or covert investigation with regards to the clinician's personal life, and so forth. At a lower level, the client may ask for the therapist's home phone number and if it is given, use it regularly for small crises or "just to talk" or may ask for a small loan or a ride to work or school. The bottom line of such interactions is often predicated on two related assumptions: (a) that the therapist is "really" willing to convert psychotherapy into sex, friendship, or other forms of intimacy and (b) that, once "found," psychotherapists should be available for gratification of the client's nurturance and dependency needs.

Given some survivors' problems in this area, an important aspect of work with postabuse trauma involves explicit discussion with the client about the nonnegotiable limits and parameters of psychotherapy (Sgroi & Bunk, 1988). These concrete statements about the overall framework of the therapeutic relationship thus serve three purposes: First, they reassure the hypervigilant client that the therapist, unlike her abuser(s), is not interested in turning one relationship into another, more exploitative one, and thus he is intentionally describing the "outer limits" of their relationship. Second, discussion of therapy boundaries sets rules for the client who seeks nontherapeutic contact, so that she is less likely to misinterpret refusal to, for example, go to a movie together as a personal rejection. Third, concrete limits and parameters protect the psychotherapist by containing the evocative aspects of treatment, thereby reducing the likelihood of major counter-transference.

What should the parameters of abuse-focused psychotherapy be? Although each therapist must decide this for herself, based both on her own orientation to treatment and her assessment of her strengths and her client's needs, the following are ground rules that the author eventually developed in his own therapeutic work with survivors.

1. Regular appointment times are specified, well in advance.
2. Regular starting and ending times are enforced for any given session with exceptions made only in times of real emergency. This means, for example, that a client who appears a half hour late usually has only a half hour session.
3. A relatively limited amount of time is allocated per session: 1 hour in most cases, 1½ hours in exceptional situations.
4. The client is seen for no more than two sessions per week, except if she or he is hospitalized or is in extreme crisis.
5. The therapist declines, in all but the most unusual cases, to give out his or her home phone number or home address, although an intermediary answering service or clinic phone number for emergencies is appropriate. When the client calls an intermediary in crisis, the therapist seeks to be briefly available (usually by phone).

If this availability becomes overused, the issue is dealt with in succeeding sessions.

6. No psychotherapy session is held if the client arrives drunk or otherwise intoxicated, except in an emergency involving danger to the survivor or others.

7. Touching or hugs are avoided for both sexes, unless obviously appropriate, and then usually only after therapy has been in effect for some time and the meaning of physical contact (i.e., an end-of-session hug) is fully understood by both parties.

8. No contact occurs outside of the therapy session (e.g., no luncheon engagements, etc.).

9. The client is explicitly informed of the therapist's "duty to warn" others and to protect the client in instances where he expresses intent to harm himself or others, such as child or elder abuse, physical retaliation, or gross suicidality. In such instances the client is aware that the therapist will call the police, contact child/elder welfare authorities, or seek psychiatric hospitalization (involuntary if need be) to prevent serious self-harm. Otherwise, the client's rights to confidentiality and self-determination are carefully honored.

10. Threats or acts of physical violence against the therapist are usually grounds for termination and transfer.

11. Finally, in instances where a direct fee is involved (e.g., private practice without insurance), clear policy is established with regard to when and how payment is to be made.

As mentioned earlier, these are a subset of all possible parameters that might be placed upon the therapeutic relationship. The specific arrangements between a given client and therapist are expected to vary.

Conclusions: The Therapeutic Relationship Revisited

As described in this chapter, there are several potential barriers to effective abuse-focused psychotherapy, primarily resulting from the psychological power of childhood maltreatment for both the clinician and the client. Additionally, as also noted in Chapter 3, treatment for the effects of abuse occurs within the same social matrix in which such victimization took place, and thus the treatment process may be compromised by equivalent social dynamics. These various impediments need not necessarily derail effective psychotherapy, however, if the client's projection of early issues onto therapy is not overwhelmingly intrusive, if treatment boundaries can be maintained, and if the clinician is sufficiently aware of (and able to control) her or his personal issues and biases.

In fact, the process of transference—when handled appropriately—can enrich the treatment process by encouraging the client to confront and directly rework abuse-based issues in the relative safety and supportiveness of the therapy session. Thus, the survivor in effective psychotherapy may (a) initially have unduly negative expectations and understandings of therapy and the therapist, which (b) slowly give way to more positive and accurate perceptions as treatment progresses and these assumptions are gradually seen to be inconsistent with the clinician's caring and trustworthiness, leading to (c) new learning about the potential for significant others to be benign and nonexploitive, despite their surface similarities to the original abuser. This process is far superior to merely being *told* that not all powerful beings are dangerous, since it allows the survivor to experience this fact *in vivo*.

The ultimate repercussions of such transferential learning can include decreased difficulties with authority, greater trust in relationships, a clearer sense of interpersonal boundaries, and the development of affiliative (rather than solely defensive or adversarial) social skills. Most basically, however, successful resolution of negative transference teaches the survivor that her abuse—as heinous as it must have been—is a historical event, not an inevitable outcome for present or future relationships.

CHAPTER 5

Specific Therapy Principles
and Techniques

This chapter introduces a number of specific procedures and approaches that the author and others have found useful in working with sexual abuse survivors. Before these tools are described, however, a point arising from the material presented in Chapter 4 should be emphasized: No "techniques" can replace the mutual respect and stable, affirming relationship offered by good generic psychotherapy, irrespective of whether or not it is abuse oriented. There are many psychotherapists who, given attitudes similar to those described in Chapter 3, provide good treatment for abuse survivors without changing their usual therapeutic style. Thus the interventions suggested by the current chapter should be seen as further sharpening or focusing of what may already be effective therapy.

An obvious corollary to this point is that use of these techniques will not necessarily make one a helpful therapist—one must already be able and prepared to listen and accept, to support, and to gently confront when necessary, all the while remaining neither too close nor too distant. Many things aid in the development of such core therapist qualities, including one's own therapy, experience in working with traumatized people, and the time and energy to introspect on "the meaning of it all." The latter point, as well as other aspects of being a therapist who works with survivors, is covered in detail in Chapter 10.

Normalization

This treatment principle is not specific to abuse survivors; it is also used with victims of other forms of violence, such as rape and wife-battering. As described earlier, many victims of socially prevalent abuse paradoxically feel ashamed, believing that they and/or their experiences were abnormal (Coates & Winston, 1983). Typical of this stigmatization dynamic (Finkelhor & Browne, 1985) are statements like "I must be weird to have had this happen" or "I feel different from everyone else—I can't tell them what happened." This sense of shame and isolation can be especially profound for the sexual abuse survivor because, in many cases, he was directly told as a child that he was to blame, that the abuse reflected something about him, and that he must keep his victimization a secret. Normalization, as might be predicted, refers to therapist interventions that help the survivor to understand that his current behavior is not "weird" or "abnormal" but, rather, an entirely understandable reaction to his childhood experience. Thus we may consider this process one of destigmatization.

Information

One of the most direct forms of normalization occurs when the therapist shares information with the client regarding (a) the high frequency of abuse in our society, thereby conveying the message that "you are not alone," (b) the abuser's and society's (not the victim's) culpability regarding the molestation and its impact, and (c) the common psychological effects of sexual abuse. The last, although admittedly focusing on what may be understood as pathology, often gives the survivor her first inkling of the fact that *abuse*, as opposed to something intrinsic in her, produced a number of the problems in her current life. Thus she may begin to understand that her reactions are, in fact, predictable responses to having been hurt by another person. Especially useful in this regard is early discussion of the symptoms of PTSD as they relate to sexual victimization and the more specific aspects of post-sexual-abuse trauma, as described in this book and elsewhere.

Information on sexual abuse may be presented in several ways. In addition to direct therapist statements (i.e., the teaching component of abuse-related therapy), the clinician may suggest one or more of the currently available books on sexual abuse. Among the best of these are Sandra Butler's (1978) *The Conspiracy of Silence*, Judith Herman's (1981) *Father-Daughter Incest*, Florence Rush's (1980) *The Best Kept Secret*, and Gil's (1978) *Growing Through the Pain*. A benefit of the last book is that it is, although somewhat brief, specifically written for adults who were molested as children.* There are also a number of

---

*As this book was going into press, a self-help manual written by Ellen Bass and Laura Davis (1988) became available. Upon first reading, this book appears to be an excellent resource for abuse survivors.

books written *by* sexual abuse survivors about their experiences, some of which (e.g., the one by Louise Armstrong) can be quite helpful. A small minority, unfortunately, are of lesser quality and may, in fact, have a sensationalistic slant—a message that obviously works against normalization.

Contact with Other Survivors

As is discussed at greater length in Chapter 8, another effective way for former victims to understand and integrate their abuse experiences is through interactions with other survivors (Coates & Winston, 1983). Whether this occurs in group therapy or self-help settings or through affiliation with abuse-oriented organizations, the net effect may include (1) the *in vivo* debunking of various social myths regarding sexual abuse (e.g., "I know what you mean. I thought it was my fault, too") and (2) a growing sense of normality derived from sharing past experiences with other group members (e.g., "You mean you sometimes feel the same way?"). Judith Herman (1981), in her discussion of the benefits of group work, notes that such survivor-to-survivor interaction

> offers a fuller opportunity for the resolution of feelings of shame and guilt . . . For while each woman fully believes herself to be a terrible sinner, she generally does not feel the same way about the others in the group. She is better able to identify ways in which the others were coerced and victimized. As one member of a group commented: 'I heard what happened to all those women. They didn't do anything wrong.' Sooner or later, each participant is able to apply the group's more tolerant judgement to herself. (p. 195)

Therapist Clarification

In addition to information and perspective provided by the clinician, books, or other survivors, certain therapist activities may serve a normalizing function. Specifically, the clinician may engage in cognitive therapy regarding the client's feelings of abnormality, shame, and isolation (Briere & Runtz, 1988c). This involves asking the client to concretely describe those thoughts or interpretations of memories that cause him to feel as if he is intrinsically bad or different from others. When these cognitions are described, for example, "What we did was nasty, and I know that people would be disgusted with me if they found out," the therapist may gently work with the survivor to disentangle the connection between bad things happening to him and his being bad.

This process does not, however, involve the therapist lecturing the client on her "illogical thinking" as much as it reflects a spirit of "why is it that when A happens to us, we often think B?" The intent of such clarification is the client's growing awareness of negative assumptions she makes regarding the meaning of the abuse, both in terms of how she sees herself and how she construes her value to others. In this way the therapist may respectfully disagree with the client's (often socially conveyed) assumptions and provide the necessary questions and feedback to permit her to reexamine these beliefs. As is true of cognitive therapy for other problems, such interventions must be accompanied by consistent support and patience, since abuse-related beliefs are often slow to change. The eventual result, however, especially in a therapeutic environment that avoids criticism or blame, may well be worth the effort. A specific form of this approach will be presented later in this chapter under the heading of "Tape Recognition."

Facilitating Emotional Discharge

Most papers and texts on the treatment of PTSD emphasize the need for adequate emotional discharge, whether the trauma be war experiences (e.g., Williams, 1980) or rape (e.g., Burgess & Holmstrom, 1979). It is now recognized that, although trauma often brings with it a tendency to avoid any feelings or events that might remind the client of his or her experience (Horowitz, 1976), release of emotion is nevertheless a necessary condition of full recovery. The restorative aspects of emotional discharge ("catharsis") were probably first truly understood during the Korean War, when "shell-shocked" (traumatized) soldiers were briefly removed from the front lines and encouraged by medics to express their fear and rage—a process that often allowed them to return to battle as "useful" warriors.

Although catharsis is easily as helpful an activity for sexually abused children (Berliner & Wheeler, 1987), there are a number of reasons why it may be less accessible to the survivor as she grows older. As indicated earlier, the victim of severe sexual abuse eventually learns to suppress the experience of painful emotion, since such distractions may interfere with the daily task of avoiding trauma and maintaining sanity. She or he develops a variety of coping strategies just to *keep* from feeling (e.g., dissociation, repression/denial, acting out, substance abuse). By learning to block out the pain, the former abuse victim invokes a short-term solution to postabuse trauma: "What I don't know (allow into experience) can't hurt me."

As presented in Chapter 6, these defenses against abuse-related feelings are typically present in full force during psychotherapy, since the client clearly understands that intense affect might otherwise be likely. Because repressed emotions are often quite powerful, and given that the survivor equates feelings with (in some sense) nonsurvival, the former abuse victim may actually believe that emotional release is dangerous. The most common fears in this regard seem to be (a) of being overwhelmed or swallowed up by intense affect, (b) of losing control and either acting on sadness (suicide) or rage (homicide), and (c) of somehow magically returning to the abuse by virtue of feeling abuse-connected pain. The first concern may present as powerful feelings of impending insanity or even, in some severe cases, death, whereas the last two are often seen as a loss of control. Unfortunately, all three may seem real to the survivor during early experiences of emotional release in therapy, when a flood of repressed, seemingly primitive feelings come to the forefront. One of the valuable lessons that therapy can bestow in this regard is that one can, in fact, feel "bad" feelings and not be annihilated or lose complete control.

Given some survivors' "dread of affect" (Blake-White & Kline, 1985) and fear of loss of control, the clinician must obviously approach the necessary task of feelings with care. She must additionally understand that the issue is not merely one of "feeling your feelings" but also one of safety and relative trust in the therapist to (1) protect the client from negative outcomes (e.g., "losing it") and (2) not revictimize her during this period of maximal vulnerability (Merriam, 1988, April).

As discussed at length in Chapter 7, the therapist herself must be prepared for the client's intense emotional responses—especially the overwhelming rage and self-hatred of some "borderline" survivors. More than one clinician has encouraged catharsis in a severely abused client only to retreat and invoke medication/hospitalization/referral upon experiencing the weight of "unacceptable" client emotion.

Inherent in this last concern is an overriding principle of work with survivors: One must convey (and believe) that all emotions are good such that emotional expression is understood as a positive thing. This holds both for what Blake-White and Kline (1985) refer to as "surface emotions" (e.g., anger and sadness) and "the stronger emotions of terror, despair, abandonment, . . . fear of pain and the fear of being totally alone and overwhelmed" (p. 397). To this latter list we might add rage, as described by Anderson (1986):

> Rage is a particularly potent emotion and probably the one that evokes the most anxiety both for the survivor and for significant others in her life, including her therapist. It is not unusual for a survivor to have violent fantasies of what she would like to do to the perpetrator, or these fantasies may be directed at herself. She may be terrified that if she allows herself to feel rage, she will be compelled to act out the fantasies . . . (p. 8)

This fear of loss of control over one's (often intrusive) impulses is common among survivors of severe sexual and physical abuse, and thus it is important to stress to the client the differences between feeling and doing: helping him to express the former while developing other ways of dealing with his need to "do something" to terminate painful affect. Specific suggestions for the latter follow in the section "Self-Control Techniques." It should be noted at this point that such affects rarely translate into action as a direct result of their being examined in therapy; more typically, acting out emerges in response to aspects of the therapeutic relationship, per se, based on the client's perception of abandonment, rejection, or judgement.

Although in many cases the survivor will not have expressed much of the affect she experiences with regard to her victimization, there exist in the case loads of most abuse specialists survivors who continually display what appear to be deep feelings yet whose emotional expression has a repetitive quality (what some therapists refer to as "the broken record syndrome"). This pattern is in relative contradistinction to the behavior of other abuse survivors in therapy who have difficulty "getting into" feelings but, after a period of time, eventually work through their repressed affect and experience a noticeable lessening of emotional pain.

Although there may be several reasons for such nonproductive emotionality, this problem most frequently arises from a distinctive form of dissociation—referred to in Chapter 6 as "as if." Specifically, the client may split off her affect from her thoughts, so that she does not have to, in fact, experience the pain she is expressing. Unfortunately she is also unable to develop emotional insight or closure during the grieving/raging process. The ultimate result of this defense may be a person who gains some momentary symptom relief from the discharge of painful affect but who cannot integrate her emotionality and thus is driven to repeat it indefinitely. Intervention approaches for individuals in this dilemma will be presented in Chapter 6. It may be noted at this point that therapist behaviors that keep the client psychologically present during intense affect and that focus on the (often chronic) cognitions that underlie repetitive emotional discharge may have a positive impact.

Final issues with regard to catharsis are the related concepts of structure and closure. The survivor's decision (whether conscious or unconscious) to allow herself the vulnerability of emotional release must be met by an equivalent commitment by the clinician to provide some elements of safety during this process. In addition to helping the client to see that no catastrophic outcomes magically follow expression of deep feeling, the therapist will ideally structure the session so that the survivor slowly works her way to emotional intensity and is then brought back down well before the end of the interview. In this way the process of catharsis is organic, in the sense that it slowly grows during therapy and remains under the control of the client. Because the session ends as it started, with the client at a baseline feeling state, there is an opportunity for reasonable closure—in the sense of discussion and integration of what transpired during the session. This debriefing prior to the end of the therapeutic hour allows the client to normalize her experience and, as one survivor put it, "regain my dignity." Such reconstitution also decreases the likelihood that the client will be embarrassed or frightened by her "loss of control" and act out or fail to return for the next session.

Disrupting the Abuse Dichotomy

As noted in an earlier chapter, one result of the victim's early attempts to extract meaning from her abuse (especially in the case of incest or abuse by a loved one) may be the "abuse dichotomy." Briefly, this dynamic, which is most commonly present in severe sexual or physical abuse, frequently proceeds as follows: "(1) I am being hurt (emotionally or physically) by a parent or someone I care about, (2) therefore either (a) I am bad or (b) he/she is. However (3) I have been taught that adults are always right and hurt you only as punishment when you are bad. Therefore (4) it must be my fault that I am being hurt, and thus it follows that (5) I am as bad as whatever was/is done to me." This dichotomy that "either I am bad or they are," especially given the added proviso that "it isn't them," may continue into adulthood in an unconscious, relatively unchanged form. Although such black or white thinking may be appropriate for the age group of the average child victim, it can be quite problematic later in life. In its more severe forms, this dichotomy may be seen as "borderline ideation," although in most cases it is far less apparent as it fuels continued guilt and inwardly directed anger.

Intervention in the client's abuse dichotomy, although effective when successful, should be attempted with care. Specifically, the therapist must "take the side" of the client (tip the balance of the dichotomy toward the victim) and yet somehow avoid the paradoxical loyalty of the survivor toward her (often still loved/valued) abuser. If handled poorly, the survivor may experience guilt at ironically, "betraying" her perpetrator by saying negative things about him, and end up defending him to the clinician—thereby potentially reinforcing the abuse dichotomy to her detriment. As Gelinas (1983) notes, in the case of incest:

> Whether immediately apparent or initially invisible, the loyalties among family members continue to operate long after childhood. If ignored by the therapist, these loyalties will function as resistance in treatment. . . . (p. 328)

How this therapeutic tightrope is walked by the clinician will vary from instance to instance. Often the message communicated to the client may be to this effect:

> It is understandable that you feel two ways about your father/ uncle/friend: there are things about him/her that you love. It is also true that he/she hurt you, and you are still feeling the pain all these years later. You don't have to give up the caring right now, or maybe ever—it's a wonderful thing about you that you have the ability to still care about him/her. What we need to do together, now or some other time, is understand what happened: what he/she did, and how you felt. Do you think you can let yourself feel what you feel about all that, and still let yourself have the good parts?

This (or an equivalent) message may take months to get across or, in some cases, may be accepted very quickly by a survivor who needs permission to have already existing thoughts or feelings. In any event, the therapist may find this perspective a hard one to communicate, based on her or his own feelings (countertransference) regarding the abuser. The therapist may, instead, find herself openly castigating the perpetrator to the survivor, hoping to lead the client into equivalent overt anger, or may slip into a "forgiveness mode," wherein the client is subtly counselled to emphasize the positive aspects of her relationship with her victimizer and essentially forget the trauma.

The tension the therapist feels to go one way or the other (hate or love, but not both) should be informative regarding the intensity of ambivalence the survivor must feel. However, as therapists, we are confronted with one overriding fact: Our job is not to punish the abuser (by proxy) but, rather, to provide an environment where the survivor can integrate her experiences and recover to the best of her ability.

Ironically, the clinician's attempt to support all survivor feelings about her victimizer often has the effect originally hoped for: The client begins to truly "see" the abuse at the point that she no longer feels she has to defend the perpetrator. As this process develops, the issue of either "I was bad or he/she was (it's me)" slowly transforms into awareness of a central fact: Abuse was *done* to me, not caused/deserved by me. Given this insight, the survivor's sense of badness may diminish while her anger at the abuser grows. This burgeoning fury may produce its own problems, as noted in Chapter 7; nevertheless, the transition from coconspirator or deserver of pain to injured (and angry) party is a healthy one.

Role-Playing

Although role-playing is not at all a new therapeutic technique, especially given humanistic approaches such as Gestalt therapy or transactional analysis, it may be especially suited to work with the sexual abuse survivor. There are two reasons for this: the survivor's readily available talents in the area of splitting parts of her awareness, and the severity of her self-esteem problems such that she may understand the sadness of her position only when observing it as "someone else." Not all survivors feel comfortable with role-playing, however, and in fact, such procedures may not be indicated for individuals whose reality contact is especially tenuous or whose dissociation is extreme. Furthermore, some clinicians' therapeutic styles are incongruent with role-playing techniques, and thus they may not choose to utilize these procedures.

The goals of role-playing in abuse-focused psychotherapy reflect the survivor's special needs: By having the former abuse victim play the roles of, and interact with, various people or different parts of herself, the intent is (1) to support the integration of the various warring (or at least isolated) components of her psyche and (2) to increase her level of self-acceptance. With regard to the former task, the client is asked to take the part of a given level or aspect of her personality and interact with its opposite (e.g., the "good girl" versus the "bad girl," or the frightened victim versus the angry retaliator). As this "conversation" progresses, often over many sessions, a rapprochement may slowly occur, wherein both parts merge to become the expression of a more flexible whole.

In the author's experience, role-playing can facilitate integration because both "sides" are directly verbalized (brought into simultaneous awareness) and thus each dissociated component is forced to acknowledge its opposite. This dialogue stimulates the development of an overbridging perspective [somewhat equivalent to Hilgard's (1986) "hidden observer"] that must orchestrate the component-to-component interaction. As awareness grows to accommodate both ego states or split-off components, the defensive value of being or knowing only one side or the other is to some extent lost (see Chapter 6 for an extensive discussion of dissociation and integration).

Similarly, role-playing may assist in the goal of self-acceptance by allowing the survivor to become "someone else" (typically not a difficult task for someone who dissociates on a regular basis) who watches and seeks to understand the survivor. To the extent that the client can (with assistance) bypass her normal self-blaming cognitions, she may begin to approximate the early tendrils of compassion for self.

Before describing specific role-playing scenarios, a point must be made: Such techniques, by virtue of their drama and support for processes akin to dissociation, should be carefully integrated into therapy. They ought to be less a matter of a single session's exercise than an ongoing dialogue over the long term. For example, it may be helpful for the "bad girl" to comment during a number of sessions (thereby allowing the survivor to verbalize her negative cognitions) and for the "good girl" to similarly rebut on a regular basis (allowing her to express hope without fear of "going too far"). Similarly, the survivor may wish to take some time in each session to formally watch herself and give herself supportive feedback when appropriate. Because such behaviors are not that distant from the survivor's (currently) maladaptive repertoire, the therapist must take an active role in keeping the client psychologically present and able to access all parts of the dialogue. Finally, role-playing exercises are probably best used after the opening phase of therapy, when the client-therapist relationship has solidified and the survivor has some sense of comfort and trust in the process of treatment. Given these precautions, therapists who work with adults molested as children often find the paradoxical notion of helpful, prescribed dissociation a useful tool.

"The Observer"

Named after a form of dissociation described in Chapter 6, this role-playing procedure is the least threatening of those outlined in this book. It is unlikely to meet with serious resistance because it involves primarily passive behavior. The initial instructions are merely for the client to watch himself in the session and to verbalize what he is thinking—in the third person. Because of his many self-hating thoughts, the survivor often begins this exercise by attempting to demean himself with pejorative self-descriptions. With the therapist's support and guidance for the more strenuous task of "objective" self-observation (e.g., to even dissociate from one's abuse-related cognitions), these verbalizations may gradually shift to a more compassionate perspective. For example, an adolescent's comments that "He looks like a wimp. He's about to pee in his pants" may eventually become "He looks real sad. He's kind of lost, and he doesn't know where to turn. He needs a friend." Such activities accomplish two goals: They facilitate the task of self-understanding with less threat (hence the third person), and they serve as a form of cognitive therapy where the client begins to substitute negative thoughts for verbalized—and therefore relatively salient—positive or caring self-evaluation.

Although the procedure presented thus far may be helpful, especially for the chronically depressed ("dysthymic") survivor, a further step is recommended for clients who appear to tolerate role-playing reasonably well. This next stage can be quite powerful, since it combines the elements described above with the opportunity for the client to directly approach the sexual abuse event, and thereby rework the feelings and cognitions that followed from victimization. This modification can additionally pave the way for another technique, described later in this chapter as "working with the inner child."

In the final stage of "the observer," the client is invited to travel back in time as an adult and "visit" herself as a child around the time of her abuse. In order to intensify this process, it is suggested that the "invisible adult" float or rest a short distance from the child and describe this child as completely as possible—detailing the room, the child's clothes, the child's facial expression, and other relevant aspects of the immediate environment.

At this point the therapist may choose to enter into the role-play, asking the "invisible adult" how the child is feeling, what the adult feels for the child at that moment, and so on, especially if the client is having difficulty with this task. It may be appropriate at this time, on the other hand, to have the adult talk to the child and have the child answer back. When this adult-child dialogue "works" (not all survivors are able to accomplish this exercise), the results may be quite dramatic, including the recovery of repressed memories or affects or the adult crying, perhaps for the first time, over the injured child (himself). As mentioned earlier, this direct access to the abused child can have additional payoffs, since the survivor may learn to more easily access parts of his experience or personality that have been "frozen" since the abuse, a skill that will be helpful in working with the "inner child" as described below.

Even if the survivor cannot manage the adult-child dialogue, he can usually describe what the child might be experiencing and may serve as an intermediary between adult and child components (e.g., "He feels all alone, he's so scared, he wonders what he did wrong"). This process, while not as dramatic as a direct adult-child "conversation," is often nearly as useful. Finally, it sometimes happens that the client cannot complete the more frightening or threatening aspects of this exercise when it is first introduced, yet he may be able to engage in such activities when he has progressed further in therapy.

Good Person, Bad Person

In addition to "the observer," perhaps the most commonly used role-playing technique for survivors is one in which the client verbalizes her self-hating and self-accepting components in dialogue form. Usually this involves the client expressing a common self-negating cognition (e.g., "You're a disgusting person whom no one would want") and the other side responding with a self-affirming statement (e.g., "No I'm not, I'm a good person who deserves love"). Although the "voice" used (i.e., first person or second person) may vary from situation to situation, it is the author's experience that the most effective cognitive restructuring occurs when the disconfirming side is spoken in the second person (i.e., "You are . . ."), thereby capturing the accusatory style of introjected negativity, while the self-supportive side uses the first person, thereby modelling affirmative self-statements that may be useful in disrupting future negative cognitions (see "Self-Control Techniques" later in this chapter).

As with "the observer" exercise, "good person, bad person" may be difficult for the client at first, especially in terms of finding positive rebuttals to (invariably available) negative self-statements. As therapy progresses, this technique may become quite easy—to the extent that it is often appropriately discontinued at some point for its failure to remain therapeutically interesting. One should not be misled, however, by early survivor boredom with this task to the extent of discontinuing it prematurely. Although on the surface this exercise appears to be almost a child's game, the survivor who enters into this experience with high motivation to address her issues will find that confronting and acknowledging one's self-hatred head-on is not easy.

Externalizing the Anger

A final role-playing scenario involves the survivor addressing her abuser *in absentia* during the psychotherapy session. Although the surface intent is to ventilate feelings regarding her abuse as if the abuser were present, this exercise can also be another way of dealing with introjected negative thoughts and feelings about self. As the survivor learns to say all the things she wishes could be said directly to her perpetrator, she becomes more able to externalize her anger, a process that often tips the abuse dichotomy further in her favor. Thus, as she tells her father, "You hurt me very badly, just to get what you wanted," she is also implying "It was your fault; I was innocent and deserved your love, not your hate."

Unlike an actual confrontation with her abuser, however, which (as noted later) can result in further enmeshment and damage, the role-play version unfolds under the relative control of the client and the therapist. Additionally, it reminds the client that although her victimization was at the hands of another person, her recovery must be her own. This lonely task can nevertheless be a freeing one, as she slowly relinquishes the hope that her abuser will redeem himself and make everything "all better."

For a number of reasons, among them the clinician's desire for the client to "understand" her perpetrator, some therapists erroneously extend the role-playing paradigm to the abuser-victim dyad. From this perspective, the survivor acts out the role of the abuser (describing why he abused her, how he felt during and after the abuse, etc.) and is thought to thereby gain a greater sense of the "human-ness" of her perpetrator. In many cases, however, perpetrator role-taking can end up being destructive. Among the possible ramifications of this practice are (a) survivor guilt at being so angry at her perpetrator who is, after all, human too, with feelings just like anyone else, (b) the survivor coming to believe that the abuser's behaviors, in the end, were not so bad, and (c) the development of premature forgiveness.

This last phenomenon occurs when the former victim (sometimes with the misguided help of her therapist) strives to understand and forgive her perpetrator as a defense against truly feeling her continuing anguish and rage. The client's interest in short-circuiting her pain in this manner unfortunately fits in well with societal pressures to "forgive and forget." Nevertheless, it is the experience of many workers in this area that the affective sequelae of abuse can resolve only when they are freely expressed and openly experienced, and that forgiveness is a long-term process that cannot be forced or arranged. Given these several issues, the therapist's attempts to integrate perpetrator and victim perspectives are typically confusing to the survivor and are likely, at best, to impede the process of therapy.

Desensitization

Desensitization is essentially a behavioral technique, typically used to reduce a client's anxious reactions to certain stimuli. It is most often applied as a treatment for phobias and other situationally inappropriate fears. In "systematic desensitization," for example, the client is taught relaxation techniques and then, while in a relaxed state, is gradually exposed (either in his imagination or in reality) to whatever it is that he is frightened of (e.g., snakes, airplane rides, etc.). Over time the repetitive pairing of the frightening stimulus with both relaxation (during which fear is impossible) and a safe therapeutic environment decreases the power of the stimulus to elicit anxiety. Thus the bond between the memories of the trauma and the fear that was originally associated with it is attenuated; this allows the client to have the memory without experiencing the (no longer appropriate) fear. Because of its effectiveness in this area, desensitization is now considered by most psychologists to be the treatment of choice for phobias and related anxiety disorders.

Since a large number of the psychological problems associated with sexual abuse also include components of anxiety, it seems logical that some form of desensitization might be useful in this area. And, indeed, clinicians have used systematic desensitization procedures to reduce the survivor's phobic responses to certain abuse-related stimuli, thereby increasing his or her level of functioning in some sexual or interpersonal situations. The major reason desensitization is presented here has to do with a related but more global phenomenon: Treatment for posttraumatic disorders often involves the repeated discussion of psychologically threatening material in a safe, supportive environment, thereby desensitizing the client to these frightening issues as therapy progresses.

The applicability of this procedure for postabuse trauma is substantial (Briere & Runtz, 1988c). Typically, the client who has developed a level of comfort and trust in the therapeutic process is invited to generally describe an abuse event in her past that is not too stressful to touch upon at that moment. During and after this task, the therapist offers empathic responses to what the survivor has experienced and gently goes over various aspects of the abuse situation with her. This discussion of issues such as "how did you feel when he said/did that," "what did he do then," and "how did you handle that" is conducted gently and carefully by the therapist, who must be prepared to terminate or lessen the intensity of the exploration if the client becomes too anxious, only to return to the topic at a later time when the client feels more in control.

In this way the client is slowly exposed to—and allowed to integrate—aspects of an event that she usually works hard (consciously
and unconsciously) to avoid. Simultaneously she learns to consider the
event in the context of current safety, support, and nurturance, thereby
gradually deconditioning the anxious arousal she usually feels when
recalling her victimization. As sessions proceed, this event and others
that previously were too "loaded" or anxiety producing to consider are
examined in greater and greater detail, so that eventually most of the
survivor's major memories and associated feelings are processed
(worked through) in therapy. Naturally, this exploration process often
stimulates "new" memories, as the client's ability to confront her history grows and as her current safety becomes more clear—material
that, in turn, is also confronted and integrated.

In addition to reducing the survivor's overall anxiety regarding her
victimization, the process of desensitization may be helpful in lessening two particularly disturbing aspects of sexual abuse trauma: dissociation and flashbacks. Given our understanding of dissociation as,
among other things, a defense against abuse-related memories and
affects, it is not surprising that the client who has learned to confront
and deal with the various aspects of her original abuse situation may
have less need to invoke this primitive response to later encounters
with abuse-related stimuli. Similarly, flashbacks, which seem to be
most prominent in cases where abuse trauma has been especially repressed, may also decrease when desensitization removes some of the
survivor's (anxiety-based) dread of memory.

Although the process of global desensitization is presented here as a
specific procedure, it is, in fact, a basic part of recovery from abuse. It
allows the client to, in some ways, take charge of her "symptoms"
(especially her intrusive memories), as well as encouraging greater
emotional and cognitive insight into the impact of victimization and
her early need to cope with such trauma. During the process of desensitization the therapist uses empathy, cognitive restructuring, and support for emotional catharsis—all helpful to the survivor as she works
toward growth and integration.

Tape Recognition

Just as desensitization has been borrowed from behavioral therapy,
"tape recognition" is a form of cognitive treatment, adapted for abuse-
focused psychotherapy. This technique, which can also be used with
survivors of "just" psychological abuse, teaches the client to identify

and deal with abuse-related perpetrator statements and inferences that have become introjected and that the survivor now believes to be her own perceptions. Before this technique is described, the problem it addresses will be presented here in greater detail.

A not uncommon consultation issue for therapists working with abuse victims is the latters' reports of intrusive thoughts, cognitions that seem akin to auditory hallucinations in their vividness—in fact, some clinicians have mislabelled them as psychotic symptomatology. For example, some survivors suddenly "hear" isolated self-condemnations such as "slut!", "bitch!" or "pig!" without obvious precipitation, often while engaged in an apparently unrelated task. Similar cognitions may be less dramatic and more integrated into the survivor's daily self-awareness, typically described as a barely noticeable running dialogue of one's inadequacies, "bad"ness, deservingness of punishment, and so on.

Such ruminations are not specific to sexual abuse victims, of course; they are also found in many depressed and/or obsessive individuals. Nevertheless, their manifestation in survivors of severe sexual molestation is often especially malignant and frequently involves a dissociated or split-off quality—experienced almost as though they were cognitive flashbacks. These thoughts frequently relate directly to the original abuse scenario and thus contain explicitly sexual or violent themes and/or direct implications regarding the victim's deservingness of abuse or exploitation.

Treatment for both the intrusive and ruminatory aspects of this problem proceeds in three phases: (a) recognition, (b) identification, and (c) "disattention."

The recognition phase is, in some ways, the most difficult, although it may eventually be a source of considerable insight for the survivor. The client is given examples of intrusive self-derogation from his actual disclosures during therapy, and it is suggested that there are many other similar instances of which he is not yet aware. The client is asked to consider that there may be two kinds of thinking: "real" thoughts, and introjects or "learned" thoughts carried over from childhood interactions with the abuser and others around the time of the abuse. Thus the first task is for the abuse survivor to monitor (pay attention to) his own negative "learned" cognitions such that it becomes clear to him that some of his thoughts are not entirely "his own."

What typically transpires, however, is that the survivor will resist this task—especially if she is primarily a ruminator and therefore has a difficult time discriminating between "real" thoughts and repetitive, introjected ones. Clients whose cognitions are more frankly intrusive and "out of nowhere" may have less difficulty accepting that an ego-alien event is occurring but may, on the other hand, be more frightened by such experiences and more likely to either deny or repress the existence of "crazy thoughts.

Thus for either version of the problem, part of the initial approach is to convince the survivor that some of her thoughts are archaic remnants of childhood maltreatment and that self-monitoring of such cognitions is important. Typically this is accomplished as therapy progresses and the therapist (followed by the client) uncovers more and more examples of this process. As a result of this "recognition process," the evidence for "learned thoughts" grows rapidly. With this increased awareness of the extent to which early perpetrator events are "alive and well" in the adult survivor, the client typically develops greater insight into the many and subtle ways in which abuse causes chronic injury. In the words of a 59-year-old woman, relatively late in therapy, "He didn't just mess with my body, he messed with my mind too!"

The second phase of tape recognition may be considered an extension of phase one, since it involves the client's understanding of the extent of his introjection of abusive communications. This stage, which the author calls "identification," is proactive; it teaches the client to anticipate and expect abuse-related introjections and to specifically identify them as such as they occur.

It is during this phase of the procedure when the actual words "tape recognition" may be used. The survivor is told something to this effect:

> The things that you say to yourself, that we call "learned thoughts," are like tapes. Just like a tape recorder, when you were young, you learned many negative ways to see yourself, from your father/ mother/boyfriend. Because you were young and had few other opinions to judge from, you believed whatever they said. The problem is those tapes are still running in your head, even though the abuse is over and you are an adult now. They play every day, as we've seen. Your job, right now, is to recognize when the tapes are playing and what they are saying. It's sometimes hard, but I think you'll find that there is something about those tapes that will allow you to spot them relatively quickly.

During this phase it is important that the survivor be counseled not to "do" anything about his or her tapes—only to become proficient at recognizing them. Some clients, especially those who are psychologically minded, will develop the tape concept to its fullest extent— including describing how the actual voice(s) on the tape are not always their own but can be, instead, the voice of their abuser or of a nonsupporting/blaming person at the time of the abuse.

The effects of the identification phase are several. It increases, for example, the client's awareness of the extent to which "old" abuse-related cognitions remain present in her or his life. This insight helps the client to perceive the extent and nature of the problem and to better apprehend the magnitude of what was done to her. Additionally, the survivor's monitoring of her introjected cognitions causes them to become, in some way, *different* from her other thoughts. As cognitive therapists point out, an important step in the client's liberation from self-derogating cognitions is her recognition of their presence and her growing ability to see them as somehow "not mine." For example, a man who suddenly thinks "I am a disgusting animal" while talking to someone will probably be less affected if he can immediately decide "that's another one of those thoughts" than he would be if he considered such cognitions to be relevant self-perceptions.

The final phase of tape recognition, referred to as "disattention," builds on the identification phase. The client is counseled at this point to alter her relationship to her introjected cognitions. Specifically, she is advised that such thoughts are deeply ingrained ("overlearned" in psychological terminology) and thus cannot be suppressed or stopped very easily. Instead, the survivor is coached to ignore thoughts that she is aware are abuse related. The client may find this instruction somewhat novel, since her typical way of dealing with intrusive negative thoughts has been either to fight them (a process that, ironically, often increases their salience) or to accept/believe them. The notion that one must, instead, learn to observe and disregard such cognitions has an uplifting effect on many survivors who, in some ways, are being given freedom to—at least intellectually—reject an albatross of many years.

As the client practices disattention, however, he often discovers that abuse-related self-evaluation is such an integral part of his identity that disengagement from such cognitions is quite difficult. The therapist may reinforce the client's attempts by likening the process to a gradual "erasing" procedure:

> Remember how we call these thoughts "tapes"? As you get better and better at knowing when a tape is playing, better at knowing that it is not really your own thoughts about yourself, and better at ignoring it, the tape becomes fainter and fainter. This is because the tape needs your agreement to stay loud. As you learn to say "Oh, there goes a tape," and not "That reminds me of how bad/ugly/stupid I am," the tape slowly erases. I don't think it ever completely disappears, but someday it may be just a whisper.

Therapeutic Restimulation

The reader may recall that "restimulation" was a term used in describing PTSD. In that context it was noted that the abuse survivor is often reminded of his abuse by various events or stimuli in the postabuse environment, leading to intense anxiety, dissociation, and flashbacks. Interestingly, a similar process can be a useful part of abuse-focused psychotherapy. In the context of treatment, and assuming that the client is not in crisis or otherwise unstable, restimulation can be used to introduce new material into therapy or to break through periods where, due to denial or repression, psychotherapy has become "stuck." As per PTSD, the procedure involves abuse-related stimuli. The intent, however, is not to produce disabling symptoms or overwhelmingly negative feelings but, rather, to bring additional aspects of the abuse into the therapy session, where it can be worked through.

Although the clinician may find any number of ways to carefully restimulate abuse issues, perhaps one of the most effective and most used is the "photograph" method. In this procedure, the client is asked to bring into the therapy session pictures of him or her taken at approximately the time of the abuse. Ideally, the survivor will bring photos not only of herself but also of herself with her family. The value of this undertaking may become apparent almost immediately, in terms of diagnosing the client's relationship to her family: Can the survivor get access to such pictures? *Are* there any pictures of the survivor as a child? Is the survivor willing to bring them into therapy? If not, why not?

Assuming that at least some photographs are available (in most cases they are), their evocative power for the client can be substantial. From the survivor's perspective, such pictures are miniature encapsulations of the abuse *as it existed then.* The former victim has, over the years, "forgotten" many aspects of her victimization and has developed a variety of strategies to bury the fear and rage she felt as a child. The experience of directly re-viewing the abuse scenario brings such memories and affects "back" (returns them to conscious awareness), where they can be worked with. Unlike their original presentation, however, these images and feelings are now recapitulated in an adult, and in a healing context.

The therapeutic exploration and discussion of abuse-relevant photos should be engaged in with care. The survivor may, to some extent, regress while making psychical contact with these artifacts of his childhood trauma, and may require relatively primitive levels of reassurance from his therapist that he is OK/safe/"still here." Other clients may take a more intellectualized and/or dissociated approach to such "stupid" or "interesting" relics. In either case, the clinician should understand the pain and vulnerability that the survivor is likely to be feeling, and should assume that she is being scrutinized for evidence that she, too, is abusive. Thus this is not the time for confrontation, interpretation, or even analysis, but rather for empathy and acceptance.

In addition to its ability to "dredge up" unconscious memories and feelings, the review of abuse-period photographs has two other obvious effects: it provides visual evidence to the client that she *was*, in fact, a helpless child at the time of her victimization (as opposed to the little adult that she might otherwise assume), and (in the case of intrafamilial abuse) it may lead to emotional insight regarding how the client and her family covered up what was an ongoing tragedy.

With regard to this latter point, many photographs of incest victims and their families superficially suggest happiness and togetherness— all members may be smiling and apparently enjoying themselves. With closer examination, however, the rigidity of this posture becomes apparent, and the "happy family" facade may seem almost garish or surreal. Especially revealing may be the presentation of the victim, who is often looking down or slightly away, appearing dazed, smiling too hard, or looking frightened. With a little prompting, the adult survivor may be able to estimate what was going through her mind at the time of the picture, including the notions that one must appear to look happy, that one's performance at being photographed may be found wanting, or, in cases where therapy has progressed considerably, a feeling of frightened rage—wanting to be part of the family and wanting to destroy it or the abuser at the same time.

The use of pictures or other restimulation devices (e.g., one's childhood teddy bear or one's father's pipe) can be sufficiently powerful, however, such that the therapist should spend considerable time and energy making the session safe and working to "bring the client back down" before the end of the session. The clinician may also wish to suggest some of the self-control techniques described later in this chapter, in order to forestall the acting out that sometimes follows a survivor's recapitulation of early abuse events (see Chapter 7 for more on treatment-related reactions).

Reframing Intrusive Symptomatology as Healthy and Healing

Of the many psychological and social problems that are associated with childhood molestation, perhaps the most disturbing ones for the survivor are those that intrude, unbidden, during everyday activities. Part of the distress associated with such "symptoms" involves the help-lessness the client feels and the associated implication that she is out of control of her behavior and, therefore, "crazy," dangerous, or both. Of these intrusive behaviors, in turn, flashbacks are probably the most aversive.

As indicated in Chapters 1 and 2, flashbacks are trauma-related memories, images, or sensations that suddenly intrude from "out of nowhere" into awareness. These phenomena are often quite vivid and, in especially severe cases, may mimic hallucinations or other psychotic symptomatology. Given the seeming pathology of such events, the reader may initially find it difficult to consider the notion that flash-backs and related psychological events (e.g., nightmares) actually repre-sent the mind's attempt to heal itself.

Horowitz (1976) and others suggest that PTSD symptoms are actu-ally biphasic: that victims of catastrophic events may cycle from a period of denial and avoidance to times when aspects of the traumatic event intrude into consciousness as flashbacks or obsessive thoughts. It is suggested here that, as Horowitz suggests more generally, this avoidance-intrusion cycle reflects a natural recovery process, wherein (a) through denial, repression, and avoidance of reminders of the trau-matic event, the survivor is able to continue to function/survive without being overwhelmed by intolerable memories and yet (b) occasionally accept bits of memory into consciousness where they can be cognitively processed and integrated—allowing the individual to become slowly desensitized to the painful affects that accompany such memories. Since flashbacks and nightmares are aversive them-selves, however, the survivor may then move into another phase of denial or repression, thereby giving herself time to "deal with" the fragments of memory she has allowed herself to confront.

This perspective on flashbacks and nightmares is inherently a posi-tive one, since it converts "symptoms" into healing strategies. It is suggested to the client that flashbacks are not evidence of loss of control but, rather, of an internal, helpful process—in fact, evidence that she can count on herself "deep down" to struggle for recovery. In the author's experience, this reversal of the client's experience from "bad" to "good" is often a powerful process—one that many survivors grasp quickly and raise often in therapy. It is likely that this acceptance of the therapist's reframe is due to the survivor's need to stay in control (as described earlier), the highly aversive nature of intrusive symptoma-tology, and the potential antidote to helplessness that such an interpre-tation provides. The author can recall several instances, in fact, where client and therapist celebrated the arrival of a flashback that contained new memories, since it introduced new material into treatment and indicated that the survivor was "ready" for information that previously was too threatening to consider consciously.

It should be noted that this analysis does not contradict other notions regarding intrusive phenomena in abuse survivors. For example, it was indicated earlier in this book that flashbacks are, in part, the result of stimulation of repressed memories by similar stimuli in the post-abuse environment. The current approach does not contradict this explanation but, instead, elaborates on it by describing under what conditions the survivor allows himself to be aware of stimulated memories. Thus, a "healing" perspective is congruent with the biphasic theory of PTSD symptoms, since both note that there are periods when flashbacks and intrusive thoughts are less common—presumably despite the continuing presence of restimulating events in the environment.

Self-Control Techniques

As noted in Chapter 3, inherent in abuse-oriented therapy are the goals of individuation and self-sufficiency. The implications of this philosophy for psychotherapy are substantial; among them is the notion that treatment should in some ways be "portable"—the client should be able to take certain skills and coping strategies away from the therapy session that will be of use to him or her in daily living. These skills are especially relevant to survivors of severe abuse, whose interpersonal problems and self-destructiveness may be reflexively triggered by a variety of events and stimuli that occur outside of the therapy session. Such triggers may include rejection or perceived abandonment in relationships, sexually laden interactions, flashbacks, criticism by authority figures, perceived helplessness or injustice, use of psychoactive substances (including alcohol), and so on. In such situations the client may choose to engage in one or more self-control techniques; coping strategies that allow her to forestall unwanted and seemingly uncontrollable acting out or impulsive behaviors.

Listed below are a number of self-control techniques that can be used by abuse survivors. These (and other) procedures are explicitly taught to the client during therapy. He is instructed to utilize whichever technique seems most appropriate when he fears impending compulsive, reflexive, or self-destructive behavior. Once these strategies are learned, the psychotherapist may remind the client of their existence at times when the clinician feels out-of-session impulsive behavior is likely (e.g., after a powerful session, during visits to parents, at Christmas or other holidays).

Grounding

The technique of "grounding," described by Blake-White and Kline (1985) and others, is a generic one; it refers to any behavior the client can engage in to feel more "here and now." Mostly used to deal with sudden dissociation (e.g., derealization, depersonalization) and/or periods of extreme affect (e.g., panic attacks, rage), grounding includes activities such as touching oneself and objects in the environment, repeating to oneself "I am here, I am real," focusing one's attention on nearby objects, talking to others, feeling one's feet on the floor, deep breathing, and the like. The survivor may also mention another grounding technique that she has used in the past—self-induced pain, via self-mutilation, hair-pulling, biting the insides of one's cheeks, and so on. Obviously such behaviors, although sometimes efficient in terminating dissociation, should not be reinforced since they encourage self-injury and imply self-punishment.

Distraction

Although this procedure may be confused with grounding in some instances, distraction is, in fact, at the opposite end of the "here and now" continuum. This technique is most useful when the survivor is caught in an internal psychological process that feeds on itself, such as panic, compulsive behavior, or self-destructive rumination. Panic attacks, for example, escalate as a function of increasing fear: I feel panic, which frightens me because it makes me feel out of control, which increases the panic, which convinces me that I *am* out of control, which is terrifying, and on and on. Distraction works to break such cycles by focusing the survivor's attention away from the process. Typical examples of distraction are reading a book, playing a concrete game (such as checkers) with someone, watching TV or listening to the radio, engaging in aerobic exercise (such as calisthenics, jogging, or brisk walking), and writing or painting.

Relaxation

This technique, whereby the client is taught to systematically relax the various parts of her body, is often effective when the client is undergoing intense anxiety or (interestingly) rage. Although "meditation" is a closely related concept and may be preferred by some clients, the tendency for this procedure to support dissociation makes it potentially problematic for some survivors. Instead, the client is counseled to "stay with" herself and to consciously work at slowing down her thoughts and reducing her bodily tension. Because this technique stresses self-control, it is often valued by survivors. A favorable side effect of this exercise, if used diligently during anxious periods, is that of systematic desensitization—the client may become incrementally less frightened of equivalent stimuli over time.

Self-Talk

A common cognitive therapy procedure is to teach the client to "talk back" to his or her negative cognitions. In actuality, this technique is far from a new idea. Just as the child may tell himself "now, don't be afraid" while walking in the darkness, or the business executive may counsel herself to "give 'em hell," the survivor may find it helpful to counter derogatory self-statements with self-affirming ones. Such self-talk is indicated at times when the client is ruminating over inadequacies, "bad"ness, or failings, and is moving toward a self-perceived need to punish self through self-mutilation, substance use, or other self-destructive behavior. Typical self-affirming statements are "I am a good person," "I can get through this," "Just because he said that doesn't mean it's true," or "I don't need to do that anymore."

"Leaving the Scene" or "Time-Out"

This technique is quite commonly used in behavior therapy and in work with violent men (e.g., wife-batterers). It has proved to be helpful to abuse survivors in three areas: control of escalating anger and subsequent violence, interruption of impulsive or compulsive behavior (e.g., indiscriminate sex, bulimic binging), and avoidance of drug or alcohol intoxication. In all three instances, the client learns to physically leave the situation where the temptation to act out resides. For example, a woman who recognizes a compulsion to flirt in a situation where she is not actually sexually interested, or where the outcome is likely to be negative (e.g., sexual aggression from the person of her attentions, or becoming involved with "another man who's bad for me") may choose to leave the party/bar while she is still able to do so. Similarly, a survivor involved in an interpersonal conflict may opt to physically leave the argument upon feeling the warning signs of impending violence. Although these solutions may appear somewhat primitive to an outside observer, those familiar with the impulse control problems of many severe abuse survivors understand the appropriateness of "leaving while you can" for some individuals.

Writing

For most clients therapy happens once or twice a week. For many abuse survivors this feels like far too little contact in a life that is fraught with difficulties. Given this apparent inequality between therapeutic supply and client demand, there is a need for an activity that encourages exploration, analysis, and perspective but that does not reinforce client dependency. Writing (or "journaling") is one approach to this problem (S. Butler, personal communication, February 1985). The client is invited to write a journal detailing his feelings, thoughts, insights, and plans—either on a daily basis or as needed at difficult times— which is then read by the therapist at some regular point in time (some clinicians read them at the beginning of each session; others review them between sessions). This procedure is more than an adjunct to therapy; it has its own positive effects, including helping the client to rely on her own support (in effect, to be her own therapist), encouraging creativity (which is growth centered rather than problem focused), and supporting the client's increasing ability to express her feelings and issues. Most important, in terms of self-control, journaling allows the client to analyze her own process at times when she might otherwise engage in impulse to reduce dysphoria. As one 34-year-old woman describes it: "My book is my friend and therapist in the night; when I'm all alone; and when I want to tear me and them apart. And this book never goes on vacation."

"Portable Therapist"

The last self-control technique described here relies, as does journaling, on the client's own ability to provide therapeutic insights and perspectives. Called "portable therapist," this activity simply involves the client asking herself "what would my therapist say?" at points of crisis or indecision outside of therapy. Obviously this technique requires that (a) the client has been in treatment long enough to guess what her therapist *would* say and (b) the client-therapist relationship is good enough that the client values and heeds the therapist's input. Given these provisos, the survivor is often able to advise herself in ways that derail potentially harmful behaviors. Thus, for example, the client who is feeling despondent and thinking about "hitting the bars" might consult her "internal therapist" and tell herself to attend an AA meeting instead. It is the author's experience that this basic procedure can be useful even with "severe borderlines" who, according to some, are theoretically unable to maintain an internal representation of the therapist long enough to receive "advice."

The self-control strategies outlined above are only a few of those that may be useful for any given client; see, for example, Gil's (1983) many helpful suggestions. Thus, part of abuse-focused treatment is the specific assessment of survivor vulnerability to abuse-related triggers and the custom development of "portable" therapeutic solutions to these potential sources of self-harm.

Working with the Inner Child

Clinicians who do psychotherapy with adults abused as children occasionally encounter what appears to be a "small child" hiding within the folds of the client's adult presentation—a child who emerges in the form of primitive behaviors, black or white thinking, or in some cases childlike speech at points of stress. This phenomenon bears close scrutiny, since many of the more impulsive or self-destructive behaviors engaged in by survivors of severe abuse have a childlike quality to them. Presented below is a brief theory regarding how the "inner child" might come into existence, as well as an approach to the therapeutic integration of this "child" into the adult personality.

Although there are multiple theories regarding the stages of normal development, most theorists agree that it progresses relatively smoothly, with each psychological and physical stage or phase yielding to the next as the child matures. Thus although we may on occasion regress to an earlier psychological stage (e.g., during play or at times of severe stress), such developmental nodes do not exist as concurrent ego states during normal adult functioning. In other words, psychologically intact adults are the *result* of developmental stages, not an amalgam of such phases.

Some survivors of severe sexual abuse, however, appear to operate from multiple, coexisting developmental states that variously influence his or her adult behavior. The primary mechanisms for this phenomenon are probably twofold: traumatic "freezing" of development and, probably more important, "splitting-off" of abuse experiences.

Traumatic freezing has been described, although in a different context, at an earlier point in this book: Because the victim must attend to the difficult task of surviving (psychologically or otherwise) ongoing abuse, she or he has little time or energy available to interact with the environment and master its surmountable challenges. Instead she becomes developmentally conservative—taking as few risks as possible and limiting her activities to those that are immediately relevant to safety and/or escape. In this context maturation is difficult, and thus the individual is, to some extent, frozen in childhood.

Although this failure to learn and grow at developmentally appropriate points in time is a serious problem, many therapists have found that the former victim can, to some extent, "catch up" on old gaps in learning, given the psychological opportunity to do so. Even more impactful, however, is the victim's use of dissociation to deal with trauma, since this primitive defense continues on into adulthood where it consistently interferes with psychological functioning. This form of dissociation is sometimes referred to as "splitting-off": abuse experiences that are too painful for the victim to accept are psychologically isolated and pushed out of conscious awareness. The net effects of this defense are whole "chunks" of childhood (and therefore somewhat primitive) experience that are separated from daily living and remain "in storage" in relatively unaltered form.

Because these split-off parts of experience consist of a gestalt of interrelated processes (i.e., abuse-specific thoughts, feelings, and memories), they have been considered by some to be discrete "ego states." From the survivor's perspective, these states emerge as sudden, intrusive changes in perspective and need. Almost literally, the severely abused adult may be "taken over" by childlike cognitions at certain points, usually when stimulated by powerful abuse-related events or issues. (The similarity of this process to that of multiple personality disorder has not escaped some writers who, probably correctly, see the various "personalities" as different abuse-related ego states.) In less extreme cases (the majority of abuse survivors) this "hidden child" will not manifest as a discrete entity but, rather, will more subtly influence the survivor toward primitive or impulsive solutions to life problems.

This analysis of the "hidden child" is well-accepted by most abuse survivors in therapy, since it meshes well with their experience of intrusive childlike feelings and demands. As a metaphor, it additionally allows the adult survivor to conceptualize, and therefore symbolically control, aspects of his behavior that have previously been both undecipherable and a source of shame and "different"ness. The stages of "working with the hidden child" are described below.

The first step in this procedure is to help the survivor to acknowledge her childlike parts. This involves presenting the material described above and working with the client to identify those aspects of her behavior—in therapy and out—that seem to come from a frightened, untrusting child. It is important, however, that all human failings not be attributed to this state; there are undoubtably things the survivor has thought or done that, abuse-related or not, do not relate to the "inner child." Thus the survivor and clinician must work to discriminate between problems that are more pedestrian abuse effects and those difficulties that are perceived as ego-alien or ego dystonic—the result of intrusion by "a different me."

Following the identification phase, the survivor is counseled to allow the "child" to describe her experience and feelings at length. The therapist may, in fact, perform therapy with this "child": asking her what she feels, why she does what she does, whether she wants to remain a child, what she thinks of herself as an adult, and so on. This process may be difficult for the survivor, and it may take considerable time before she can actively participate in this exercise. Among other activities the clinician must work to normalize the client's experience of not having a seamless, integrated ego and to reassure the survivor that it is not "silly" to "talk to yourself."

This is, of course, in actuality a form of role-playing, where the survivor takes the part of her dissociated experience. During this phase, the client may behave in a childlike manner and may appear to be responding from a relatively primitive perspective. It is important that the therapist understands two issues here: (a) if the survivor is, in fact, accessing his split-off gestalt, he *will* appear childlike, at least initially, and (b) given the complex of interpersonal difficulties described in earlier chapters, the survivor may act as if he were being the "child" when, in fact, he is using the process as an opportunity to avoid confronting important issues. In the latter instance, the client's behavior may appear to be a parody of childhood, and little emotional work will transpire. This is, of course, a danger of any procedure that is in any way "magical"; the survivor may use it to avoid the real world.

Typically both of the above will occur: the survivor will have accessed, to some extent, aspects of her "inner child," and the anxiety of this experience may cause her to titrate the process with regression and "as-if" defenses (see Chapter 6 for more on the latter form of dissociation). Since, in fact, there *is* no actual "inner child," the survivor's tendency to play fast and loose with this exercise is understandable. Nevertheless, especially in the case of severe, compound abuse, these isolated ego states can be quite potent and should be approached as such. The cognitive exercise of "speaking as the child," whether totally accepted by the client or not, may nevertheless accomplish the task of accessing formerly dissociated material and bringing it into conscious awareness.

In summary, working with the "child" is a way to break through archaic dissociative defenses and thereby integrate repressed childhood memories, affects, and cognitions with adult understanding. Through the process of "acting as the child," the survivor speaks the previously unspeakable and thus updates old perceptions and desensitizes primitive emotionality. As these split-off parts of the client are worked through, their ability to motivate primitive/archaic behaviors lessens, and the "child" loses its status as a discrete entity. Finally, by using the metaphor of the hidden child, the therapist further normalizes what to the survivor is a frightening aspect of postabuse trauma.

Some Final Comments on Abuse-Related Psychotherapy

As was noted at the beginning of this chapter, and despite the various methods and techniques presented above, probably the most important components of psychotherapy with abuse survivors involve its most generic aspects: (a) a therapist who is caring, nonexploitive, and reliable and (b) a therapeutic environment that fosters self-awareness, self-acceptance, and individuation/independence. Thus the corrective interpersonal experience of abuse-focused psychotherapy is as much about *how* the therapist is as it is *what* she says. In this regard, one should not be overly concerned about which of the specific procedures described in this chapter one uses at a given point in therapy. Far more important is one's adherence to the basic philosophy and approach to abuse-oriented treatment as outlined above and expanded upon in the remaining chapters of this book.

CHAPTER 6

The Specific Problem of Client Dissociation During Therapy

Psychotherapy, in some ways, represents a paradox for the sexual abuse survivor: On the one hand, she has been victimized and exploited in the context of an interpersonal relationship, yet on the other, it is suggested that her best chance for recovery may be to engage in a similar situation where, she is told, she should "trust" that further abuse will not occur.

From the survivor's perspective, there are several communalities between her abuse and psychotherapy: Both involve a form of intimate relationship with an authority figure who is likely to be a male (especially if she consults a psychiatrist), both can be emotionally painful, and both demand vulnerability. These similarities, in combination with the survivor's almost reflexive hypervigilance and general distrust, make it very hard for some former abuse victims to (a) attend psychotherapy and (b) stay there. It is with regard to the latter point that this chapter is written: Just as during her abuse the victim used dissociative strategies to psychologically "leave the scene" of her trauma, so may the adult survivor dissociate from the psychotherapeutic process at times of stress or perceived danger.

As discussed in this chapter and outlined in Chapter 1, such dissociative behaviors can be unconscious defensive strategies and yet autonomous "symptoms" as well, and can emerge in either primitive or more sophisticated forms. Some dissociative states may be obvious to the client, the therapist, or both, whereas others may be considerably more subtle and may not be recognizable as dissociative by either member of the psychotherapy dyad. Whatever its form, extreme or chronic dissociation can have a negative impact on treatment: The client may, for example, "miss" relevant material, avoid important emotional tasks, or "dilute" the therapeutic relationship—each in an unconscious attempt to ensure continued psychological survival in what is mistakenly, but understandably, perceived as a potentially abusive situation.

Given the frequency of dissociation in abuse-related psychotherapy (as one client stated, "I wasn't really here for the first couple of months, you know") and its impact on the treatment process, this phenomenon is addressed in detail in the following pages. First, seven common forms of client dissociation are presented and their typical impacts on treatment are noted, and then a general approach to dealing with therapy-based dissociation is discussed.

Disengagement

Disengagement is probably the most simple and most common form of dissociation. Utilized by most people on occasion, this defense (sometimes referred to as "spacing out") involves a cognitive separation of the individual from his environment at times of stress. This disengagement from the external world is not to be confused with daydreaming or distraction by other thoughts or affects. Instead, the individual withdraws into a state of neutrality, where thoughts are seemingly "placed on hold." During such times he may be temporarily unresponsive to conversation or questions, although he will usually "snap out of it" if the questioner persists in seeking his attention. Most periods of cognitive disengagement are relatively brief, ranging from a few seconds to usually less than several minutes, and the depth of the dissociation is typically shallow.

As opposed to most nonvictimized persons, the survivor of severe molestation may slip in and out of disengagement many times a day, apparently in an attempt to titrate the stress of daily living down to manageable levels. These frequent and brief "time-outs" are often not recognized as such by the individual, who may be surprised to hear from others that she is inattentive during discussions or other interpersonal interactions.

The defensive aspects of cognitive disengagement reside in the survivor's ability to psychologically attenuate disturbing or threatening stimuli—whether they be internally generated (e.g., flashbacks, painful memories, intrusive thoughts) or encountered in the interpersonal environment (e.g., real or perceived danger, boundary violations). Like many other psychological defenses, disengagement usually occurs as a function of unconscious decision making: The individual perceives a potential threat and "decides" to cognitively withdraw as a protection against (a) sustained anxiety and other painful affects commonly associated with trauma and (b) further (conscious) awareness of danger.

Since disengagement is rarely planned at the conscious level, and since its net effect is to decrease awareness, the survivor may not "notice" that she is dissociating until after the fact—if at all.

The primary impact of disengagement in therapy is that the client may "miss" important insights or opportunities for self-confrontation while "away." Such interference is especially likely in the early stages of abuse-oriented treatment, when the survivor is most fearful of the therapist and therapy, although it may reemerge as a problem at later points of stress.

Detachment/Numbing

As opposed to disengagement, detachment does not require the survivor to mentally "leave the scene"; instead, he or she figuratively "turns down the volume control" of negative feelings associated with certain thoughts, memories, or events, so that the latter may be engaged in with less emotional pain. This defense, like disengagement, is used by most people at one time or another as a way of handling acute stress, grief, anger, or other aversive states. Typically in the survivor, however, detachment (also referred to as "numbing") serves as a primitive protection from *old* pain (i.e., the trauma of child abuse) or as a regular defense against affective responses to current abuse-related events (e.g., the numbness frequently associated with prostitution or chronic physical abuse in marriage).

Although sometimes adaptive in dealing with acute or immediate psychological trauma, recurrent or sustained forms of detachment (as is found, e.g., in chronic PTSD) can interfere with the psychic processing of painful affect in the recovery process. In its chronic incarnation, this numbing may result in an individual who is psychologically removed from her feelings (especially negative ones) and who may, in fact, be relatively unaware of feelings per se. Such people, especially if they have had access to "higher" (university) education, may present in an intellectualized manner, using verbal and analytic skills to turn subjective (personal) distress into "objective" (impersonal) data. Typical statements of clients whose use of detachment is automatic and largely unconscious may include "I feel dead inside," "I don't feel bad about what he did—I understand that he must have been a very disturbed and alienated person," or "I know in my head that I must be upset, but I can't feel it."

The primary effect of detachment on psychotherapy is that the client may fail to accomplish emotional learning and integration. By keeping painful feelings out of consciousness during cognitive processing of abuse issues, the survivor avoids actually experiencing psychotherapy as a whole (i.e., thinking *and* feeling) person. The net result may be someone with exceptionally good "insight" into the various aspects of her victimization, perhaps even into her own reactions and accommodations to the abuse, who nevertheless continues to feel suppressed and unacknowledged rage, sadness, and fear with regard to these events and her role in them.

Observation

This dissociative phenomenon is often described by clients as "watching" oneself engage in an interaction, as opposed to actually participating in it. In this sense, "observation" has much in common with the depersonalization and out-of-body experiences found in abuse survivors and other PTSD sufferers. The primary difference between the current defense and these other dissociative states is that whereas the latter occur as relatively sudden, discrete episodes, observation is a chronic pattern of avoiding the direct experience of stressful events. The client will frequently describe a feeling of calm or affective neutrality, which can be traced to a sense of being "outside of oneself looking in" and therefore not directly threatened by whatever potentially frightening stimulus is present. Thus observation may also be understood as another pathway to detachment, where separation from affect is accomplished by, at least metaphorically, distancing oneself from the stressor.

In the therapy session observation serves to divorce affect from thought in much the same way as does detachment. As an observer of psychotherapy, rather than as a participant, the client can be relatively uninvolved in the treatment process and thus less "touched" by it. The problem with this solution to therapy-based emotional pain is, of course, that by removing one's self from treatment, one cannot benefit much from the process. Luckily for most survivors, the observer defense is less frequently used as treatment progresses, especially if, as described later, the clinician actively addresses this problem during therapy.

Postsession Amnesia

A frequent experience of therapists working with survivors of severe abuse is that their clients seem to approach some sessions as if they had never been in earlier ones. The client may, for example, not recall important material uncovered in the previous therapy meeting, may deny that the clinician ever said certain things, or may cover "new" ground that was identically addressed in one or more earlier sessions.

These and similar behaviors can be understood in several different ways: (a) it may be assumed that the client is unable to maintain "object constancy" from session to session, and thus she is, in fact, beginning anew in each session; (b) it may be that the client was inattentive in previous sessions, as a result of various dissociative defenses, and thus did not "receive" information that was available at a given point in time; or (c) it is possible that the client has, for whatever reason, forgotten what transpired in certain therapeutic interactions.

Although all three of these dynamics may operate in the abuse survivor (with the first being perhaps least likely), the third notion—that of "forgetting" recent therapy material—often underlies what appears to be session-to-session discontinuity. Specifically, just as psychogenic amnesia is understood to be a dissociative phenomenon in current diagnostic systems (i.e., DSM III-R), so too may the client use this dissociative technique to eliminate threatening material from memory during the treatment process.

Thus, for example, the client might not recall an insight developed in the previous session that her father did not, in fact, truly love her or may repress newly accessed memories of having taken money or candies for "not telling" about an abuse episode. In the former instance postsession amnesia protects the survivor from confronting the full extent of her exploitation and betrayal, whereas in the latter case it may forestall guilt arising from the belief that she "gained" from her molestation.

Finally, postsession amnesia can serve to break up the flow of the therapeutic process for the survivor, allowing him to (a) control (titrate) the intensity and rate of treatment and (b) moderate the extent of closeness or dependency on his therapist. In this regard, the discontinuity of therapy that arises from amnesia is, in fact, the "planned" outcome.

"As If"

This defense is perhaps the most sophisticated form of dissociation found among sexual abuse survivors. Deployment of this protective mechanism in therapy can result in a client who appears to be present during treatment, who engages in spontaneous, "real"-appearing affect (e.g., tears, anger), but who never seems to improve or gain emotional insight into his or her experience (e.g., the "broken record" described earlier). Careful examination of such individuals, however, may reveal that their participation is "too good to be true," and that there is a subtle sense of unconscious "playacting" about their presentation. It may appear, for example, that the survivor is an excellent performer of a script that requires one to act "as if" they were a client, with all the attendant emotions and behaviors that that role requires.

The relative sophistication of this defense lies in its subtlety: "As if" may interfere with the treatment process without either the clinician or the client being aware of it. The underlying unconscious strategy appears to be the following: I cannot allow myself to experience the pain and fear that go along with confronting my abuse, and the process of psychotherapy itself is frightening (especially given my previous experience with the results of intimacy). However, I want to be "good" for this powerful other, and I want to believe that I am involved in a process that will help me. Therefore, I will play the part of myself being in therapy: I will get angry, cry, remember things and report on them, but it won't be me—it will be me playing the part of me. The difference between these two states is enough to keep me safe and to keep me in control.

It has often been noted that therapy with "borderlines" may superficially progress quite well early in treatment, but later sessions may stall as it becomes clear that the client wasn't "really" working in therapy after all. Although such outcomes may derive from a number of different sources, one frequent factor appears to be the "as if" defense described above, especially when such clients are survivors of sexual abuse. In these instances the client may be understood as attempting to "survive" psychotherapy—not trying to trick the therapist or undermine the treatment process per se; rather, attempting to be present and not present, a "good girl" and yet still safe.

Shutdown

Elaine A.

Elaine is an obese, 31-year-old woman who has been in therapy for six months. As a child she was a victim of extensive sadistic abuse, involving, among other activities, long periods of being tied to a bed, raped with various objects, and burned with cigarettes.

Elaine appears to be doing quite well in treatment and is already gaining some control over the flashbacks and dissociative periods that have plagued her adult life.

During her current session, however, Elaine becomes more and more unresponsive and psychologically distant, apparently in response to a recent memory of her childhood torture. At one point her eyes roll up into her head, her eyelids flutter, and she begins moaning and crying. Her arms are rigidly folded across her chest, and she slides off her chair into a "fetal" position on the floor. Elaine is nonresponsive to her therapist's questions as she slowly rocks back and forth and side to side. After about 15 minutes, she gradually "returns" to the room and sits back on her chair. She remains withdrawn, however, and it is not until her next session that she is able to discuss her experience, which she characterizes as falling into a "black hole" of terror and seeming loss of volition.

Whereas "as if" is a relatively complex form of dissociation, client "shutdown" is extremely primitive. Typically invoked when the client feels out of control or unable to avoid overwhelming affect, this mechanism involves psychological withdrawal into a mute, nonresponsive state during treatment. Although it shares many features with disengagement, "shutdown" is not a retreat into neutrality; it is an autistic wrestling with frightening cognitions or affects, motivating a need to stop "being." As with other defensive strategies, this dissociative mechanism occurs on a continuum: ranging from diminished awareness of the clinician, self, and the psychotherapeutic environment to extreme withdrawal with attendant rocking and moaning or crying. The obvious intent of such behaviors, over which the client often feels no conscious control, is sensory "shutdown" and escape from an immediately threatening environment. That a person would experience such elemental terror or pain during psychotherapy emphasizes the seriousness of her injury. That she would feel the need to engage in such primitive behaviors and yet not physically escape the therapy office underlines the radical sense of helplessness and dependency the survivor may experience.

Total Repression

This last form of dissociation differs from the other types described in this chapter in that it does not occur as a function of treatment per se. Nevertheless, it has a substantial impact on therapy with many survivors. Specifically, as noted in Chapter 3, a small proportion of survivors totally dissociate themselves from memories of severe childhood victimization—typically reporting long "blanks" in their memory for early life events. This total repression of abuse is, obviously, hard to identify or "prove" when it occurs, since the majority of clients who dissociate in this way deny being abuse survivors in the first place. Most clinicians who specialize in abuse, however, have clients who they are relatively convinced were sexual abuse survivors, despite their clients' claims to the contrary.

Among the frequent signs of repressed sexual abuse seem to be (a) certain feelings and behaviors during sex (e.g., sudden disgust, anger, or fear; arousal to aggression or pain; abrupt crying or fighting during intercourse for no discernable reason; unexplainable aversion to or craving for sexual contact; intrusive sexual fantasies or flashbacks involving the original abuse); (b) a tendency to become involved in destructive and/or degrading relationships; (c) chronic disturbing dreams; (d) extreme, unexplainable reactions to films or books describing sexual abuse or rape; (e) "strange feelings that something bad happened to me when I was young"; (f) dissociative behaviors, in addition to the hypothesized repression, especially disengagement and "as if"; and (g) a general personality style reflecting brittleness, self-destructiveness, pseudosexuality, and compulsive behaviors. While none of these indicators, alone, guarantees the presence of an abuse history, the presence of several should alert the clinician to the possibility of "unremembered" childhood sexual victimization.

Dynamic Tension Between Dissociation and Psychotherapy

The major impediment of dissociation to effective psychotherapy is the fact that one acts in direct cross-purpose to the other. A major goal of abuse-focused psychotherapy is integration: the simultaneous awareness and availability of thought and feelings, of "contradictory" ego states. Dissociation, on the other hand, is specific in its drive for *dis*-integration. Detachment serves to hypertrophy thought and deny affect, "as if" can involve the reverse, and disengagement separates the person from her outside world. "Multiple personalities" and other forms of splitting go even further, *dis*-integrating various parts of awareness so that all are incomplete. The ultimate dissociation, total amnesia, removes entire segments of memory from awareness. The bottom line of each of these defenses is equivalent: "I don't want to know completely, I don't want to be entirely aware . . . ignorance may not be bliss, but it's far better than realization."

Psychotherapy, of course, implies the contrary. It assumes that complete self-awareness leads to self-acceptance, as the client comes to reject the myth of personal "bad"ness. Thus the therapy session may figuratively resemble a battleground: The therapist invites the client to truly see and understand, while the client works (through various dissociative defenses) to avoid what he believes to be dangerous self-knowledge. Paraphrasing a 52-year-old actor, midpoint in therapy: "I don't trust you or me enough to open doors where I've locked in monsters. I'm supposed to believe you that this will help, but you can't help me if you're wrong."

Intervention

The major principle involved in working with treatment-based dissoci-ation is as follows: Dissociation, like other defenses, should be re-spected and not discounted. Instead, the client's attention is drawn to his defensive behavior, and assistance is offered in reducing his current dissociative state to its most minimal, yet effective, level. If dissocia-tion continues, it is assumed that this self-protective mechanism is appropriate for the moment, and the therapist works to reduce the client's immediate level of stress.

Fortunately, it is often the case that the client's therapy-based disso-ciative behavior is, to some extent, reflexive, and thus she may be able to reduce this impediment to treatment with only minor difficulty. For this reason the two major therapeutic responses to dissociation empha-size awareness and control. For the purpose of discussion, these will be referred to as "process feedback" and "self-monitoring."

"Process feedback" refers to the therapist's continuing attention to the possibility of client dissociation (signalled by behaviors such as fixed or "glazed" eyes, sudden flattening of affect, long lapses between words, seemingly "unreal" responses, or excessive intellectualization) and her gentle reminders to the client when such dissociation occurs. This feed-back is not expressed punitively or in a negative manner but more in the manner of a team member informing her partner of an impending prob-lem. Typical examples might be, "Jim, are you still with us?" or "Sarah, you seem to be spacing out. Is something going on?" Inherent in the clinician's comments, regardless of their content, should be the message that dissociation is not a "bad" response, only one that should be moni-tored for its immediate appropriateness. In fact, punitive or castigating therapist reactions in this area often *increase* client dissociation, as the survivor struggles to get further away from abusive contact.

Upon being informed or reminded of dissociation by their therapists, most clients are able to (at least temporarily) terminate disengagement, detachment, or observation. If the client continues to have problems "returning" (especially in the case of disengagement or observation), the interventions described in Chapter 5 under "grounding" may be appropriate. Similarly, clients who become too detached may benefit from support for catharsis and "feeling your feelings" as described earlier. In many cases such intervention may merely consist of frequently asking one's client "What are you feeling now?" "How does it feel when you say that?" or "It looks like there's a feeling way down there. Do you know what it is?"

Less easily confronted, as might be expected, is the "as if" defense. In many cases this form of dissociation may go unnoticed by either therapist or client. Even when detected, however, "as if" may be difficult to derail, since it is not always clear exactly what it is that the client is doing. Perhaps the most effective intervention is simply to educate the client about "as if," point out to him instances where it may be occurring (this should always be phrased tentatively, since a process this subtle may be misidentified), and work with him to "make the session real" in any way that seems to work. Among the latter possibilities are (a) grounding techniques, (b) increased focus on feelings, and (c) gentle reminders that therapy is for the client, not the therapist. Given the ambiguity of this defense and the lack of clear "solutions" to its presence, it is reassuring to note that "as if," like other treatment-based dissociative events, tends to decrease as psychotherapy continues over time—especially if dissociation is directly addressed during treatment.

"Shutdown" is undoubtedly the most frustrating and, in some cases, the most frightening of the dissociative responses. Not only is the client "not home" to receive therapeutic (therefore verbal) contact, the drama of a psychologically absent person may prove overwhelming to some clinicians. Common labels used for such client behavior include "catatonic," "regressed," and "psychotic"—all descriptions that imply extreme negative prognoses. Thus, as described in Chapter 7, perhaps the first intervention the therapist may wish to consider is the decatastrophizing of his own cognitions. "Shutdown" is a dissociative defense, not a psychotic break. Even when untreated, it is self-limiting —most instances of this phenomenon last for minutes; few endure for an hour.

It is the author's additional experience that most clients are not totally "absent" during shutdown. There is often a part of the client's awareness (i.e., a "hidden observer") that remains focused on the environment for protective purposes and thus is somewhat accessible to the therapist. The clinician may find it helpful to talk to this part, even though the survivor appears nonresponsive. Typically, the therapist's statements at this time should be reassuring, normalizing, stress reducing, and nondemanding of response. The client may be told, for example: "We've gone far enough, today, now we just need to get you back together for the outside world," or "Bill, it looks as if you've got a lot of stuff happening in there. I think what we should do is spend the next 20 minutes or so just being silent, letting it be peaceful in here."

Finally, the clinician should be alert to the possibility that what appears to be "shutdown" is, instead, volitional nonresponse. The client may, in other words, be engaging in an instrumental behavior to alter the therapist's behavior. She may, for example, be fearful of the material being discussed or may be angry at the psychotherapist for real or imagined failings.

"Shutdown" is best discriminated from active nonresponse in terms of the client's awareness of her environment. Shutdown may manifest with glazed, fixed, or closed eyes, rocking, rigid or tense muscles, and other signs of involuntary withdrawal; volitional nonresponse may involve glaring, turning one's head away or downward, sudden nonverbal responses to further therapist statements, a grim or stubborn-appearing mien, and other evidence of ongoing awareness. Although volitional responses are important too, they should be approached differently, as has been outlined in previous chapters.

Because abuse-focused therapy actively involves the client in the recovery process, a final aspect of intervention relies on the client's "self-monitoring" of her dissociative processes. The survivor slowly learns to recognize times when she is reflexively distancing herself from frightening stimuli or splitting her consciousness into compartments to avoid "knowing" what she would rather avoid. As she becomes more aware of (a) the safety of psychotherapy and (b) the archaic quality of many of her fears, such treatment-related dissociative episodes and processes become increasingly ego-dystonic and lose much of their reinforcing quality. At this point, when the survivor no longer "needs" dissociation to protect her from therapy, the frequency and intensity of these defenses usually diminishes.

As opposed to other forms of dissociation, however, total repression cannot be directly addressed by techniques such as process feedback or self-monitoring. Since the client, by definition, denies that any abuse transpired during childhood, therapist confrontation or advice regarding abuse-related defenses is inappropriate. In fact, the repressed survivor is liable to see therapy as a power struggle if, from her perspective, the therapist tries to convince her of something that she "knows" is false.

Because this fundamental disagreement between client and therapist is potentially disconfirming of the survivor's sense of reality, the therapist is advised to "tread softly" with such individuals—especially since the therapist may, in fact, be wrong. In the author's experience, such instances of repressed abuse often resolve themselves as treatment progresses. In such cases the client eventually comes to recall more and more repressed events as therapy gradually lowers her unconscious resistance and increases her trust. In this way the abuse history is "reconstructed" during the process of therapy such that assessment and treatment become indistinguishable (Steer, 1988, April).

Alternatively, other explanations for the client's clinical presentation may emerge, including the possibility of severe physical or emotional maltreatment or, for example, a father who continually sexualized (but never technically "molested") his daughter. In either event the helpful aspect of treatment is the therapist's willingness to "go with" the client's perspective while, at the same time continually remaining open to the likelihood that more severe sexual child abuse actually transpired.

CHAPTER 7

Teasing the Dragon:
The Fruits of Confronting
Severe Abuse

Several Eastern teaching philosophies contain the following story: A person, for whatever reason, disturbs a slumbering beast, usually a tiger or a dragon. The beast upon awakening becomes angry and dangerous. The person thus finds himself faced with a conflict: to hang onto the beast (by the tail) means temporary safety but also exposure to a frightening ride and continual danger; to let go is to stop the ride but also to become immediately vulnerable.

This chapter is about this dilemma as it relates to work with more severely injured abuse survivors: "Awakening" the survivor's often repressed or suppressed awareness of extreme childhood trauma may cause her to feel and appear as if she is "getting worse" while in treatment. As psychotherapy supports the gradual uncovering of previously repressed memories, the client's concomitant increase in painful affect changes her relation to her therapist and may motivate what seem to be primitive, disorganized, sometimes even "crazy" behaviors—responses that others may label as "acting out," "deterioration," or "decompensation." Such reactions may lead the clinician to question the further use of exploratory or abuse-focused therapy with such a "fragile" or problematic individual.

Initially the therapist's task seemed clear: to foster increased awareness and integration of child abuse experiences by assisting in the "reworking" of abuse-related memories. However, as she is confronted with the fruits of this recapitulation (client rage, regression, dissociation, etc.), the therapist may feel that something Bad has happened—that she has gone "too far," stimulated decompensation, or otherwise instigated a catastrophe by opening the Pandora's box of her client's past. Unfortunately, because many mental health professionals do not want to know about sexual abuse and/or believe that such material should be avoided whenever possible (Summit, 1988), the clinician's peers or supervisors may reinforce her greatest fears: that she has gone somewhere that she shouldn't have ("with, of all people, a borderline") and that now she has to "pick up the pieces."

This chapter presents a different perspective. It acknowledges that, as described in Chapter 6, severe childhood victimization is often experienced by the survivor as "chunks" of unintegrated, sometimes disremembered pain, fear, and self-hatred, which nevertheless exerts a strong, albeit unconscious, negative influence over her adult functioning. Given the client's denial and dissociative defenses, it is assumed that therapy must necessarily work to bring such material into the open, where the client can view it, reunderstand it, and eventually integrate it into adult awareness. This process of therapeutically replaying old abuse memories, however, typically releases a gestalt of feelings and thoughts appropriate to an injured, frightened child. These (often ego-dystonic) reactions may seem quite "scary" to the adult client and, in some instances, her therapist. Fortunately, if done well, with sensitivity and at the correct pace, abuse-focused therapy can *take advantage* of these responses, work directly with the hurt, confused child, and assist in the development of a more whole and less "symptomatic" individual.

The solution to having the "tiger by the tail" is therefore to hang on, to stay with the client until she is through with what she has to do—no matter how uncomfortable or frightening the ride may be for the therapist. In contrast, it is likely that a therapeutic approach that fosters the client's continued avoidance of her abuse memories, or only superficially addresses them, will not result in significant improvement. As noted by Blake-White and Kline (1985),

> Many therapists and incest victims believe that bringing the repressed material to the surface makes the client worse. They see her exhibiting acute anxiety and expressing suicidal ideation. They believe that, forgotten, the problem will disappear. It is the authors' contention, however, that the problems never disappear; they continue to manifest themselves in serious depression, panic attacks, "free-floating" anxiety, and angry outbursts. (p. 397)

Abuse Characteristics and Treatment-Related "Deterioration"

In a chapter such as this one, where severe abuse-related problems are discussed, it is important to restate that (a) not all sexual abuse victims sustain major long-term trauma and (b) of those whose abuse-related problems persist into adulthood, not all present with severe personal or interpersonal difficulties. Given this variability, we may also assume that not every sexual abuse survivor in therapy will "get worse before she gets better." What, then, determines whether an individual in treatment will progress fairly evenly, with, perhaps, only minor setbacks or brief periods of increased dysphoria, or instead, despite what is often an initial facade of relative psychological health (e.g., MacFarlane & Korbin, 1983), will experience extensive psychological disturbance prior to further improvement?

Although, as noted in previous chapters, the complexities of child maltreatment make it difficult to know what exactly is traumagenic and what is not, certain characteristics of the original abuse experience nevertheless appear to affect client response to "uncovering" in abuse-related therapy. In this regard we may ask what aspects of sexual victimization produce especially high levels of denial, repression, dissociation, and so forth, such that integration is especially low (i.e., the "chunks" are especially large), and thus therapeutically revealed material appears especially "new" and threatening.

Extreme Abuse

Clinical experience and at least one research study (Herman & Schatzow, 1987) suggests that the adult whose childhood included especially severe abuse is more likely to repress such events and may respond more extremely to therapeutic restimulation of these memories. Among the characteristics of such abuse may be early onset and extended duration (e.g., ongoing victimization from age 3 to age 13); incest, especially at the hands of a parent; use of physical violence by the abuser (e.g., physically forced intercourse, concurrent beatings); multiple perpetrators, either within the family (e.g., instances where both parents molest the child) or in "sex rings" (Burgess & Grant, 1988); and more intrusive acts (e.g., oral, anal, or vaginal penetration).

Concurrent Psychological Abuse

As traumatic as sexual abuse may be, these effects may be intensified and augmented by psychological and emotional maltreatment. Chronic verbal punitiveness, frequent criticisms and insults, emotional neglect, and other forms of nonphysical abuse produce their own long-term effects (e.g., Briere & Runtz, 1988b; Hart & Brassard, 1987; Rosenberg,

1987) and appear to have specific impacts on children's reactions to concurrent sexual victimization.

By conveying to the child that he or she is "bad," "no good," or "worthless," such maltreatment increases the victim's sense of having deserved the molestation and of not having warranted any better form of treatment. These and similar messages increase the victim's sense of shame and guilt at having been abused and underlie her perception of maltreatment as an appropriate response to her "bad"ness—conclusions that may motivate the repression of molestation experiences. This desire to unacknowledge sexual abuse may be especially high if the victim was, in fact, *punished* for reporting abuse or for expressing abuse-related pain. The author has, for example, encountered a number of clients who were beaten for telling others of their abuse or who were forced to engage in painful or humiliating activities (e.g., holding Tabasco sauce in one's mouth, eating soap, kneeling on bottlecaps for hours) as "punishment" for crying, resisting, or trying to escape during or after sexual molestation.

Pseudoparticipation

In a significant proportion of cases victims of sexual abuse are trained or forced by their perpetrators to initiate or respond to sexual behaviors. This may range from being told to ask for sexual contact and/ or to respond to sexual abuse with expressions of pleasure to being taught to "seduce" the abuser or others (e.g., siblings or friends). Some perpetrators, in fact, have been known to devote considerable attention to sexually arousing their victims so that, in the words of one molester, "She's tied to me forever by her own feelings of pleasure; she becomes part of it too." After repeated experiences of this kind, some children become prematurely sexualized—actually seeking out sexual contact and in some instances deriving some physical pleasure from it.

Although such behaviors are still clearly abusive, regardless of the child's eventual "participation" or response, adults with backgrounds of pseudoparticipation are prone to feelings of extreme guilt and responsibility (Sgroi & Bunk, 1988). During psychotherapy recall of these experiences may be incomplete or nonexistent, as the survivor seeks to avoid not only the memories themselves but also intense feelings of self-disgust and self-blame. Additionally, the therapist's comments vis-à-vis the perpetrator may come to be consciously or unconsciously understood by the survivor as statements about herself, since she believes that she shares the blame for the abuse.

Ongoing Abuse

When an adult presents to a psychotherapist with issues involving childhood sexual abuse, it is frequently assumed that the victimization itself is in the past. Unfortunately, for a small number of adults (e.g., approximately 5–10% of the author's lifetime survivor case load) and a larger group of older adolescents, the victim is still "involved" with at least one of her perpetrators. In many cases this situation involves the client's father or stepfather or a family friend who has become the client's "sugar-daddy." In almost every instance the survivor initially keeps this relationship from the therapist, feeling ashamed and fearing rejection or ridicule. This secret can be quite destructive, however, as the survivor's guilt escalates and as she continues to withhold "the truth" from her therapist.

Ongoing abuse stimulates repression and nonintegration of earlier molestation for several reasons. First, abuse memories may be even more threatening for the ongoing victim than for others, since they remind her of her current, extremely guilt-inducing situation and emphasize its abusive and exploitive basis. Second, the client's ongoing relationship may, in her mind, retroactively imply earlier participation and consent, and thus the client's normal anger toward her abuser may be turned toward herself. Finally, given the level of avoidance she must marshal to "overlook" or tolerate her ongoing/current abuse, the survivor may become extensively involved in denial and repression, producing a brittle facade that is highly vulnerable to "danger" from awareness-building interventions of any kind.

Sadistic and/or Ritualistic Abuse

Because of all types of sexual abuse this last form is least often described and most distressing to hear about, sadistic/ritualistic abuse has only recently been understood to any extent by therapists. Nevertheless, it is now becoming clear that this especially malignant type of victimization is considerably more frequent than previously thought, and that the terror, horror, and pain associated with such acts may cause them to be repressed quickly and completely by the victim.

Sadistic abuse refers to acts engaged in against a child by an adult who derives sexual pleasure by inflicting pain or degradation. Examples of such sexual torture are burning and mutilation during a sexual assault (including cutting of genitals and nipples, carving of words or symbols into the skin, use of electrical drills or surgical instruments, etc.); insertion of dirt, feces, insects, or various other objects into the vagina and/or anus; and the victim being tied, restrained, or bound for extended periods of time, during which various sexual acts are performed.

Ritualistic abuse differs from sadistic abuse (in those cases where both are not present simultaneously) in that the former is done in the context of "spirituality" or occult religion, rather than solely for sado-sexual pleasure. Perhaps most commonly, adult survivors of this form of abuse describe black magic or satanic rites, where the child victim is part of a ceremony involving desecration and sexual debasement. Examples of such activities include the child being forced to publicly masturbate with a crucifix; ceremonial gang rape by all (or a privileged few) of the male members of the cult; ritualized sexual interactions where the victim symbolizes "Good" or "innocence" and thus is sexually defiled and/or "converted"; sexual contact with or dismemberment of a family pet; demands that the child drink blood or urine or eat vile substances; and ritualistic ceremonies where the child is stripped of clothing, tied to a crucifix or platform, sexually molested, and led to believe that she is about to be sacrificed.

Survivors of such practices are often triply injured: (a) these acts are so abhorrent that the victim often cannot conceive of herself without reference to her torture and degradation, and thus may unconsciously believe that she is as "bad" as whatever was done to her (Briere, 1988); (b) abuse in the context of "supernatural" or occult events may lead the victim to perceive the world from a magical perspective, including the notion that omnipotent evil beings or spirits are always present and preparing to harm her (especially if she "tells"); and (c) memories of her victimization may be so sketchy and yet so horrible that they are discounted by her therapist as fabrications or, at best, examples of delusional thinking (Strieff & Bitz, 1988, April).

Impact on the Psychotherapeutic Process

In combination or separately, these various intensifiers of abuse trauma often have a common effect: They cause the survivor to especially fear the past and to avoid activities that trigger painful memories. As noted in Chapter 6, the survivor thus finds himself in a double bind: Therapy that may eventually offer relief from the frightening and painful abuse-related symptoms also involves, by nature, the very recapitulation of childhood trauma he seeks to avoid. Viewed from this perspective, we must appreciate the bravery entailed in being a psychotherapy client for such individuals. Further, we may then understand the "extreme" or "abnormal" reactions to therapy that frequently arise from this dilemma. Presented below are several of the most problematic of these responses.

Heightened Transference

Transference, as noted in Chapter 4, involves client reactions to her therapist that are, in fact, projections of earlier experiences with significant others in the client's life. As was also noted, given that the abuse survivor's childhood was generally aversive, such transference is likely to be negative or at least highly ambivalent—producing sudden angry, hurt, or stereotypically sexualized responses to relatively neutral clinician behavior or stimuli. These responses, if not handled appropriately, may serve to impede the process of treatment, as well as potentially stimulating negative countertransference in the psychologically vulnerable therapist.

Severe sexual abuse may produce more transferential problems than otherwise would be expected, an outcome that, in turn, can easily result in escalating difficulties as treatment progresses. Specifically, the client with a history of extreme maltreatment may be especially unable to integrate her childhood trauma with adult awareness, given the high levels of denial and repression she has necessarily had to invoke. For this reason her responses to replaying these experiences in therapy may be especially archaic and childhood specific. To the extent that the client thus may briefly "become" the abused child at points in therapy, the therapist is proportionately more likely to be seen as a parent and/or abuser.

The frequent effect of this involuntary return to childhood is a highly ambivalent, emotionally intense client-therapist relationship, where transferential affect and "acting out" is especially common. Typical responses include periods of unwarranted rage at the therapist for imagined or minor "sins"; cycles of idealization and devaluation; excessive need for approval, with concurrent expectations of rejection; over-attachment and, in some cases, intrusion into the therapist's personal life; adversariality, manifesting as manipulativeness; and intrusive sexualization of the therapeutic relationship.

In addition to transferentially based behaviors, however, there exists an entirely separate domain of responses that arise from the nonintegration forced by severe abuse—the client's extreme reaction to abuse-related memories and affects as they emerge during treatment.

Self-Destructiveness

The sexual abuse survivor's tendency to turn anger and self-hatred into self-injurious acts is described throughout this book. As presented in Chapters 1 and 2, this self-destructiveness often occurs during periods of abuse-related dysphoria, when depression, self-blaming thoughts, and inwardly directed anger are especially prominent. It should not be surprising, then, that the resurgence of memories and feelings that frequently transpire during abuse-focused therapy may also stimulate some survivors' potential for self-harm, especially if denial and repression had previously been high.

At the most immediate level, this self-destructiveness may manifest as dissociated, seemingly reflexive, minor self-injury during the psychotherapy session. Examples of such low-level self-mutilation include distracted scratching of one's hands, arms, or chest while discussing stressful material, clawing at one's scalp or neck, hitting one's head or fists against a nearby wall, or poking at oneself with objects such as pencils or paperclips. More frequently, however, the need for self-injurious behavior may peak minutes or hours after emotionally intense sessions, especially if previously avoided or repressed memories were processed.

A common scenario in this regard is presented below, as we consider a client described in earlier chapters.

Alice B.

As the reader will recall, Alice is a young woman who had recently been admitted to a psychiatric hospital for her third time, during a severe dissociative reaction. She has a long history of self-mutilatory episodes, as well as a total of five suicide attempts. Although Alice was not forthcoming about childhood victimization, her roommate reports that Alice, her younger sister, and (later) a friend were repeatedly sexually abused by her father over four consecutive years, until his eventual imprisonment (her sister contracted syphilis and child welfare authorities were notified).

After Alice is discharged from the hospital, outpatient appointments are arranged. Fortuitously, one of the nurses on Alice's unit is aware of the implications of sexual abuse trauma and ensures that her outpatient therapist has experience with abuse survivors. Alice is initially reluctant to attend therapy sessions, stating "there's nothing wrong with me that I can't take care of." As treatment progresses, however, she becomes quite involved. Her therapist discovers that Alice has very few memories of her abuse and is very reluctant to talk about her past. Using an approach similar to that advocated in earlier chapters, the clinician slowly and gently facilitates the recall and partial integration of several previously repressed abuse memories and works to counter Alice's pervasive self-blaming cognitions.

During her 37th session, Alice develops a powerful flashback, reexperiencing an occasion when her father forced her to have oral-genital contact with her sister. She becomes highly agitated and distraught but slowly calms down as her therapist places the event in context, repeatedly stresses her blamelessness, and applauds her progress such that "You were able to have that important memory." Because of the power and disruptiveness of this flashback, however, her therapist schedules another session for two days hence, elicits Alice's evaluation of her psychological state ("I'm OK, just a bit grossed out"), and reminds her of several self-control techniques that she had used in the past to counter self-mutilatory impulses.

Alice does not appear for her next appointment, and her therapist is later contacted by an emergency room physician. He reports that Alice has made a suicide "gesture" involving ingestion of approximately 10 of her mother's low-dose tranquilizers (Xanax). Upon discharge from the emergency room, Alice attends a session with her therapist and describes the hours following their last session. After leaving the office, she had "wandered around downtown" in a seemingly dissociated state for several hours. She states that "The next thing I knew, I was with Andy [an abusive ex-boyfriend] in his apartment, smoking 'crack' [a highly potent form of cocaine]." She then relates having sex with Andy's friend, crying and calling him names during and after intercourse, and then somehow returning to the streets, "all the time with bad thoughts running through my mind." She has no memory of how she later ended up at her mother's house ("I don't even like her") or of taking her mother's pills.

Alice continues in therapy and slowly recovers further memories and "little kid" feelings, although never again at the intensity of her earlier experience. The following 6 months of treatment were difficult, however, marked by periods of depression, unfocused anger, and two more cocaine binges, along with a temporary return to her ex-boyfriend Andy.

Many aspects of Alice's story typify the incursion of self-destructive impulses into abuse-oriented therapy. First, although her current behavior occurred within the context of psychotherapy, the activities she engaged in were ones she had used many times in the past. Second, her acute episode of self-destructiveness was anteceded by an intrusive, abuse-specific memory, as opposed to just happening "out of the blue."

Third, much of her behavior occurred during a dissociative episode, as is often the case when the survivor is struggling to somehow "deal with" unwanted awareness (i.e., her forced sexual contact with her sister).

Finally, Alice's self-injurious behaviors were those frequently seen in abuse-related "acting out": suicidality (of low lethality in this case), substance abuse (the substances of choice usually being alcohol and stimulants such as cocaine or amphetamines), and seemingly indiscriminate but, in actuality, often specifically degrading or hurtful sexual behavior. Also frequently present is self-mutilation, although in Alice's case there may not have been the time or the opportunity for this behavior, which usually occurs when the survivor is alone and after some rumination.

Not a major factor in Alice's case, except perhaps in terms of her low lethality suicide attempt, is a last quality of some abuse-related self-destructiveness: self-injury as a method of influencing or communicating to one's therapist. Thus, as noted in Chapters 1 and 2, suicide attempts, self-mutilation, or "high-risk" activities can be a form of interpersonal behavior for some survivors, allowing them to say or demand things that they believe cannot otherwise be said or asked for (Runtz & Briere, 1986). For instance, Alice's suicide attempt may have been, in part, a way to tell her therapist about how much abuse memories hurt and how bad she "really" feels or to punish the clinician's exploration of abuse material so that it would not happen again.

"Deterioration"

In addition to those behaviors that are manifestly self-destructive, some survivors more generally appear to "get worse" at points in abuse-focused therapy. As noted earlier, such "deterioration" may suggest to the clinician (or it may be suggested to her) that uncovering treatment is contraindicated or that the therapist is mismanaging treatment. While, obviously, there are times when "uncovering" is inappropriate (e.g., with highly unstable clients or during periods of extreme stress or crisis) and some therapists may, in fact, "mismanage" a difficult clinical situation, in many instances of work with sexual abuse survivors an increase in symptoms or dysphoria may indicate that treatment is progressing as it should.

As described earlier, the process of confronting and integrating long-repressed memories implies, at minimum, psychological discomfort. Repression and denial serve as defenses against the painful affect which would otherwise accompany full awareness. Thus, recall of repressed or dissociated material must necessarily include a resurgence of distress, although perhaps not always at its original (abuse period) intensity. The most frequently reported problems that arise during abuse-oriented therapy are increased anxiety and depression and "new" PTSD reactions.

The anxiety reactions most commonly associated with uncovering repressed abuse material appear to be free-floating anxiety, fearful preoccupation, and panic attacks. "Free-floating anxiety," present in many individuals to some extent, refers to a general sense of fearfulness that cannot be "pinned down" to any one cause. This reaction may be quite substantial for the survivor whose unconscious awareness of abuse issues has been restimulated by psychotherapy or other abuse-relevant events. Such fearfulness is often experienced as free floating because the relevant material is still partially repressed, and thus the survivor is unclear as to why she is so anxious. In addition, the very process of psychotherapy is diffusely threatening, since it implies potential for further awareness of aversive events.

This sense of impending danger frequently manifests as a general fearful preoccupation—the survivor becomes increasingly afraid of the future, anticipating any number of painful/disastrous outcomes. Thus, rather than being consciously frightened by recent or upcoming abuse recollections, the client may describe increasing fears of death by disease or assault, thoughts that one's house might burn down, that an earthquake might ensue, or that loved ones might be in danger. More basically, of course, the abuse survivor is beginning to process abuse-period affects, the most common of which is fear or perceived vulnerability.

In addition to vulnerability, abuse-focused therapy may restimulate the survivor's childhood experience of lack of control. This sense of frightening helplessness often emerges in the form of panic attacks: sudden episodes of intense fear that escalate as a function of their intrusiveness and seeming uncontrollability. As many individuals with "anxiety attacks" will attest, one of the most powerful precipitants of such episodes is the growing fearful expectation that another one will occur. From the survivor's perspective, this process may develop as follows: (a) the sudden emergence of abuse-related memories, feelings, or responses during therapy is frightening, both in terms of their unpredictability and their actual content; (b) along with concomitant free-floating anxiety, this intense fear of one's own thoughts and affects is, itself, seen as further evidence of loss of control, leading to (c) an escalating spiral of fear stimulating fear, panic attacks, and other extreme anxiety states.

As has been noted in Chapters 1 and 2, survivors of sexual abuse are especially prone to depression, as well as anxiety. This tendency to respond to stress with dysthymic mood is often exacerbated during psychotherapy, where the survivor's usual defenses against abuse-related dysphoria are ideally lessened. As she comes to confront the full extent of her victimization, and more fully experience its results, the psychic pain that accrues from such awareness typically becomes more obvious. As a result, the client in abuse-focused therapy may report periods of increased dejection, isolation, "neediness," or hopelessness.

Finally, psychotherapy of abuse trauma may trigger, in some individuals, a resurgence of PTSD-like reactions, including increased flashbacks, dissociative episodes, nightmares, and sleep disturbance. This is undoubtedly because, just as PTSD symptoms can be restimulated by similar events in the posttraumatic environment, abuse-related problems often intensify when therapy "reminds" the client of childhood victimization. These reminders, in turn, can produce intense emotional and/or physical reactions during treatment, such as panic attacks, intense self-disgust, waves of nausea, or sudden headaches, the majority of which terminate when the session ends or the focus of discussion changes.

Together these various therapy-associated problems may engender a "crisis of faith" for the client, whose initial fears regarding psychotherapy and self-examination may appear to have been justified. Fortunately, these affective and cognitive signs of distress are not always extreme, and most typically recede over the course of treatment. The rate at which this remission occurs is, of course, a function of the extent and severity of the original abuse trauma, as well as the pace of therapy and the extent of the client's current psychological resources.

Although the survivor of severe abuse may temporarily "feel worse," however, she is often also aware of simultaneously feeling stronger. This latter experience may derive from two related processes. First, the lessened need to "not know" about one's abuse appears to free up emotional and psychological energy otherwise involved in active repression (Freud, 1959/1920), allowing greater awareness, free attention, and interaction with the "here and now." Second, the experience of confronting one's greatest fears and yet of not being annihilated can foster a growing sense of mastery and self-efficacy. As a 27-year-old actress with a history of severe (sibling) sexual abuse concluded, "It's true that I'm having a bad time these days, but I've never been so alive, either."

Treatment Implications

The treatment implications of "teasing the dragon" are thus twofold: On the one hand, the occasional intensification of symptomatology can produce "acting out" and self-destructiveness; on the other, the process of "getting worse before you get better" is a natural one, which should not be overdramatized or pathologized. In the former case, the clinician must work to keep the client safe—providing structure and support up to and including brief psychiatric hospitalization, if necessary. While in no way overlooking the need for such heroic interventions in isolated instances, however (the author has, for example, admitted or helped to admit to hospital a number of suicidal abuse survivors), it should be stressed that clinician "co-panic" (becoming as frightened and losing as much perspective as one's overwhelmed client) is a not infrequent phenomenon.

In such instances the therapist may catastrophize her client's difficulties, seeing him as an immediate danger to himself or others or as gravely disabled. In the therapist's attempt to protect all involved (including, perhaps, herself vis-à-vis a civil suit), the client's confidentiality may be violated, psychiatric medications may be started or increased, and hospitalization may be initiated. While each of these options has its place (although major medications such as the neuroleptics are, in the author's experience, rarely helpful in the long term), they are all potentially stigmatizing and may easily communicate to the client that he is sick, out of control, and getting worse.

There appear to be, in fact, a small subset of "severely borderline" abuse survivors who have unnecessarily become chronic psychiatric patients. These individuals are typically prescribed chronic antipsychotic medications and are often hospitalized several times per year with diagnoses such as "schizophrenia," "major depression with psychotic features," or "atypical psychosis" (see, e.g., Beck & van der Kolk, 1987, cited in van der Kolk, 1987). Although the lives of such individuals are chaotic and fragmented, they often cling tightly to their psychiatric role and identity—choosing (in the absence of helpful, long-term psychotherapy) sedating drugs and highly structured, controlling environments over living with abuse-related pain. The clinician who overreacts to client "deterioration" with inappropriate medication or hospitalization may find a willing partner in some abuse survivors, who have learned to rely on immediate (but temporary) medical/psychiatric solutions to otherwise aversive psychological states.

In contrast to some clinicians' overreaction to client distress, other therapists unconsciously utilize the exact opposite defense when confronted with escalating dysphoria or disorganization: They deny any evidence that the survivor is in unusual pain or experiencing greater psychological difficulties. As a result, such clinicians often fail to moderate the pace or intensity of treatment, despite their client's obvious increased distress. Although the motive for this unresponsiveness is usually benign (i.e., the therapist's anxiety that the client may, in fact, be "getting worse"), it is frequently perceived by the survivor as abandonment ("You don't care how I feel, just like my father/mother/ uncle didn't") or incompetence ("You don't know what is happening to me—you're not in control of this process"), either of which may stimulate further dysphoria and "decompensation."

This last scenario illustrates a final point with regard to therapy-based increases in client disturbance: Although helpful treatment does not overemphasize the survivor's pathology or underestimate her strengths, it also recognizes the psychic disequilibrium which often accompanies exploration of severe abuse trauma. Thus the clinician must be prepared to slow the pace of treatment, provide greater structure, or utilize other therapeutic interventions that allow the client to remain safe and psychologically present during the especially "rough" points in her therapy.

In summary, the uncovering of repressed abuse trauma during psychotherapy can produce temporary increases in various types of client "symptomatology," which may lead the client or therapist to assume that something has gone wrong. This chapter suggests that such "downturns" are, in fact, to be expected in the treatment of severe abuse trauma and frequently do not reflect actual deterioration. The clinician is counselled to (1) keep the client safe by whatever means are necessary, (2) continue to evaluate the appropriateness of her interventions, including the possibility that a temporary decrease in therapeutic intensity is indicated, and yet (3) avoid unnecessary stigmatization or other processes that imply that treatment is failing or that the client is too "sick" to help. Instead, the positive aspects of intensified symptomatology are stressed, including the implications that the client is beginning to "open up" to psychotherapy and the likelihood that favorable outcomes (e.g., increased awareness and psychological strength) are also present.

CHAPTER 8

Family and Group Therapies

The focus of this book is clearly on the basic psychotherapy dyad—client and therapist—as opposed to other types of treatment. Other forms of therapy are also quite useful in work with abuse survivors, however, especially to the extent that they incorporate a broader social or interpersonal focus. For this reason, two other treatment modalities—family and group therapy—are presented in this chapter. Coverage of the former is less extensive than that of the latter, given (a) the author's experience that family therapy has less relevance to the adult survivor than does group treatment and (b) the dearth of available information on nonsexist, non-victim-blaming approaches to abuse-focused family treatment. For information on an additional form of treatment, that of couples therapy for the survivor and her/his partner, the reader is referred to an excellent article on this topic by Wendy Maltz (1988).

Issues Involved in
Abuse-Focused Family Therapy

A perusal of older articles on intrafamilial child abuse, especially in social work journals, reveals the extent to which family therapy has been seen as a treatment for child maltreatment and its effects. Recent writings, however, have focused more on individual or group treatment—especially in the case of sexual abuse. This switch in modalities probably reflects, to some extent, the frequent failure of traditional family therapy to either (a) stop abuse from occurring or (b) help the incest victim to recover from her trauma. The poor record of earlier forms of family treatment does not, however, necessarily suggest that some form of family-based intervention would not be helpful with abuse victims or survivors, especially in the context of concomitant individual psychotherapy (C. Lanktree, personal communication, November, 1987).

The relevant questions for an abuse-specific approach to family therapy are the following: Should the family be involved in the victim's treatment in the first place? How about the intrafamilial offender? What about the relationship of the nonoffending parent and siblings to the survivor?

These issues are somewhat controversial in the sexual abuse field, especially in terms of the role of the incest perpetrator. Traditional "family systems" clinicians, who tend to view incest as a family dysfunction rather than an act committed by one individual against another (e.g., Anderson & Shafer, 1979; Lustig, Dresser, Spellman, & Murray, 1968; Maisch, 1973) obviously believe that family therapy is the treatment of choice, ideally with the offender present. Other clinicians, who believe that incestuous fathers are "sick" individuals who can "recover," may stress the importance of reconciliation between the perpetrator and the victim during or after treatment. In contradistinction to these views, it is suggested here that the sexual abuser forfeits the possibility of reconciliation by virtue of his actions against his victim and that the vast majority of victims do better, and are safer, when their therapy and their future lives do not include their abusers. For a well-articulated, opposing position, the reader is referred to two chapters by Gelinas (1988a, 1988b) in a recent book by Sgroi (1988).

The current position is predicated on several points. First, experience with sexual abuse survivors suggests that once incest has occurred, trust in the perpetrator by the former victim becomes improbable, regardless of the passage of time. In fact, the goal of some therapists to "reconstitute the family" may be largely an impossible one, at least on a psychological level. (It is the author's experience that most impassioned courtroom pleas to "bring the family back together" are initiated by the offender, rather than the victim.) In a similar vein, the survivor's anger at her abuser is very unlikely to disappear as a function of his apology or successful "treatment," nor is it likely that his continued presence will cease to stimulate abuse-related pain. This is as important for the perpetrator to understand as it is for the former victim to accept without self-blame. Finally, there are few data that support the notion that child molesters are reliably able or willing to cease their abusive behavior, even after being caught and/or treated (Quinsey, 1986), and thus the victim's continued safety cannot be assured.

In the case of most abuse survivors, the issue is not whether the family can be "reconstituted," since she or he is usually already living away from the family home. She may, however, feel pressure from family members, friends, or therapists to "forgive and forget," to accept the abuser back into her life. Some clinicians express this as a clinical goal: to "put your victimization behind you" by "letting go of your rage." The implication is, of course, that if the survivor could "work out her issues with her father" (and, it is sometimes hinted, relinquish her selfish claims to continued injury), she would be a healthier person. However, as noted earlier, recovery from sexual abuse can take years, and pressure for "forgiveness" usually serves to stifle pain and anger that should be expressed.

The notion that incest can preclude a further relationship between the abuser and the former victim is not primarily a blaming one. Were there good evidence that further interaction between the survivor and her perpetrator aid in the recovery of the former victim, many clinicians would probably be in favor of it. Instead, most postabuse interactions between abuser and former victim are characterized by perpetrator denial, intellectualization, blaming, or "technical" apologies, along with the potential for even more abuse, as opposed to victim experiences of rage, guilt, and, in many cases, ambivalent needs to both gain vengeance and, paradoxically, to seek "father-ness."

This last survivor issue—the desire for nurturance and support from one's abuser while, at the same time, feeling hatred toward him or her—typifies a frequent issue in abuse-oriented treatment: Many father-daughter or father-son incest victims experience real difficulty letting go of their need for a father who was not an abuser. In the (by definition) absence of such a person, the survivor may become enmeshed in a cycle of continually seeking "fatherly" behaviors from her or his abuser—a self-defeating process that keeps the survivor tied to the perpetrator and increases the likelihood of revictimization. Obviously, activities that encourage this hurtful bond—as opposed to facilitating the acknowledgment of loss and resultant grieving (e.g., "I guess I never really had a true dad, not like I wanted")—are frequently counterproductive.

Nonoffender Family Therapy

Although therapy with one's perpetrator present is, at best, unlikely to be helpful, there are often times when treatment effectively includes the nonoffending parent and siblings. As noted earlier in this book, intrafamilial sexual abusers may victimize other members of the family as well, through wife-battering, emotional and/or physical abuse, molestation of the victim's siblings, or by setting a general family tone of authoritarianism and adversariality (e.g., deLang & Goodson, 1988, April). In such a setting scapegoating, further abuse, and neglect by "nonoffending" members is common. Thus although the primary abuse transpired at the hands of the molester, the incest survivor may have substantial issues with—and anger toward—other family members. Since extent of familial support appears to impact on the survivor's ultimate psychological health (e.g., Wyatt & Mickey, 1987), intervention in such dysfunctional family systems can be of considerable long-term benefit.

Especially salient for the survivor, in many cases, are feelings of abandonment by the nonoffending parent (e.g., "Why didn't she do anything? He hurt me a lot, and mom never did a thing"). This sense of betrayal can be so strong that, as many clinicians discover to their dismay, the former abuse victim feels greater antipathy for her (typically) mother than for the incest perpetrator. This reaction is probably the result of two major dynamics: First, the survivor, like other members of North American society, has been raised to expect unconditional protection and nurturance from the mother, regardless of that parent's own problems or endangerment; second, the nonoffending parent is, by definition, less threatening and safer to hate.

With regard to the first issue, clinical experience, as well as recent research (e.g., Russell, 1986), suggests that the nonincestuous parent is frequently not cognizant of the abuse, although she may know that "something" is wrong. Even in those instances where she is aware, it is often the case that she is a psychologically or physically battered wife (Herman, 1981), a sexual abuse survivor herself (Goodwin, McCarthy, & DiVasto, 1981), or otherwise psychologically or physically incapacitated (Finkelhor, 1980). Thus she may be unlikely to serve as an optimal guardian for her children—especially against her husband, whom she may desperately need to believe incapable of sexually abusive acts against her family and/or whom she may fear as much as do her children.

Because of these secondary factors, the focus of the survivor's therapy, at some point, may be family sessions involving the former victim, the nonoffending parent, and any siblings. In these sessions the survivor is allowed to ventilate her feelings of abandonment and rage yet, nevertheless, is encouraged to hear clearly other family members' situations or perceptions at the time of her abuse. The therapeutic tasks are generally (a) to facilitate communication between family members, without excessive blaming or scapegoating (e.g., Gelinas, 1988a), (b) to explicate the many adaptive and defensive responses that the family engaged in to deal with the violence around them, and (c) to assist in the "restructuring" of family relationships away from abuse-related authoritarianism and toward mutual support (C. Lanktree, personal communication, February, 1988). As was noted for her response to the perpetrator, the client is not expected to short-circuit her anger with premature forgiveness. Nevertheless, it is the author's experience that the anger dynamics are different in the case of the "abandoning mother" or coabusive siblings (if sexual abuse did not occur there as well) and often are more subject to eventual reconciliation.

Successful work in this area—for example, reconnection of the mother-daughter dyad or renewed communication between siblings— often has other salutory effects on the survivor, including decreased isolation and a greater sense of belonging to a caring family unit. Secondarily, by rediscovering family support sans the abuser, the survivor may come to see her perpetrator as ultimately less important and as not necessarily representative of her family's feelings about her. As one survivor noted, after a particularly fruitful family session, "I thought they alll hated me, but they never really did. A lot of it had to do with dad, and how he twisted things around, and how we were afraid to put our anger on him."

Confronting the Abuser

Often debated is the advisability of having at least one session where the survivor and perpetrator are both present. The purpose of this meeting is for the client to directly tell her molester about her experience of the abuse, how she was injured by his actions, and how she feels about the perpetrator at present. Therapists who support the use of offender confrontation during treatment note the benefits of "breaching the secret," both in terms of the client formally externalizing her anger and guilt, as well as the opportunity that this process offers to place some closure on the abuse. Opponents to confrontation note the frequently negative and verbally assaultive responses of abusers in such sessions and question the ultimate value of such conflictual interactions.

The current author finds validity in each perspective. It is clear that if not well-structured and controlled, survivor-abuser confrontation sessions can become highly destructive events, wherein the abuser further damages the client. On the other hand, if orchestrated carefully, such sessions may be quite helpful for those survivors for whom such action is a major issue (Agosta & Loring, 1988). The most critical determinants of a positive outcome are (a) the *survivor's* (as opposed to the therapist's) desire for this confrontation; (b) her being prepared well ahead of time (e.g., through role-playing) for the fact that the abuser is very unlikely to admit his culpability and/or truly apologize (a persistent fantasy of many survivors); (c) her definite understanding that the confrontation session is entirely and solely for the survivor, allowing her to "say what must be said," as opposed to convincing (or even "helping") the abuser; (d) some level of agreement from the perpetrator, if possible, that he will try to listen—or at least remain silent—rather than attacking the client or defending himself; and (e) perhaps most important, the survivor being sufficiently advanced in her recovery that she has the internal resources and stability required to undergo such a stressful event. With regard to the last, the therapist may choose to discourage the rageful survivor who is besieged by intrusive memories from "having it out with dad" and instead may focus on additional treatment and greater understanding before any such activities are undertaken.

In summary, when abuser confrontation is successful, it yields many of the same benefits that accrue to the mourner at a funeral: It allows the release of affect which salves the grief entailed in loss (e.g., of the father-daughter relationship) and provides a formal ending and closure (i.e., of the abusive relationship) so that a "new," more positive life may begin.

Permanent Separation

A final issue with regard to family members is what may be called "parentectomy." This refers to intentional, permanent separation from one or both parents because of their continuing abusiveness and the extremely low likelihood of eventual rapprochement. While this procedure is advocated for most instances involving the molester, it may also be necessary with regard to the remaining parent. In the latter case, this radical action may be warranted when the "nonoffending" parent directly and consciously defends the molester and negates the survivor and/or where said parent, herself, has engaged in physical or emotional abuse without remorse or intent to change.

Although a "parentectomy" is likely to improve the survivor's general mental health, it nevertheless extracts an unavoidable price. Such psychological surgery results in permanent unfinished business: The survivor not only can never make total peace with her abuser, she also can never complete her war with him or her. Her anger lives on, although usually attenuating over time, and some parts of the wound usually remain tender.

Group Therapy

In addition to family therapy with nonoffending members, group therapy is often a powerful adjunct in the treatment of post-sexual-abuse trauma. This modality is briefly outlined here, and the reader is referred to more comprehensive presentations by Blake-White and Kline (1985), Cole (1985), Cole and Barney (1987), Courtois and Leehan (1982), Goodman and Nowak-Scibelli (1985), Gordy (1983), Herman and Schatzow (1984), Lubell and Soong (1982), NiCarthy, Merriam, & Coffman (1984), and Tsai and Wagner (1978).

As described in earlier chapters, group therapy has certain advantages over individual psychotherapy alone (Johnson, 1985). Most writers in this area specifically stress the benefits of lessened isolation and stigmatization, reduced shame, the development of early interpersonal trust, and identification with a supportive network of other, similarly injured individuals. Additionally, participation in such groups offers the survivor the opportunity to help as well as to be helped—a process that supports self-esteem and lessens the sense of being a deviant, passive recipient of treatment.

Although there are obviously many principles that apply to group therapy with any client population (see, e.g., Yalom, 1975), certain issues and parameters are especially relevant to work with survivors of severe sexual victimization. The most important of these are outlined below.

Screening

Because of the variable psychological functioning found among sexual abuse survivors, most therapy group leaders require that prospective members attend a pregroup evaluation interview. This meeting allows the group leaders to assess the client's level of psychological disturbance and her or his ability to withstand the stress of group treatment. The philosophy of this screening process is perhaps best articulated by Cole and Barney (1987):

> The screening interview includes a reciprocal exchange of information. Emphasis is placed on the fact that both therapist and potential group member must make a decision about the interviewee's participation in the group. Thus the survivor's ability to be a part of the decision-making process and act on her own behalf is underscored, as is the therapist's responsibility to set limits and "do no

harm." The prominent themes in a survivor's life, taking care of oneself and appropriate (or inappropriate) exercise of responsibility by authority figures, are relevant even in this early context. (p. 603)

Although the minimal criteria for group participation varies from therapist to therapist [Tsai & Wagner, e.g., advocate accepting "all women who report a molestation experience and wish to participate in a group" (1978, p. 426), as do NiCarthy et al. (1984)], many workers in this area suggest screening out individuals who are (a) either chronically unstable or currently in crisis, (b) currently abusing drugs or alcohol, (c) psychotic, or (d) suicidal.

Although the current author has no quarrel with any of these exclusion criteria per se, he would remind the reader that these screening parameters are similar to the major long-term effects of sexual abuse, as described in Chapters 1 and 2. Thus if taken to their extreme, these criteria might successfully screen out most victims of severe abuse, leaving only those with less need for treatment. For this reason the following strategy is suggested.

1. Carefully evaluate each client for the presence of the above difficulties, as well as any other relevant concerns.
2. Determine the actual extent of each problem (e.g., there may well be a considerable difference between the group functioning of a severely suicidal person versus one who has passing suicidal thoughts, or between a woman who occasionally uses recreational amounts of cocaine and a heroin addict).
3. Determine whether such negative factors, in combination with any specific strengths (e.g., good impulse control), are likely to interfere with each particular client's individual response to group therapy. If the answer is yes, the client should be referred back to her individual therapist until a later point in time, when she is more ready for the stress of a group experience. The answer may be no, however, if the prospective member is not psychotic, out of touch with reality, substance addicted, overly impulsive, or obviously unable to interact appropriately with others. Additionally, even these problems may not rule out a survivor's participation if the group is specifically designed for such issues (e.g., a group for addicted incest survivors). Thus, at least from the author's perspective, group "screening criteria" should be seen as advisory, as opposed to mandatory. The ultimate question the therapist must ask herself is: Does this client have sufficient inner resources and few enough interfering factors

that she could attend this group without becoming a casualty of the treatment process?

Concurrent Individual Psychotherapy

As noted earlier in this chapter, the process of group treatment is inherently a stressful one for abuse survivors. Not only does the client have her own painful memories to disclose and to work on in front of relative strangers, she must also listen to painfully detailed accounts of other members' betrayal and victimization. The effect of these group experiences is often escalating anxiety and anger and restimulation of abuse-related flashbacks and intrusive thoughts.

This high level of stress not only requires careful attention to group process and specific timing of interventions for each group member, as described by Cole and Barney (1987), but also suggests the need for concurrent individual psychotherapy. Of the many abuse groups that the author has supervised, perhaps the most common negative outcomes have involved survivors whose internal resources have been overwhelmed by powerful group processes and who have had no external (nongroup) therapeutic supports to call upon.

Such individuals additionally often demand (or elicit) a disproportionate share of the group's attention and may become disruptive as a result of their dysfunctional interpersonal behavior. By virtue of their monopolizing the group's attention and agenda, these clients may eventually become ostracized and/or attacked by other group members—leading to further alienation and distress. In most cases this "fallout" from group is clinically manageable but requires that the therapists become personally involved (e.g., Courtois & Leehan, 1982), thus violating the important group therapy maxim of "equal attention for all."

For this reason many clinicians insist that group members also have regular outside psychotherapists (Cole & Barney, 1987; Goodman & Nowak-Scibelli, 1985; Gordy, 1983; Herman & Schatzow, 1984; Lubell & Soong, 1982). This division of labor allows the survivor to gain from the social interaction, feedback, and support of group psychotherapy and yet have an individual therapist who can devote her full attention to the client and her more pressing needs and issues. Thus although leaders of "high functioning" groups—where all suicidal, substance abusing, and "emotionally unstable" clients have been screened out—may not feel the need for a concomitant therapy rule, therapists of most abuse groups (e.g., in mental health centers, drug treatment facilities, psychiatric inpatient units, or postincarceration settings) are well advised to make this a requirement.

Other Ground Rules

In addition to concomitant individual psychotherapy, it is usually a good idea to introduce a few other ground rules at the onset of group therapy. The most common of these are as follows:

1. *Attendance.* Members should try to attend every session of the group, especially if it is closed and/or short-term. It is often further requested that if a member is considering dropping out of group, that he or she return one last time to share that decision with the group.
2. *Confidentiality.* Participants are asked to refrain from discussing the group with nonmembers, both in terms of the material disclosed during sessions and the identities of the group participants.
3. *Outside contact.* Some clinicians (e.g., Goodman & Nowak-Scibelli, 1985) request that participants not socialize outside of group meetings, whereas others (e.g., Herman & Schatzow, 1984) place no constraints on outside contact. The argument in favor of noncontact is that the neediness and interpersonal dysfunctionality of some abuse survivors can produce occasional intense and disruptive interactions outside of group, where they cannot be controlled by the group leaders. Such interactions, in addition to being potentially injurious to the members involved, may also have negative impacts on the group's functioning. Examples of such behaviors are clients who make repetitive and unwanted phone calls or visits to other group members, members coercing other members into sexual contact, and subgroups of members having "councils of war" regarding disliked other members. Although the current author does not advocate a "no contact" rule per se (among other things, such rules are virtually unenforceable), it is recommended that clients be asked to forego sexual relationships with group members, at least during the tenure of the group, and that, most important, any significant contacts between group members that occur outside of group be brought into the next session where they can be discussed.
4. *"Air time."* A final recommended ground rule is that all group members be allowed a certain amount of uninterrupted time per session to speak about their issues, concerns, or feelings. This may be ensured by having all members begin each session with a brief presentation of how their week went, how they are feeling now, and so forth. Other groups have a "no interruption" rule, whereby any

member is deemed to have the right to speak without being cut off by another member. Finally, in groups where the leaders take an active role, the clinician may specifically keep track of who has or hasn't spoken in a given session and may ask silent members if there is anything that they wish to discuss. Regardless of how this rule is enforced, the bottom line should be that all members have the right to speak—that silence is no longer being forced upon them, and that the group cares that they have a chance to participate.

Group Composition

Although it is clear that abuse groups should consist of only males or only females [see Fair (1988, April) for an opposing perspective], should usually be run by clinicians of the same gender as the members and should not combine early adolescents with older adults, most other mixtures of clients seem to work equally well together. Herman and Schatzow (1984), for example, conclude that "prospective group members' motivation and positive expectations seemed to outweigh other factors such as age, race, sexual orientation, or diagnosis in predicting a successful group outcome" (p. 3).

The only provisos that might be added to this assessment are that optimal group dynamics are probably most likely when (a) less verbal members are balanced by a number of more verbal ones, (b) one or two members are "advanced," in the sense of having already dealt with many of their abuse issues in previous psychotherapy, (c) all group members are at *roughly* equivalent levels of psychological functioning, and (d) the total number of participants per group ranges between 5 and 10. As to the last point, groups with fewer than 5 members often appear to drag or, paradoxically, become too intense, whereas groups larger than 10 often deprive individual members of needed "air time" and frequently fail to coalesce into a functioning entity.

Number and Duration of Sessions

A review of the limited literature on sexual abuse groups reveals a considerable diversity in the number of sessions considered best for abuse survivors, although most authors agree on the length of each session (1½ to 2 hours). Two writers, for example, describe group programs consisting of either four or six meetings in total (Tsai & Wagner, 1978; Cole, 1985), whereas, at the other end of the continuum, Lubell and Soong (1982) and Courtois and Leehan (1982) suggest 19 and over

24 sessions, respectively. The advantages of small numbers of sessions appear to be their economy (both in terms of time and money), their goal orientation, and the sharp focus on abuse-related issues they offer. Such groups are likely to be conceptualized as partially didactic and as serving as a prelude to other, more extensive forms of treatment (Tsai & Wagner, 1978). Longer groups, on the other hand, allow the members to learn about one another, to build group cohesion and a sense of trust, and to work through abuse-related interpersonal problems (Courtois & Leehan, 1982).

Although the optimal number of sessions may thus vary according to the goals of treatment, as well as the setting in which therapy is taking place, the author has found that 10 to 12 sessions (the average number cited in the abuse group literature) is often most effective— allowing enough time for group cohesion to occur, and yet not so extended that intra-group conflicts and habitually dysfunctional behaviors supersede abuse-related concerns.

Group Structure

There are several basic types of group structures, different combinations of which may be adapted for work with abuse survivors. Most basically, these can be summarized as "open" versus "closed," and "programmatic" versus "nonprogrammatic."

Open abuse groups begin at a specific time, but continue for an indeterminate number of sessions. Because these groups are ongoing, members typically rotate in and out of them as needed. One client, for example, may enter the group at session 7, stay for the next 10 sessions, and then leave, whereas the next client might enter at session 9 and stay until session 35. The advantages of such groups include (a) their flexibility of membership, making them ideal for psychiatric hospitals or residential settings where clients enter treatment at different times and (b) the opportunity for new members to learn from "old" ones who are familiar with the group process and who can provide helpful information and feedback.

Although open groups have several positive attributes, some survivors are unsettled by the shifting membership of such groups and may report never feeling entirely safe. A commonly expressed concern in this regard is that open groups do not foster a sense of community, where survivors can grow to know and count upon each other. Closed groups, on the other hand, do offer this opportunity for group cohesion. Such groups begin and (hopefully) end with the same members, usually after a predetermined number of sessions. Understanding and trust between group members thus becomes a major issue, as does heightened communication. Successful groups of this sort take on "a life of their own" in many instances and may become central support systems for their members. Despite these obvious advantages, however, closed groups also have several potential weaknesses, including the effects of client dropout over time (in most instances one or more members leave prior to the official end of group) and the duress of "waiting lists" for survivors who were not present at the beginning of the group but who nevertheless would benefit from immediate group therapy (Blake-White & Kline, 1985; Cole & Barney, 1987).

Programmatic groups proceed according to a predetermined plan, wherein each session has a specific focus and in some cases specific exercises. These groups are almost always closed and tend to be shorter than nonprogrammatic ones. Cole (1985) and Tsai and Wagner (1978), for example, list the goals and activities of each of the four to six sessions of their groups, and Herman and Schatzow (1984) have specific instructions for sessions 1, 2 to 5, 6 to 9, and 10. Most programmatic groups follow some version of the following schema: Early sessions focus on introductions, description of ground rules, didactic information on sexual abuse (both orally presented and in the form of reading lists or handouts), summary disclosures of molestation, and the development of group cohesion and identity; middle sessions are devoted to extensive discussions of individual group members molestation experiences, with support and feedback from other members and the group leaders; and final sessions work to develop a sense of closure on the experience, including the sometimes difficult work of termination.

Nonprogrammatic groups, while usually remaining structured in terms of specific starting and stopping times, "air time" limits for each participant, and occasional prescribed "homework" assignments (e.g., Courtois & Leehan, 1982), nevertheless are less subject to strictures regarding the appropriate content of any given session. The topics of each meeting are more typically determined by the participants, given the overriding assumption that the general context will still be members' abuse experiences and their ramifications. Most open groups are, of necessity, nonprogrammatic ones, since it would be inappropriate for new members to enter a group halfway through a programmed series of sessions. Some long-term closed groups, however, are also nonprogrammed, especially if one of the group goals is the working through of abuse-related interpersonal problems.

In the author's experience, both programmed and nonprogrammed groups "work"; the choice of which type to use is primarily a function of the goals of treatment, the setting in which it will occur, and the time available for therapy. Short closed groups usually function best in a programmed mode, whereas long-term groups, whether open or closed, are often most effective if the agenda for each session is participant determined.

Session Structure

In addition to its structure across meetings, the abuse group also has form within sessions. Most groups begin with each member speaking briefly about his or her life since the last session and about how he or she is feeling at the present moment. This activity gives each member a structured opportunity to share with the group, as well as allowing the group leaders to ascertain who may need special attention. After this exercise is completed, the group typically moves on to whatever discussions have been planned (in programmatic groups) or are generated by the participants' opening presentations (in nonprogrammatic ones). At the end of each session the group process is recapped by the members or the leaders: Significant points are reemphasized and a more global perspective on the group's process is offered, usually stressing communalities of experience. Also at this time many therapists repeat the opening exercise: Each member, in turn, makes a brief statement on how the group went and how they are feeling.

The intent of these activities is twofold. First, anxiety is lessened by providing a predictable structure within each session. Participants know they will have several opportunities to speak but that the focus of the group will then move on to other speakers. The predictability of this routine reassures the participants that the process is under control and therefore is relatively safe. Second, the internal structure of the session allows for closure, giving the members a sense of completeness. By "wrapping up" each session at its end, the therapists in some sense imply that the process is finished for that moment and thus is no longer as threatening as it might otherwise be. In the words of one group member: "The wrapup kind of closes the book until next week, so I can feel like, OK, let's move on to the next thing I have to do."

In contrast, a session where intense disclosures continue until the allocated amount of time runs out, at which time all members unceremoniously depart, is quite likely to remain anxiety provoking well beyond the end of the session. This anxiety continues partially because there has been no "official" end to the experience, and there is seemingly no one to rely upon to keep it constrained and therefore safe. In the author's experience, such poorly structured groups encourage acting out between sessions, as group members attempt to control their dysphoria by any means possible.

Termination Issues

As was noted in Chapter 2, many sexual abuse survivors have experienced lives dominated by abandonment and maltreatment, leading them to become hypersensitive to these issues later in life. It is therefore understandable why for some individuals, termination of group therapy can be a major stressor. The very aspects of group that are most attractive to the survivor, for example, a supportive network of understanding people and the opportunity to discuss issues intensely meaningful but difficult to share with nonabused individuals, become the most hurtful as they are seemingly taken away as group ends.

For this reason termination issues are best introduced well before the end of group therapy, just as the "last day" should be known to all from the outset of treatment. Additionally, most groups devote the last one or two sessions to discussions of what was gained by the members, "where do we go from here," and good-bye saying. Some group leaders (e.g., Herman & Schatzow, 1984) further suggest that members make a small list of people they can call upon for further support after the end of group, in addition to their regular outside psychotherapists. Other, open-ended groups simply remind the terminating member that the group is ongoing and that she can "drop in, visit, and report her progress" whenever necessary (Blake-White & Kline, 1985, p. 402). Finally, as per Gordy (1983), the group may decide to have a reunion session several months after the termination of group, thereby lessening the members' sense of immediate loss.

Regardless of what interventions are used to deal with termination issues, however, three principles are usually present: (a) an ending date is specified well in advance, either for the member (in the case of open groups) or for the group itself (for closed ones), (b) frequent reminders that group participation is for a finite period of time are built into the group process, so that members may prepare themselves well in advance, and (c) the last sessions of group are "ceremonialized" (Herman & Schatzow, 1984), including devoting considerable time for leave-taking, thereby providing closure on the experience.

CHAPTER 9

Client Gender Issues

Throughout this book reference is made to both male and female sexual abuse survivors, as if the results of victimization and its ultimate treatment were equivalent for both sexes. This approach has been intentional, based on recent data and clinical experience that much of post-sexual-abuse trauma manifests equally in males and females, and that treatment approaches appropriate for one sex are usually applicable to the other. It appears, for example, that the various symptom subscales of the Trauma Symptom Checklist (TSC-33; Briere & Runtz, in press,b—see Appendix 2), including Dissociation, Anxiety, Depression, Anger, and Sleep Disturbance, do not differ significantly between male and female sexual abuse survivors (Briere, Evans, Runtz, & Wall, 1988; Urquiza & Crowley, 1986, May), nor do indices of sexual satisfaction, family environment, or self-concept (Urquiza & Crowley, 1986, May). Similarly, a UCLA study indicates that male abuse survivors may display psychological symptom patterns roughly equivalent to those of female survivors (Kelly, MacDonald, & Waterman, 1987) and may produce similar MMPI profiles (McDonald, Kelly, and Waterman, n.d.).

This probable equivalence in how males and females experience post-sexual-abuse trauma makes sense, suggesting as it does that all humans can be hurt by extreme stressors, regardless of gender. For example, PTSD symptoms such as flashbacks or restimulation occur after severe trauma in both men and women, as does postabuse depression or dissociation. The data available in this area therefore support the notion that although males may retrospectively report more enjoyment of molestation at the time it transpired (Finkelhor, 1979a; Maltz & Holman, 1987) and may report it less frequently to others (Briere et al., 1988), they are no more immune to its negative effects than are female survivors.

Obviously, however, males and females *are* different in various respects, partially as a result of social training to behave in sex-role "appropriate" ways (Bem & Lenney, 1976; Spence & Helmreich, 1978). As these differences relate to sexual abuse, it is clear that the sexes are socialized differently with regard to sexuality and aggression, responses to victimization, and expressions of emotional pain. These variations, in turn, can impact on how the survivor deals with the effects of abuse and how she or he will respond to psychotherapy.

Sexuality and Aggression

As noted in Chapter 3, ours is a society that tends to socialize men to be sexually aggressive and women to be nurturant, passive, and relatively easily victimized. In fact, the very motives for sexual contact are thought to be different for men and women: Men are, to some extent, socialized by their peers, media portrayals, and other cultural forces to use sex as a vehicle for dominance, self-assertion, and immediate pleasure (e.g., Malamuth & Briere, 1986), whereas women are trained more than men to see sex as a way to build a relationship, ensure protection and safety, express affection, and experience loving contact.

Although there is little reason to believe that such cultural prescriptions are based in real gender differences in sexual needs or behaviors (despite recent "sociobiological" theories of human sexuality), these disparate sex roles *are* real in terms of how people, as social beings, see male versus female sexuality. These roles, in turn, can easily affect how individuals who suffer sexually related trauma respond to such injuries. Most notably, such social messages probably have significant bearing on why females who have been sexually abused are prone to revictimization, whereas male sexual abuse survivors are more likely to become sexual abuse perpetrators.

As noted in Chapters 2 and 3, the female sexual abuse victim may come to see sex as a potentially dangerous endeavor that, nevertheless, can be used to achieve other goals. Among these other outcomes are exchange for wanted commodities, such as money, shelter, or security, limited control over powerful (male) others, and satisfaction of unmet needs for affection, contact, and avoidance of loneliness. Learning early in life that her sexuality is one of her most precious social commodities, some female survivors especially strive to appear "pretty," seductive, or desirable to men, both through use of makeup and sexually provocative dress, and by stereotypically "feminine" behavior. Unfortunately, not only do such activities have the effect of verifying to the survivor that she is only as good as she looks or performs sexually, they also, especially when combined with trained passivity, place her in greater danger from predatory males in her environment.

Males who have been sexually victimized as children, on the other hand, have not had that experience in the context of social training to be passive, ornamental, or a sex object. Whereas victimization can be construed almost as an aspect of the female role, it does not in any way support social notions of masculinity (Maltz & Holman, 1987). Instead, males are encouraged from childhood to be strong, assertive, and aggressive—traits that are antithetic to the concept of victimization (Johanek, 1988; Stukas, 1988, April). Thus the growing boy's sense of masculinity is often impaired by his abuse, since victimization implies weakness and being *done to* rather than *doing to.*

As well as social proscriptions against a male "allowing" himself to be victimized, many male survivors struggle with the fact that their sexual molestation happened at the hands of another male. The combination of "weakness" implied by victimization and the fact of sexual contact with another man (regardless of the victim's nonconsent) is likely to lead the male victim—and many of those around him—to believe that he is homosexual. In a society as homophobic as is ours, this belief may engender panic and self-disgust beyond that associated with sexual molestation per se. A minority of males, however, perhaps especially those for whom the sexual molestation was perceived most positively and for whom sexual arousal was a major factor, may translate early abuse into a later homosexual or bisexual orientation (Johnson & Shrier, 1987; Maltz & Holman, 1987; Simari & Baskin, 1982). Kelly et al. (1987), for example, found that one-third of their sample of male sexual abuse survivors labeled themselves as other than exclusively heterosexual.

The meaning of these findings remains unclear, however, since homosexuality is now appropriately understood as a normal psychosexual phenomenon (see, e.g., DSM III-R) which does not appear to be explainable on psychological grounds alone. Nevertheless, it is likely that an undetermined number of individuals have the propensity for either heterosexual or homosexual orientation, the determining factor one way or the other being childhood experience.

In either case, the developing male child may strive to reaffirm the power or masculinity he believes was compromised by his abuse—potentially leading to high levels of sexual aggression against others. As one adolescent male reported: "Some time when Thomas was doing that stuff to me, I said to myself: 'When I get older, I want to be the one who does it, not the one who gets it.'"

Thus one result of sexual molestation may be its impact on adherence to prevailing sex roles (J. Brickman, personal communication, April, 1983). In the case of females, early sexual abuse may train and support later pseudofemininity and pseudosexuality, since victimization is congruent with parts of the female role. Other parts, such as social expectations of female "sexual virtue" are, of course, compromised, such that the survivor may be seen by others as "easy" or "sluttish" and as unworthy of respect. Male victimization, on the other hand, violates male sex role requirements regarding invulnerability, thereby motivating in some individuals behaviors thought to bestow masculine power, such as aggression against others (Johanek, 1988). In both cases, ultimately, the sex-role-related effects of abuse are parodies of true sexual identity—just as sexual victimization, to some extent, reflects an exaggeration of social rules regarding sexual interactions.

Reaction to Abuse-Related Emotional Trauma

As with sexual and aggressive behavior, male and female survivors often differ in their expression of abuse-related trauma. Most males in our society grow up learning to suppress verbal expressions of pain or discomfort, a process that often keeps male survivors from sharing their abuse or its effects with others, and that may delay or negate their access to psychotherapy. Females, on the other hand, are more likely to be reinforced for communicating their feelings to others. This expressiveness can have positive ramifications for the female abuse survivor who, as noted in earlier chapters, is likely to benefit from catharsis and emotional insight during therapy. The "downside" of this ability to express emotionality is that such women are likely to look "worse" than equivalently injured males and may, in fact, be labeled (and discounted) as "histrionic" or "overly dramatic."

This equation regarding the expression of emotional pain is reversed, however, when it comes to *acting* on abuse-related dysphoria. Common messages to males in our culture, for example, are "Don't get mad, get even" or "When the going gets tough, the tough get going." Unfortunately, victimization-based anger frequently generalizes to a wide variety of interpersonal situations, producing male survivors who "get even" with any number of supposed combatants. This tendency toward acting out, but not verbally expressing, one's trauma applies not only to male sexual abuse survivors but also to men who have suffered physical abuse during childhood (e.g., Pollock, Briere, Mednick, & Goodwin, 1988, August). In each case the net result may be a person who suffers considerable psychic pain but who is unable to communicate it to others. He may, instead, convert his hurt, frustration, and helplessness into escalating anger and act this affect out through physical violence or other destructive activities.

Implications for Response to Therapy

These sex-role-related processes have obvious implications for the survivor's behavior and reactions during abuse-oriented psychotherapy. As suggested earlier, however, such gender differences relate more to the *process* of treatment than to what actual techniques are utilized. In this regard, male and female differences in expressivity, range of emotional responses, freedom to be vulnerable, and responses to psychic pain determine, to some extent, how issues are presented, how the client responds to them, and how the therapist-client relationship develops.

Survivors Who Are Perpetrators

The first gender-related issue that impacts on psychotherapy is whether the survivor is, himself, a perpetrator. Most research indicates that males who engage in molestation are more likely to have been sexually abused as children than are nonmolesters (e.g., Gebhard, Gagnon, Pomeroy, & Christensen, 1965; Johanek, 1988; Langevin, Handy, Hook, Day, & Russon, 1985; Rokous, Carter, & Prentky, 1988, April). Equivalent data have not been found for females—partially because the vast majority of sexual abusers are male (Finkelhor, 1979a; Runtz, 1987; Russell, 1983b; Wyatt, 1985). Because of this increased potential for sexual aggression, the author suggests that male survivors presenting for psychotherapy services be informed of (a) the therapist's duty to warn potential victims, both at the time of screening and/or at any point in which it is disclosed during therapy and (b) his or her ethical responsibility to report to police any person who admits to being a child abuser. Further, even if the police have been informed and the molester remains "on his own recognizance," most therapists (i.e., those without specialized training in treating offenders) should probably avoid working with male survivors who are also perpetrators. Instead, the clinician's best option may be to refer the abusing survivor to programs that specialize in treating perpetrators—the most effective of which also address the client's own abuse history.

The above constraints may appear harsh to the reader, who may correctly note that men whose abusiveness is partially an outgrowth of their own molestation experiences deserve treatment as much as do any other survivors. Further, he or she may point out that such a policy may serve only to keep male survivors from disclosing their molestation activities in order to receive or continue therapy. The author does not disagree with either point and only notes that (a) the therapist must do the best she can to report and confront child abuse whenever it is disclosed, and (b) therapy with males who are molesters is very difficult work, requiring the clinician to be both a police officer and a healer. Furthermore, in many cases, sexual abusers do not stop molesting children merely because they are in treatment unless, of course, they are in prison or residents of a "closed" (locked) treatment facility.

Expression of Emotion

Assuming that the above advice is heeded, those sex-role-related concerns that remain involve the actual process of therapy. Of these perhaps the most primary relate to differences in male versus female awareness and expression of emotions. As noted earlier, the female sex role tends to support emotional expression whereas the male role discourages it. Combined with cultural expectations that males should be tough, strong, and aggressive and, therefore, able to resist victimization, these social forces especially encourage male survivors to avoid reference to their molestation and to suppress emotional expression of their trauma. In addition to denial of the matter of their abuse, as well as its effects, males are prone to greater intellectualization of their experience. The latter phenomenon may result in, for example, someone who speaks at length on the sociocultural or psychodynamic basis of victimization but who rarely describes the personal impact of his own abuse.

The male survivor's tendency to deny, suppress, and/or intellectualize his abuse history has obvious effects on his ability to express feelings regarding his trauma. This disability, in turn, reduces the amount of catharsis and emotional insight he is able to accomplish during treatment. Additionally, the male survivor's frequent choice of action over affect may result in higher levels of treatment-related acting out, or impulsive "solutions" to long-standing problems (Stukas, 1988, April). For these reasons the therapist working with male survivors must devote more attention to emotional expression than he or she would with the average female survivor. Specifically, successful treatment involves increased focus on the survivor's hidden feelings of shame, hurt, and fear regarding his abuse and greater attention to defenses such as denial, intellectualization, or precipitous action.

Interestingly, because males in our society are less likely to be punished for anger or expressions of hostility, this is one emotion that the therapist typically does not have as much trouble "freeing up." In fact, for many male survivors of severe abuse, anger becomes the *primary* (or only) emotion available for expression (Stukas, 1988, April). Such men actively funnel less "masculine" responses, such as fear, guilt, shame, or powerlessness into the single affect of rage, which can then be triggered by a wide variety of interpersonal stimuli.

This conversion of pain into anger is so automatic, for many men, that the therapist may have to work at length to help them recognize the simultaneous presence of nonangry feelings. Furthermore, when these "weaker" emotions are brought into the survivor's awareness and are verbalized, the clinician often spends considerably more time normalizing them than would be necessary for a female survivor. Among the messages that the therapist should convey are reassurances that sadness and fear are normal responses to victimization for any person, irrespective of gender, and that emotional expression is not antithetic to true masculinity. Also, it may be suggested to such clients that anger can serve as a defense against feelings of vulnerability, and he may be encouraged to examine the "softer" feelings which hide behind his rage.

In contrast to the male experience, female abuse survivors have been trained to avoid anger and express only the less threatening affective domains, such as sadness or fear (Agosta & Loring, 1988). We need only consider the multiple pejorative words for an angry woman in our society, in contrast to the relative absence of such words for equivalent males. Given these cultural constraints on women, the therapeutic agenda may reverse: While supporting the female survivor's expression of psychic pain, the therapist may also encourage the release of otherwise suppressed anger. As noted earlier in this book, this does not mean that the clinician should attempt to force the client into premature angry feelings. It may be appropriate, however, for the therapist to gently confront the female survivor at times when it appears that angry responses are being inhibited and/or replaced with feelings more "appropriate" to her sex-role. Thus just as the male may use anger to defend against "weaker" feelings, so may the female survivor invoke dysphoria to avoid feeling the more "aggressive" affects of anger or rage.

In addition to emotional expression, male and female survivors frequently differ in their response to power or control issues during psychotherapy. How these issues are manifest, in turn, depends to some extent on the sex of the therapist. The fact that such behaviors vary according to therapist gender highlights the transferential and counter-transferential aspects of psychotherapy with former abuse victims.

Power Dynamics: Male Therapist, Male Client

Power dynamics are perhaps most obvious when the therapist is male, partially because he is likely to be of the same gender as the client's perpetrator. Male survivors frequently attempt to go "one up" or "one down" with male therapists, according to their assessment of their own vulnerabilty and that of the clinician. In the "one down" mode the client may present as passive or eager to please. There is the frequent sense that the therapist is seen as a potentially dangerous father figure, who must not be challenged and who may require pacification. Although such clients may appear amenable to treatment, based on their "good" presentation, their (often hidden) distrust can inhibit therapeutic progress. For this reason trust issues should be addressed frequently with acquiescent male clients, and tentative attempts at greater self-determination should be reinforced. For example, the passive male client may be encouraged to disagree with the therapist, and the therapist may seek to be especially egalitarian with him. The messages that the clinician seeks to convey are that (a) the client is not in danger from his therapist, (b) independence of thought and opinion are good things and will not be punished, and (c) the therapist's gender will not keep him from understanding or caring.

In obvious contrast to the "one down" male client are those who strive to dominate interactions with their male therapist. Such clients are frequently challenging, verbally aggressvie, and likely to present a front of invulnerability. These "hypermasculine" reactions usually represent compensations for fearfulness and thus reflect many of the same concerns felt by the "one down" client. Specifically, the survivor who seeks to be "one up" hopes that a threatening or disinterested demeanor will forestall therapist aggression or negative judgement, as well as, in some instances, prove to the clinician that he is "still a man" despite his molestation history.

The aggression and hostility expressed by such clients also represent, however, a watered-down version of their rage against their childhood perpetrators—a process that is a positive sign, since it implies that (a) the therapist is seen as more safe than the original abuser and (b) the client is able to experience and discharge at least some related affect. It is suggested that the angry survivor, regardless of gender, is often healthier than the acquiescent or passive one and thus has a better "prognosis." Treatment interventions with such clients should not punish challenging or angry behaviors as long as they do not escalate into physical aggression. Instead, the therapist must work hard to control his countertransferential anger or sense of injury and consistently convey acceptance of the client's affective responses. Such acceptance, of course, does not preclude gentle confrontation and clarification of angry expressions that actually mask fear or sadness.

Power Dynamics: Male Therapist, Female Client

Female survivor responses to male therapists are not as clearly delineated as those of male survivors with regard to dominance of the therapeutic interaction. Specifically, as per the previous section on female socialization, women who were sexually abused as children rarely seek to be "one up" to male therapists, especially in terms of threatening, blustering, or aggressive behavior. As noted in Chapters 1 and 2, however, their historically appropriate adversarial view of male-female interactions is usually in force during therapy with male clinicians.

Some female abuse survivors seek to exert control over the psychotherapy session in the same ways that they do in other interactions with powerful males, using sexual or "feminine" behaviors to barter for acceptance, attention, and the like. This style of relating is, in important ways, different from that of the male survivor: While the male may attempt to dominate the session, the female survivor is often more invested in emotional survival. Stated differently, whereas the male survivor may try to fight, the female survivor often assumes she would lose a battle and instead seeks to "buy off" or ally with her assumed assailant.

The above scenario is, of course, a generalization: There are women survivors who are extremely aggressive (even quite violent) in treatment and males who are acquiescent and eager to please. Nevertheless, the general trend is for abuse trauma to heighten existing sex-role prescriptions regarding relations within and between the sexes such that males are trained to convert dysphoria to aggression and females are taught to groom and maintain powerful males for protection and support (Brownmiller, 1975).

The therapeutic implications of this role ownership for female survivors in treatment with male clinicians are significant. By virtue of his male stimulus value, the therapist may be blocked from making real therapeutic connections with his female client. He is, in a sense, asking the female survivor to forget that he is a male, with all the power and dangerousness that she associates with that gender. Thus even the most nonexploitive, caring male begins treatment with female survivors of severe abuse at a disadvantage: Until he proves otherwise (if he can), he is likely to be seen as someone to service, maintain, or vilify rather than someone who can assist. Further, even his assistance may be relatively unhelpful, since it may reinforce the notion that "mental health" is a gift bestowed upon a subordinate female by a powerful male with whom she is intimately connected.

The above analysis does not always hold, of course. Many female sexual abuse survivors have been significantly helped by male therapists. It is important to note, however, that in most of these instances the survivor was not extremely damaged by her abuse (i.e., was healthy enough to see an "exception to the rule" of male dominance), the therapists in question were not predatory, and the above issues were confronted, in some form, at various times during treatment.

As to the last point, there are several principles that should be attended to when male therapists see female abuse survivors in treatment. First and foremost, the clinician must be healthy enough, sexually and interpersonally, such that he does not see female clients as potential objects for gratification of power, closeness, or erotic needs. Thus he should be clear regarding the boundaries between himself and his client and should not use her in any manner, including voyeuristic titillation or self-flattery.

Second, he must be willing to assume that he is initially disabled by his gender stimulus value—that he must do extra work merely to arrive where competent female therapists begin (although female-female combinations have their own problems, as noted later in this chapter). The clinician who overlooks this point will also overlook the fact that his client has been trained by victimization to placate and maintain males, often to her own detriment. As a result of this denial, he may subsequently be surprised by the "transference" issues which "suddenly" arise.

Third, he must pay especially close attention to the client-therapist relationship, carefully reinforcing independence and self-affirming responses and gently discouraging, by nonparticipation, survivor behaviors that appear focused on the therapist's needs or well-being rather than her own.

Lastly, the therapist must be willing to take a clear stand against male sexual aggression and male social privilege relative to females. This last proviso is necessary because if this gender configuration is to work, the therapist must clearly convey to the client that he is not "one of the boys" and that the "boys" are wrong about her and other women. This position should not, obviously, be used by the clinician to assert a "holier than thou" status relative to other men (as sometimes occurs

among self-proclaimed "new" men) but, instead, is articulated so that
the male clinician's "side" or position vis-à-vis abuse is clearly understood by the survivor.

Power Dynamics: Female Therapist, Male Client

When the therapist is a woman and the survivor is a man, the dynamics
that emerge are often a composite of those described above for male-
male and male-female dyads. On the one hand, the male client may
seek to dominate the therapist (go "one up") or respond to her as if she
were a mother figure (go "one down"). On the other hand, he may
become seductive, seemingly responding to the clinician solely in
terms of her sexual stimulus value. In many instances the first and the
third patterns are combined: The client behaves in a controlling, sexualized way, both flirting and challenging the therapist's status as "boss."
     Male survivors (as well as other male clients) who respond to female
therapists in the latter manner are often utilizing one of two related
tactics. First, they may seek to reduce the threat posed by the woman
clinician by accessing traditional rules regarding male-female relationships—hoping to negate her therapeutic power by placing her in the
traditional role of sex object or subordinate. Typical statements by
such clients are "I'm sorry, I didn't hear what you said. I was distracted
by your legs," "Doctor, I think I'm falling in love with you. I can't get
therapy from someone I feel this way about," or even "I can't believe you
said that to me. Would your husband let you talk that way to him?"
     The male survivor who responds in a sexualized or hypermasculine
way may be attempting to compensate for the fact that he was sexually
victimized by a man. Expressing this history to a woman may prove
embarrassing for some men, who believe that their female therapist
will see them as less masculine because of their victimization and the
gender of their assailant. By responding to the clinician sexually or in a
"macho" fashion, the client thus may communicate his desire to be seen
as strong and virile rather than as a "wimp."
     As opposed to the use of aggressive behavior to neutralize or impress
the therapist, some male survivors, as noted earlier, respond to her as if
she were an idealized mother. The client may regress during therapy,
speak or act in a childlike fashion, and/or grow especially dependent as
treatment progresses. Motivation for this response may be twofold.
First, the choice to see the seemingly powerful clinician as a mother
figure makes her safe and changes the agenda from one of working on
one's issues to that of developing a source of (often much desired)
nurturance and comfort. Second, by converting therapist to mother, the

male survivor robs her of her power and credibility as a professional, given his typical view of mothering as a primitive, stereotypically feminine act.

Thus, whether through sexualization or maternalization, some male survivors seek to decrease the threatening aspects of therapy by changing the role of the female therapist. Because (in addition to its irritating qualities for the clinician) this alteration is defensive, focusing the therapeutic process away from self-examination, it should be persistently discouraged. The message to be conveyed is that resolution of the male survivor's trauma will not be accomplished by exerting control over others or by strategically attenuating the impact of treatment. This message may be difficult for the client to apprehend completely, given the proddings of the male sex role to deal with anxiety through direct action or manipulation of the environment. The ultimate outcome may be quite positive, however, if the client can come to see his therapist not in the traditional guise of "woman" (lover or mother) but rather as a respect-worthy guide to greater awareness and decreased pain.

Power Dynamics: Female Therapist, Female Client

Most writers on the treatment of sexual abuse effects suggest that this therapeutic pairing is the most advantageous (e.g., Herman, 1981; Blake-White & Kline, 1985) in the sense that female survivors are thought to be less defensive in therapy and female therapists may be most empathic and least likely to victimize. Although this generalization fails in many specific instances, it has some overall validity based on male and female sex roles. Nevertheless, some potentially disruptive dynamics occur in this dyad as well. Most frequently these relate to ways in which the female therapist is seen as representing other, less positive women in the survivor's past.

As is also true for male survivors, women with abuse histories are prone to seeing female therapists as mother figures. The mother-child relationship appears to have more salience for female survivors, however, especially in terms of perceived abandonment and psychological abusiveness.

Issues reflecting perceived maternal failure are well known to therapists who work with female incest survivors—although the father was the actual perpetrator, the mother is frequently most hated, apparently because she is seen as abandoning the survivor by not protecting her from abuse. As described earlier, this blaming of the mother for the father's behavior is usually technically unfair, although it is psychologically "true" for the survivor. This sense of having been abandoned, in turn, is often projected onto the female therapist, who may be simultaneously punished for her symbolic sins as well as tightly grasped to prevent what the survivor perceives as further betrayal.

Conflicts arising from the client's earlier psychological maltreatment by her mother are also quite common among female-female therapy dyads, even in those where sexual abuse was not present. The mother-daughter relationship is especially likely to be strained or adversarial, however, when sexual abuse is present in the home. As described in Chapter 3, such families are often characterized by tension, hidden injuries, skewed loyalties, and reverberating victimization (victims subsequently maltreating others).

Although the mother is frequently unaware that her daughter is being sexually victimized by her husband or boyfriend, she may sense that some unusual connection between the two exists. Especially in cases where the abuser is maltreating the mother as well, this "special" relationship may produce maternal jealousy, and the child may be punished or treated in an adversarial manner. Additionally, the mother (often an abuse survivor herself) may be psychologically abusive to the child independent of her partner's treatment of her. In either case such maltreatment typically consists of rigid and contradictory rules regarding acceptable behavior, frequent criticisms and insults, and very little emotional support.

This maternal maltreatment often has substantial impacts on how the survivor perceives the female clinician. She may be especially sensitive to what she believes to be critical or rejecting comments by her therapist, and she may make erroneous assumptions about the clinician's lack of empathy or caring for her. These cognitions may fuel reactive and defensive behaviors by the client, who is afraid to be vulnerable and yet desperately needs nurturance. Examples of such client behaviors are extensive quizzing of the therapist regarding her credentials and treatment approach, extreme negative reaction to constructive feedback, testing of the therapist's commitment to her through various forms of acting out, and what appears to be an almost paranoid suspicion about the clinician's motives for various statements or behaviors.

The last power dynamic to be described here involves the client's perception of the female clinician as a peer and therefore as either a competitor or, paradoxically, as irrelevant. With regard to the former, the adversarial focus of many abuse survivors may cause them to see all women as competition for male attention. Thus, for example, the client may verbally or nonverbally compare her own attractiveness to that of her therapist, the results of which may influence her subsequent inter-actions with the clinician during therapy.

If the therapist is perceived as more attractive to men, the client may exhibit jealousy or bitterness and may suggest that psychotherapy is unlikely to be successful. On a milder level, the client may make numer-ous comments such as "How would someone like you know how I feel" or "If I had your body, I wouldn't be desperate either." If the client views herself as more physically attractive, she may subtly (or otherwise) use this "advantage" to nullify what she sees as her therapist's greater power. For example, she may discount clinician concerns about her compulsive sexuality or extreme male orientation by implying that, being less attrac-tive to men, the therapist is merely jealous about the client's greater status in a stereotypically feminine hierarchy. Similar comparisons may be made about the client's versus the therapist's relationship status, with the assumption that the possession of a man is a sign of success.

Finally, the survivor's often extreme male orientation (Herman, 1981) may cause her to devalue female therapists totally on the basis of their gender. Such clients may express disappointment that they "got a woman" as a therapist, since they believe that women are less impor-tant, powerful, or valuable than men and thus are less likely to be effective or interesting in therapy. This dynamic, incidentally, may create conflicts for those who assign clients to therapists (e.g., in clinics or counseling centers), for the client's insistence on a male therapist is quite possibly evidence of her need for a female one.

The various issues that arise in some female-female therapy dyads are thus primarily based on the survivor's familial, social, and abuse-related training with regard to other women. The female clinician must therefore view client reactions in these areas as largely transferential and as information on fruitful areas for therapeutic attention. Such behaviors should additionally indicate to the therapist the importance of frequent clarification and support in work with such individuals. The therapist will typically work to alter her client's view of women and therefore of herself. Through her encounters with a strong and caring female role model who affirms the value of woman-ness, the survivor may slowly take back those parts of her identity that were distorted or negated by her victimization.

Summary

As indicated in this chapter, although sexual abuse impacts on males and females in many of the same ways, the survivor's gender frequently affects how such abuse-related trauma will be expressed and acted upon. Further, it appears that if the survivor seeks out psychotherapy, the sex of his or her therapist will additionally affect the course of treatment. These gender issues reflect the fact that sexual abuse occurs within a cultural context and highlight the importance of considering sex role socialization, along with clinical issues, when working with sexual abuse survivors.

CHAPTER 10

Therapist Issues

Working with sexual abuse survivors can be a gratifying experience for the psychotherapist. The opportunity to help someone grow through and past major psychological trauma can feel like a gift, one that bestows optimism and a sense of meaning to one's work. There is a "dark side" to such endeavors, however. The seemingly unending stream of anguished stories one listens to session after session, the personal impact of reliving other people's pain, and the frequent non-support of traditional mental health systems can very easily have negative effects on the clinician and, therefore, potentially on her clients. Over time, the therapist may experience a growing sense of helplessness, anger, and disillusionment with the human condition, leading to what is sometimes called "burnout." As noted by Summit (1987, December): "The usual anchors of training, authority, wisdom, and professional standards are elusive and contradictory for the sexual abuse specialist, and there is a compelling tendency to burn out, to abandon child advocacy or to rely on the client for reassurance and reward" (p. 2). This final chapter is therefore written about the therapist herself. The most common pitfalls associated with this type of work are described and a number of remedies are suggested.

Isolation

Whether employed within a mental health center, a psychiatric inpatient unit, or in private practice, the clinician working with sexual abuse survivors is prone to feelings of isolation. This is partially due to the nature of the work—it is difficult to share with others the actual experience of listening to client A as she describes her first violation at the hands of a formerly cherished father, or of Client B who was assaulted with a broomstick and then told to "clean up the mess."

Psychotherapy with victims is a relatively autistic process, a closed system where the therapist absorbs the client's pain and often is unable to fully unburden it to others. Many readers of this book, for example, are likely to have had the experience of discussing a particularly horrendous or saddening session with other therapists, only to find that their co-workers didn't seem to have "enough" appreciation of the client's experience or of the therapist's reactions to it. Although some of this problem may reside in the ironically low level of supportiveness present in many mental health settings, there is also another process at work: Some of the experiences of those who treat survivors of violence just can't be completely shared with anyone else. Not only is this truism salient with one's co-workers, it is also quite relevant to the therapist's home environment. As difficult as it may be to unburden oneself of "abuse stories" with other clinicians, it is almost impossible (and probably unfair) to do so with one's family, friends, or lover. The net result of this incommunicability is often a sense of working alone, without support.

Beyond the general sense of isolation experienced by anyone who listens to horrible stories on a regular basis, there is a separate process inherent in work with sexual abuse survivors: A society that discounts abuse and its effects will also discount those who work with abuse victims. The therapist's concerns about a given client may be dismissed by others, who summarize their understanding with statements such as "She sounds pretty borderline to me" or "You've got to take this kind of patient with a grain of salt." The clinician may also find herself being paternalistically quizzed about the truthfulness of her client's statements, and it may be suggested that she is being "hooked" or "pulled in" by the client.

These subtle or overt disconfirmations of the clinician are frequently exacerbated when, as is often the case with survivors of severe abuse, the client makes a suicide attempt, acts out during a session, or starts to make frequent phone calls to the clinic. At such times the tendency of many clinicians to see abuse reports as manipulations or attention-getting devices is reinforced, and it is often hinted to the therapist that he is "mismanaging the case" or "losing control of therapy." Such feedback, by nature of its implication that the therapist isn't controlling the client well enough, is strongly authoritarian and thus is antithetic to effective treatment of postabuse trauma. More generally, however, traditional responses to abuse survivors and those who would help them tends to drive the therapy underground: The clinician stops discussing abuse cases with her peers and supervisors and may strive to keep the client and therapy more or less a secret. Thus the therapist finds herself cut off from standard resources and support systems at a time when she needs them most.

Impact of the Material

In addition to the isolation felt by many therapists who work with abuse survivors, there is also the impact of the actual content of therapy. Therapeutic work with former sexual abuse victims routinely involves dealing with violence and cruelty at a level that most people would find incomprehensible. Repeated exposure to disclosures of victimization, exploitation, and resultant self-destructiveness and rage can slowly produce a PTSD by proxy in the listener. It is not unusual, for example, for clinicians to report an increase in violent or distressing dreams as they work with abuse survivors or other victims of violence, nor is it uncommon for some therapists to become hypervigilant about personal danger in settings where they had previously felt unafraid (e.g., at parties, in empty streets, or even in relationships).

It is the author's impression that the clinician's therapeutic empathy, ironically, makes her especially vulnerable to personally incorporating the trauma expressed by her client, thereby creating a secondary victim of the therapist. Predominant signs of this process include increased irritability, free-floating anxiety, decreased ability to appropriately deal with stress, increased difficulties in personal relationships (including decreased sexual or romantic interest), and a general sense of being helpless to "fix" the pain and suffering around her. More basically, repeated contact with victims of violence often diminishes the therapist's belief in a just world, as was described earlier with reference to survivors. This often emerges as extreme cynicism and either chronic anger at or helplessness about "the system," most combinations of which are detrimental to therapy and to the therapist.

Because abuse-related material can slowly impair one's perspective regarding survivors, it is not uncommon to find workers in this area who are either over- or underinvested in their clients. Those who underinvest have, in most cases, dissociated from their client's trauma; similar to some abuse survivors, they become numb to what might otherwise invoke anxiety, anger, or depression. These clinicians may appear coolly professional or relatively disinterested in their client's history or pain. They may often come to see survivors as "cases" and respond to them in an unnecessarily detached or clinical manner.

Finally, in order to create the maximal psychological distance from their clients' pain, such therapists may become invested in finding ways in which the abuse survivor can be understood as having caused or deserved her present predicament.

Their counterparts are those who overinvest, therapists who become extremely involved in their clients, often transcending the limits of appropriate therapist-client relationships. Such workers can frighten survivors with their intensity and personal involvement or may become highly parental and rescuing, to the extent of taking clients home with them, driving them to job interviews, lending them substantial amounts of money, or seeing them in therapy many times a week. Their therapy style may become lecturing or advice giving or they may become so uncritically supportive of their clients that they fail to confront or discuss inappropriate or destructive behavior. In addition, such clinicians may express extreme anger at perpetrators, all parents, or all males and may frequently attempt to push their clients into equivalent affective states. Ultimately, they may come to believe that only they truly understand their client and thus only they can treat her successfully.

This type of behavior, although understandable in light of the clinician's experience, is nevertheless nontherapeutic. It addresses the therapist's internal state rather than the survivor's current experience and often has the effect of infantilizing the client and/or encouraging her dependence and regression. In extreme cases the relationship ceases to be therapeutic and, instead, becomes intensely personal. At this point the therapist has violated boundaries and misused the survivor's vulnerability in much the same way as did her childhood perpetrator.

Effects on the Therapist—Revisited

As outlined above, it is clear that psychotherapy with abuse survivors is a double-edged sword for the clinician. On the one hand, the work is obviously of great value and the benefits to the client are potentially immense. On the other hand, such treatment is typically slow going and the impacts on the therapist can be significant. Because it directly taps basic human concerns about responsibility, safety versus danger, and love versus betrayal, child abuse can evoke adverse reactions in many therapists, responses that can easily interfere with treatment.

As described in this chapter, the work itself is often traumatizing, especially when one's case load consists primarily of survivors. Clinician empathy, as noted earlier, may support the therapist's internalization of the former victim's injury. In addition, the prevalence of child victimization in our society—whether it be sexual molestation, physical maltreatment, or emotional abuse—usually means that the therapist herself has points of psychic vulnerability based on painful childhood experience. Thus, client trauma may open up old wounds in the clinician and cause her to lose perspective.

Finally, our culture trains therapists, just as it does victims and abusers. This socialization may interfere with the development of a healthy, nonvictimizing environment in psychotherapy. Instead, the unprepared clinician may act out victim or perpetrator roles to some extent, often despite his or her best intentions.

A major result of these various forces is stress on the therapist as she or he tries to maintain objectivity during the psychotherapy process. To the extent that he is successful, the client may grow while the therapist slowly weakens. If he is unsuccessful, both client and clinician will suffer. The following section offers the possibility of a third option: activities and interventions that help to center and support the therapist, thereby permitting him to assist others while he himself grows stronger.

Remedies

One's Own Therapy

It is probably a good idea for any mental health worker to have undergone psychotherapy as a client. Not only does therapy reveal to the clinician what being a client feels like, it also helps her to understand and control what might otherwise be nontherapeutic responses to her client's disclosures and behaviors. As helpful as therapy may be for the "average" clinician, it becomes even more important for those who work with abuse survivors. Specifically, as noted above, one's unresolved childhood experiences are likely to stimulate countertransferential reactions to abuse-related client material. Psychotherapy, by virtue of its emphasis on self-awareness and the working through of personal trauma, can therefore help the clinician to see her client more clearly and to respond less defensively to client behavior during treatment.

Among the issues that the therapist in therapy should confront in this regard are (a) the tendency to impose his own abuse-related perceptions (such as helplessness or authority issues) onto his client, (b) his potential for defensive responding to client anger and criticism, as if the client has suddenly become his childhood abuser, (c) his need to control restimulated anxiety during therapy by keeping the client from addressing the full extent of her or his victimization, and (d) his own abuse-related identification with the aggressor, which might lead him to support the actions of his client's perpetrator. More generally, the task for the therapist-as-client is, of course, to come to terms with his childhood such that he no longer projects early injuries onto others—most notably his clients.

In addition to one's own abuse, therapists whose psychotherapy also examines gender issues (e.g., "feminist" or "consciousness-raising" approaches) may have the opportunity to confront the effects of traditional sex-role socialization on their behavior as clinicians. For males this may involve the development of empathy for women and children, the opportunity to learn how to relate intimately to others without the intrusion of sexual issues, and the chance to examine how he too has been socialized to victimize others (e.g., via sexual coercion, excessive competition, or the use of threat of violence to control those with lesser social power, such as one's wife or children). Female therapists, on the other hand, may learn to confront socially trained passivity and related assumptions regarding the appropriateness of male dominance and may discover the cognitive shift required to identify with her female client's strengths rather than with her fears or helplessness.

Finally, her own psychotherapy can provide the therapist with an ongoing sounding board during her work with survivors. Unlike supervision alone, such therapy allows the therapist-as-client to explore in depth her reactions to her clients' victimization histories, and to do so in light of her own personal history and issues. This process offers the therapist an opportunity to remain centered and focused during particularly impactful and/or personally confusing sessions with her client. A beneficial side effect of this process is that such sessions may serve as a source of stimuli for the clinician's own therapy by restimulating repressed or forgotten childhood memories and by the sustained attention to abuse-related concerns that working with survivors demands.

Sharing the Load

In addition to one's own psychotherapy, the difficulties involved in working with survivors can be lessened by regular consultation with other abuse-focused clinicians. Unlike interactions with those who question the validity of abuse and its effects, "debriefing" a particularly intense session with a like-minded therapist can decrease the sense of isolation and responsibility associated with this work.

As clinicians in this area will attest, an important part of this process seems to be, within the limits of confidentiality, the sharing of "horror stories" with one another. To the outsider such interactions may seem likely to intensify the worker's stress, since one might assume that each therapist would "take on" the other's worst experiences. Instead, this activity frequently produces a paradoxical calming effect and often serves to restore perspective. The clinician typically rediscovers that she is not alone in this task, that others are grappling with equally disturbing scenarios, and that this sort of work is surmountable and survivable. Graphic descriptions of one's client's victimization undoubtedly also serves as a form of catharsis, as the clinician struggles against treatment-based dysphoria. Interestingly, friends and loved ones who witness this unburdening often comment on the "negativity" of the process—not understanding that what appears to be group self-flagellation, or even competition for the "worst" story, is actually, among other things, reassurance that "I am not alone in this," "other people's clients are equally distressed," or even "I am not doing something wrong by being privy to such pain."

As useful as such informal sharing is, it is quite important that therapists who work with survivors of violence also have regular, scheduled sessions with a consultant or clinical supervisor who is experienced with former abuse victims. Usually occurring on a weekly basis for 1 to 1½ hours, the consultation session is an opportunity for the clinician to regularly discharge painful affect regarding his various "cases," to examine the impact of such work on his own psyche, and to hear useful suggestions and perspectives from the consultant regarding what to do next. By virtue of their predictable regularity, these sessions come to be relied upon by the therapist, who knows that within a few days or hours he will have someone to share with and, if need be, lean upon.

It is difficult to emphasize enough the importance of regularly scheduled consultation sessions for those who work with abuse survivors. In the author's opinion, this is one of the most important mechanisms that an agency, clinic, or hospital administration can offer its therapists if they wish to decrease the rate of burnout and increase the quality of service. Similarly, it is suggested to those in private practice that they actually hire a clinical consultant who will meet with them on a regular basis, in the same way that they might hire a receptionist or accountant or rent a phone.

Beyond the salutary effects of debriefing and consultation, networking with workers in other settings and locations can also be quite helpful. This may be accomplished by having monthly or bimonthly meetings with abuse therapists from other local centers, during which time mechanisms for transfer of clients, interagency disputes, and common endeavors can be discussed. Such settings also have the positive effect of decreasing the insularity of a given treatment center—by listening to the similar concerns and experiences of workers in other agencies or clinics, clinicians from a given location are less likely to feel like the only experts on survivor treatment in the city and may be less prone to adopt a seige mentality with regard to contact with other helpers.

On a broader scale, networking should include attendance at state, provincial, or national conventions on child abuse, such as is offered by the Children's National Medical Center in Washington, D.C., or the University of New Hampshire in Durham. Attendance at such meetings often engenders a feeling of being part of a movement to help survivors and almost inevitably solidifies one's sense of identity as an abuse specialist. Additionally, this form of networking allows the clinician to see the "big picture" with regard to the amelioration of child maltreatment and its effects, a process that often lessens the perceived seriousness of individual disappointments or political bickering back home.

Mixed Case Loads

It is the author's recommendation that, no matter how much one chooses to specialize in the treatment of abuse effects, no clinical case load should consist totally of victims of violence—let alone solely sexual abuse survivors. Continual and exclusive work with people who have been intentionally injured and/or exploited by others is almost guaranteed to twist one's perceptions, in and out of therapy. Most typically, as described earlier in this chapter, such exclusivity results in views of the world as inherently dangerous, relationships as usually adversarial, and the future as often bleak.

These distortions in perception, along with the emotional impact of a continual "diet" of deeply injured clients, can combine to produce therapists who are especially pessimistic and, in some sense, "shell-shocked" by their profession. For this reason most successful (i.e., helpful *and* healthy) clinicians include some relatively high functioning, nonabused clients in their case load. Such clients are often more free to be creative and engaging than survivors of severe abuse and are usually far less demanding of the therapist's time and energy. Work with these people ideally reminds the therapist that, among other things, some parents are not harmful to their children, growth is as important as recovery, and psychotherapy can be a more immediately helpful endeavor.

Social Partitioning

As is also true for some other professions, clinicians tend to interact socially with other clinicians. Given the social isolation sometimes associated with being an abuse-focused therapist, workers in this area may especially limit their contacts to others who treat abuse survivors and devote much of their time to thinking and talking about victimization. The positive aspects of restricting one's social circle include not having to defend one's work to others, having friends and lovers who understand what one is going through with difficult abuse clients, and the general warm feeling that accompanies relationships in a close-knit, movement-oriented community. Unfortunately, as reinforcing as such connections may be, chronic preoccupation with abuse-related issues and abuse-focused co-workers can have negative consequences, much in the same way as occurs when one's case load is restricted to survivors.

Perhaps the most important of these effects is on the therapist's world view. By relating more or less exclusively to other abuse-specialized psychotherapists and spending much of one's time discussing abuse, the clinician may easily come to believe that child abuse is everywhere and that everyone is either a victim, a perpetrator, a therapist, or all three. A major impact of this assumption is the tendency to see violence or tragedy in all things and thereby miss the many opportunities to love, laugh, act "silly," and appreciate beauty around him or her.

This process, which can reverberate and amplify within an abuse-focused social group, may interfere with the therapist's ability to regenerate her excitement about life and may foster cynicism and, eventually, helplessness. Ultimately, by virtue of the power of abuse-related issues and the therapist's reflexive tendency to remain with others who share her commitment, some clinicians extend the emotional impact of their work to the majority of their waking hours. To the extent that this occurs, the therapist is even more prone to the problems outlined in this chapter.

The solution to overinvestment in abuse issues is not to blame oneself for caring so deeply, nor is it to abandon the field. Instead, the clinician is advised to "partition" her or his life: focus on victimization during one's work and try to live a "regular" life outside of it. Thus, although consultation, debriefing, and networking are antidotal to burnout during work, different approaches are indicated when one is not working. Over the years the author has found three remedies that appear to be especially useful in this regard: (a) reduce abuse-related discussions and activities during social and nonworking hours,

(b) become involved in noncognitive and physically demanding activities, and (c) take "mental health breaks."

The first suggestion implies a different approach to socializing with friends. The therapist is counseled to widen her social circle—intentionally seeking out friendships with artists, craftspersons, playwrights, and other people who live lives substantially different from one's own. Similarly, social activities with other therapists should explicitly avoid extended shop talk sessions and, instead, be approached as opportunities to relax, enjoy one another, and have fun.

The second recommendation reflects the notion that psychotherapy is primarily a cognitive task, involving words, thoughts, and ideas as vehicles for emotional growth. Because of this, some psychotherapists become overdeveloped cognitively: tending to want to analyze and intellectually "understand" much of what they encounter. This predisposition to thinking rather than acting or feeling can dominate one's daily life and may cause the clinician to forget that he is a living organism who has inherent needs for physical exercise and, possibly, adventure. When unmet, these needs may produce a chronic dysphoria—a process that is obviously antithetic to recovery from the stress of treating abuse trauma.

For this reason the clinician may choose to engage in physically demanding activities on a regular basis, such as daily walks, running, hiking or racquetball. Many therapists have noted that aerobic activities are very effective "thought interrupters," allowing the clinician to finally stop thinking about the worst sessions of the day. Regular exercise has been shown to decrease stress levels and to inhibit subsequent overreaction to stressful events as well.

The last suggestion involves "mental health breaks." This term refers to intentional interruptions of one's occupational routine in order to allow recovery from work-related stress. As this concept relates to abuse therapists, it is recommended that psychotherapists take relatively frequent (e.g., bimonthly) "minivacations" of several days, preferably out of town, during which time little or no attention is paid to abuse. Although this regimen might appear extravagant to clinic administrators, the author's previous experience as an agency clinical director taught him that burnout, excessive sick days, and excessive staff conflict could often be reduced by pro-actively intervening in work-related stress. For example, a therapist who takes a "three-day weekend" every one to two months may be considerably less likely to require more days in sick leave and may be more able to work efficiently with abuse survivors in the time that she does spend in the clinic.

Macro-Interventions

The final remedy presented in this chapter may be less intuitively obvious than those described thus far. It approaches the stressfulness of work with abuse survivors not just by lessening the load or by providing more resources, but rather by increasing the meaningfulness of the intervention process. Specifically, one of the major stressors involved in helping victims of violence is the fact that such work is primarily reactive—we strive to help those who have been hurt, all the while knowing that many more are being victimized even as we do so. As a well-known community psychologist once said, psychotherapy is like pulling drowning people out of a river, never having the time to go upstream and stop whoever is pushing them in! Knowing that she can never catch up with the abusing process, the clinician is stuck helping those who have already been injured. This awareness can be demoralizing and can easily lead to feelings of inadequacy and helplessness.

Thus the last recommendation to be offered here is to travel upriver. Rather than concentrating all of her efforts on treating abuse trauma, the clinician may experience some real satisfaction in broader ("macro") prevention efforts as well. Since the sexual victimization of children is, to some extent, the result of a violent culture, such efforts may involve a variety of social interventions, ranging from public education or working with action groups for legislative change to involvement in antisexism curriculum changes for grades 1 to 6 or public demonstrations against pornography. Additionally, the therapist may choose to do research on the causes or effects of child abuse or write papers or books on sexual victimization for mental health workers. Whatever the activity, the sense that one is directly addressing the problem—rather than solely treating its effects—can be a powerful antidote to feelings of helplessness.

Summary

This chapter has been about the process of helping sexual abuse survivors as it impacts on the therapist. It has been suggested that the clinician, as a human being, both brings her own issues into treatment and is affected by the pain she confronts during that process. As a person, as opposed to a mere therapeutic instrument, the therapist must understand her strengths and limitations and should not deceive herself that psychotherapy is anything but a subjective, highly personal process. Because of this, it is the psychotherapist's responsibility to her client—and to herself—to remain psychologically healthy and to be relatively aware of her own defenses and behaviors as they interact with the client's. If this can be accomplished, such treatment will benefit not only the client but the therapist as well.

APPENDIX 1

Psychological Testing and the Sexual Abuse Survivor

Because of the relative recency of mental health's involvement in child maltreatment and its effects, published psychological testing data on sexual abuse survivors is quite sparse. Interest in this area is increasing rapidly, however, since abuse-specific psychometric results might allow psychologists to (a) identify previously undetected sexual abuse survivors by virtue of their responses on standardized tests and/or (b) determine the extent and type of abuse-related effects in individuals already identified as having been molested in childhood.

This appendix is offered to stimulate such interests, although the research in this area is preliminary, and we are not yet at the point where we can describe one or more survivor "profiles" per se. Instead, the following information—restricted to two psychological tests (the MMPI and the Rorschach)—is meant merely to be an update for the psychologist who wishes to know what, in fact, is known or hypothesized about the psychometrics of postabuse trauma.

The MMPI

It is the author's experience that clients with severe sexual abuse histories are likely to present with MMPI elevations on scales 4 (Pd) and 8 (Sc), followed by, in some cases, a high 2 (D) and/or 9 (Ma). The few studies in this area appear to support this generalization, typically finding disproportionately high numbers of 4-8 profiles in clinical samples of survivors (MacDonald, Kelly, & Waterman, n.d.; Scott & Stone, 1986; Tsai, Feldman-Summers, & Edgar, 1979), although not inevitably

so (Meiselman, 1978). Additionally, Caldwell and O'Hare (1975) indicate in their excellent *A Handbook of MMPI Personality Types* that
women with 4-8 profiles frequently report "a seductive and ambivalent
father" and "a high frequency of incest" (p. 94)—important confirmation
of this association since the authors were studying MMPI responses as
opposed to abuse survivors per se.

With regard to the modal 4-8 profile found among female sexual
abuse survivors in their clinical sample, Tsai et al. (1979) summarize
the following known concomitants of a 4-8 MMPI pattern:

> 'a) a history of poor familial relationships; b) problems stemming
> from early establishment of an attitude of distrust toward the
> world; c) poor social intelligence and difficulty in becoming emo-
> tionally involved with others; d) sexuality seen as a hostile act
> through which anger is released; e) low self-concept; and f) a charac-
> teristic pattern of choosing men inferior to themselves in relation-
> ships.' The authors note that 'Such features of the 4-8 profile in
> general are consistent with observations made about women in
> therapy who were sexually molested in childhood. . . .' (p. 414)

In addition to a 4-8 scale configuration, it is the current author's
impression that the MMPI responses of adults molested as children
frequently contain an unusually high number of "critical items," especially in terms of sexual issues (item #s 20, 37, 69, 74, 133, 179, and 297)
and familial discord (item #s 21, 96, 137, 212, 216, 237, and 245). These
items may be endorsed by nonsurvivors as well, of course, and thus may
only be suggestive of sexual abuse.

The Rorschach

As miniscule as are the MMPI data on sexual abuse survivors, even less
has been written on their Rorschach responses. At the time of this
writing, only two studies were readily available in this regard: one
comparing 17 psychotherapy clients with a history of incest to
17 matched control clients with no such history (Owens, 1984), and
one study contrasting 37 women sexually abused before age 9 with
43 women first abused between ages 9 and 16 and 72 women with no
history of abuse (Zivney, Nash, & Hulsey, 1988).

Owens (1984) found that former incest victims indicated more "interpersonal problems, poor self-esteem, and anger" (p. 606) on the
Rorschach than did nonabused clients, as witness their reduced Tex-

ture (FT, TF, T), Popular (P), and Reflection (Fr, rF) responses, as well as their elevated Bl (blood) content. Owens also found fewer Whole (W) and Organizational Activity (Zf) responses among incest survivors, although he did not directly interpret these results.

In an excellent study of sexual abuse effects as a function of age at first victimization, Zivney et al. (1988) found that those molested before age 9 displayed a pattern of "disturbed cognition, damaged self, and preoccupation with themes of primitive supply and transitional relatedness" (p. 99) relative to those abused at age 9 or over. Specifically, the former group presented more pathological scores on the following indices: 1) M− plus DEV. VERB. plus FABCOM; 2) MORBID plus PERS. REFERENCES; 3) Y plus YF plus FY; 4) FOOD plus CLOTHES plus X-RAY plus ABSTRACT; and 5) H plus Hd/A plus Ad, with low X+%.

The author's experience with survivor Rorschach behavior approximates the findings presented above, especially with reference to unusual content categories or especially "ideographic" (Exner, 1974, p. 304) responses. Among those that appear to be more prevalent among survivors of severe sexual abuse are An (anatomy), Bl (blood), and Sx (sex)—responses that seemingly mirror the client's early experiences with aggressive or violent sexual events.

ROOM TO BREATHE

<u>6</u> <u>9</u>   <u>E</u> <u>I</u>   <u>8</u>   <u>8</u>   <u>8</u>

V   V | V

| Year born | 1ST 2 letters of Mother's 1ST name | Month of entry to JMH SoN (1) (8) | Year of entry to JMH SoN (88, 89, 90, 87) |

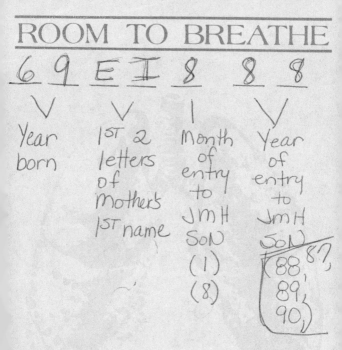

BROWARD GENERAL MEDICAL CENTER
1600 S. Andrews Ave. • Ft. Lauderdale, Florida 33316

APPENDIX 2

The Trauma Symptom Checklist (TSC-33)

Although the vast bulk of research surveyed in this book indicates long-term effects of childhood sexual abuse, the measurement systems used in these studies are, in fact, of variable quality and are typically borrowed from other areas and applied to abuse victims. In a recent "National Symposium on Assessing the Impact of Child Sexual Abuse," the invited participants frequently concluded that the use of generic assessment instruments as measures of abuse effects is problematic, and that new, abuse-specific measures should be developed (e.g., Berliner, 1987, April; Briere, 1987, Apirl; Conte, 1987, April; Finkelhor, 1987, April).

As the author noted at that symposium, abuse impact measures may be divided into "construct" versus "symptom" approaches. The former attempts to relate aversive childhood experiences to clinical phenomena already thought to exist in the general adult population, such as "Hysteria," or "Neurosis." Such constructs represent hypotheses about underlying processes that are thought to produce certain symptoms or problems and that are assumed to be present when these symptoms occur. Although the construct approach has real value (e.g., it may allow us to examine the relationship between existing psychological disorders and key childhood traumas such as incest), it may be problematic or misleading if either (a) the construct itself is a poor one (i.e., does not represent a "real" phenomenon) or (b) sexual abuse effects do not directly correspond to the specific pattern of disturbance associated with the construct in question.

As opposed to the "construct" approach, the "symptom" perspective restricts itself to observable, reportable problems, such as poor appetite or periods of depersonalization, and examines their variation between

Therapy for Adults Molested as Children

abused and nonabused subjects. Given our incomplete understanding of abuse effects, this method allows the available data to describe the exact pattern of difficulties associated with a molestation history. Such symptom items are either interpreted individually or are summed with similar items to form homogenous scales (e.g., "anxiety" or "somatic preoccupation"). The only instance where such scales might include diverse types of problems would be when certain patterns of symptoms have been empirically shown to covary with sexual abuse per se such that a summary score would reflect the extent of postabuse trauma.

This appendix presents one of the first attempts to create an abuse scale of this second type, that is, the Trauma Symptom Checklist (TSC-33; Briere & Runtz, in press,b). The TSC-33 was designed to be a brief, abuse-oriented instrument of reasonable psychometric quality that can be used in clinical research as a measure of traumatic impact, primarily (but not exclusively) in the area of long-term sexual abuse effects. This instrument consists of 33 symptom items, each of which is rated for frequency of occurrence on a 4-point scale (see page 190). These items may be read to the subject (as in the study reported here), or administered as a "pencil and paper" test (as per Cole, 1985). Combinations of TSC-33 items are then summed to produce five symptom subscales: "Dissociation," "Anxiety," "Depression," "Sleep Disturbance," and a summary subscale of those items most commonly associated with sexual abuse—"Post-Sexual-Abuse Trauma—hypothesized" (PSAT-h).

Method Used to Develop the TSC-33

Items for this scale were derived from two sources: the contents of a "Crisis Symptom Checklist," shown in an earlier study to be a reasonable predictor of clients' sexual abuse history (Briere & Runtz, 1987, July), and additional symptoms frequently reported in the literature on long-term child abuse effects.

The resultant 33 item scale was administered to 195 female crisis clinic clients during their intake interview, a sample described in detail in another study (Briere & Runtz, 1986). Briefly, 133 of these women had childhood histories of sexual victimization (sexual contact before the age of 16 years, initiated by someone at least five years older), whereas 62 had no such history. The mean age of the nonabused and abused groups was 29.6 and 26.3 years, respectively and there were no marital status differences between groups. Within the sexual abuse group, 77% had experienced oral, anal, or vaginal penetration as a child,

61% were victims of incest, and the average duration of sexual abuse was approximately 6 years.

Results of Study

As indicated in Table 1, 23 of the 33 items were endorsed to a greater extent by sexually abused than nonabused crisis clients, assuming a minimum univariate probability level of $p < .05$. A discriminant function analysis of this relationship was highly significant, $\chi^2(33) = 92.63$, $p < .0001$.

Analysis of the internal consistency of the five TSC-33 subscales indicated reasonable reliability (see Table 2), with an average subscale α of .71, and α for the total TSC-33 being .89.

The individual subscales and total TSC score discriminated well between sexually abused and nonabused clients, with the possible exception of Depression (see upper portion of Table 3). Discriminant analysis indicated that the weighted combination of subscale scores was substantially predictive, categorizing approximately 79% of all clients correctly in terms of sexual abuse history ($Rc = .53$; $\chi^2(5) = 63.16$, $p < .0001$). Univariate analysis supported the discriminant results, indicating that the total TSC-33 score was considerably higher for sexually abused than nonabused clients. Transforming the univariate F value per Wolfe (1986) and utilizing Rosenthal and Rubin's "binomial effects size" equation, we can estimate that being sexually abused increased the probability of having an above-average TSC-33 score in the present study from approximately 30% to slightly over 70%.

Data from Other Studies

In addition to the findings reported here, two other recent studies have examined the performance of the TSC-33 in discriminating sexually abused from nonabused subjects (see the lower portions of Table 3). These are (a) a study of sexual and physical abuse effects among university students (Cole, 1985) and (b) a study by Briere et al. (1988) which evaluated sex differences in the effects of sexual abuse on clinical subjects.

In Cole's study of university students, the majority of subscales and the total TSC-33 score were found to be higher for sexually abused than

Table 1. TSC-33 Item Differences Between Sexually Abused and Nonabused Clients

No.	Item	Nonabused (n = 62)		Abused (n = 133)		ANOVA		DFA
		$\bar{x}$	S.D.	$\bar{x}$	S.D.	$F(1,193)$	p	$\underline{c}^a$
1.	Insomnia	1.26	1.00	1.56	1.15	3.10	ns	.15
2.	Restless sleep	1.27	1.15	1.97	1.02	18.10	.0001	*.37*
3.	Nightmares	0.68	0.94	1.42	1.12	20.52	.0001	*.39*
4.	Early morning awakenings	0.98	1.09	1.26	1.24	2.30	ns	.13
5.	Weight loss	0.81	1.11	0.84	1.22	0.04	ns	.02
6.	Isolation	1.81	1.10	2.00	1.03	1.43	ns	.10
7.	Loneliness	1.90	1.10	2.00	1.02	0.37	ns	.05
8.	Low sex drive	1.44	1.22	1.33	1.22	0.27	ns	−.04
9.	Sadness	1.94	1.05	2.09	0.96	1.04	ns	.09
10.	Flashbacks	0.71	1.03	1.44	1.15	17.98	.0001	*.37*
11.	Spacing out	0.65	1.06	1.20	1.13	10.68	.0013	*.28*
12.	Headaches	0.97	1.02	1.49	1.13	9.31	.0026	*.26*
13.	Stomach problems	0.94	1.10	1.30	1.17	4.29	.0396	.18
14.	Crying	0.87	0.98	1.16	1.01	3.49	ns	.16
15.	Anxiety attacks	0.87	0.91	1.18	1.15	3.48	ns	.16
16.	Temper problems	0.76	0.92	1.20	1.09	7.81	.0057	.24
17.	Getting along with others	0.48	0.76	0.91	1.00	8.90	.0032	*.26*
18.	Dizziness	0.37	0.66	0.76	0.91	9.14	.0028	*.26*
19.	Passing out	0.00	0.00	0.12	0.43	4.91	.0279	.19
20.	Hurt self	0.26	0.65	0.68	1.02	9.12	.0029	*.26*
21.	Hurt others	0.34	0.63	0.62	0.88	5.23	.0233	.20
22.	Sexual problems	0.29	0.69	1.11	1.23	23.64	.0001	*.42*
23.	Sexual overactivity	0.05	0.22	0.32	0.73	7.93	.0054	.24
24.	Fear of men	0.52	0.84	1.60	1.19	41.92	.0001	*.56*
25.	Fear of women	0.15	0.40	0.55	0.82	13.49	.0003	*.32*
26.	Excessive washing	0.06	0.40	0.44	0.94	9.27	.0027	*.26*
27.	Inferiority	1.52	1.14	1.92	1.08	5.86	.0164	.21
28.	Guilt	1.61	1.09	1.94	1.06	3.93	.0490	.17
29.	Unreality	0.50	0.86	1.12	1.13	14.70	.0002	*.33*
30.	Memory problems	0.73	0.89	1.09	0.97	6.26	.0132	.22
31.	Out of body experiences	0.39	0.75	0.70	1.04	4.50	.0352	.18
32.	Tension	1.74	1.09	1.94	1.00	1.57	ns	.11
33.	Trouble breathing	0.42	0.78	0.70	0.94	4.18	.0423	.18

[a]Discriminant structure coefficients, considered meaningful (italicized) when $/c/ \geq .25$.

Table 2. TSC-33 Scale and Subscale Characteristics

Subscale	No. of items	α	Subscale composition (item nos.)
Dissociation	6	.75	10, 11, 18, 29, 30, 31
Anxiety	9	.72	12, 13, 15, 18, 24, 25, 26, 32, 33
Depression	9	.72	1, 4, 5, 8, 9, 14, 20, 27, 28
PSAT-h	6	.72	3, 10, 22, 24, 29, 30
Sleep disturbance	4	.66	1, 2, 3, 4
TSC-33 (total)	33	.89	1 to 33

nonabused subjects, with the two remaining scales (Dissociation and Anxiety) showing trends in the same direction. Other analyses (not included here in the interests of brevity) indicated that the TSC-33 was an even more powerful predictor of physical abuse effects within this college sample.

The Briere et al. (1988) study examined the joint effects of gender and sexual abuse history on TSC-33 scores in a sample of male and female crisis center clients. No sex differences were found for subscale scores or for the total TSC-33, both in terms of the total sample and within the sexual abuse group. There were, however, major differences between sexually abused and nonabused clients, as indicated in Table 3.

Discussion

The data presented in this appendix suggest that the TSC-33 is a brief, relatively reliable instrument that demonstrates reasonable predictive validity in the area of long-term sexual abuse effects. Although the TSC-33 appears to be a fair discriminator of sexually abused versus nonabused subjects, however, this instrument is not intended to be a "litmus test" for the presence of childhood sexual victimization. Some subjects in the validation study, for example, reported low levels of symptomatology despite having been molested as a child, whereas other subjects were highly symptomatic but denied a sexual abuse history.

Additionally, it should be noted that the current results are relatively preliminary, and do not, in fact, represent normative data. Thus,

Table 3. TSC-33 Scale and Subscale Differences Between Sexually Abused and Nonabused Adult Subjects from Three Studies

Study	Subjects	TSC-33 Scale	Abused		Nonabused		ANOVA		
			n	x̄	n	x̄	F	df	p
Current study	Crisis intervention center outpatients, females only	Dissociation	133	6.31	62	3.34	24.73	1,193	.01
		Anxiety		9.95		6.03	29.58		.01
		Depression		12.19		10.24	4.23		.04
		PSAT-h		7.78		3.34	63.48		.01
		Sleep Dist.		6.21		4.19	16.55		.01
		Total (TSC-33)		39.97		27.26	38.69		.01
Cole, 1985[a]	Nonclinical university students, males and females	Dissociation	113	3.43	114	2.60	3.30	1,212	.07
		Anxiety		4.49		3.66	2.76		.10
		Depression		6.64		5.40	5.14		.02
		PSAT-h		3.15		2.31	5.23		.02
		Sleep Dist.		3.79		3.03	6.34		.01
		Total (TSC-33)		19.85		16.00	6.58		.01
Briere et al. 1988	Crisis intervention center outpatients, males and females	Dissociation	40	6.83	40	2.80	24.62[b]	1,75	.01
		Anxiety		9.65		5.73	20.03[b]		.01
		Depression		14.10		10.10	15.21[b]		.01
		PSAT-h		7.80		2.93	44.98[b]		.01
		Sleep Dist.		6.88		4.35	16.98[b]		.01
		Total (TSC-33)		43.80		28.25	26.98[b]		.01

[a] Data used with permission of author.
[b] Analysis of covariance (covariate = subject age).

TSC-33 results should not be interpreted clinically at this point, although the application of this scale in abuse-effects research is strongly encouraged. As further investigations are conducted with this instrument, it is likely that usable norms will follow, thereby increasing its clinical utility in the future.

In the interest of this measure's potential future value, the author includes here and elsewhere (Briere & Runtz, in press,b) seven additional "experimental" TSC items, which may (a) increase the reliability of the Sleep Disturbance scale and (b) allow the assessment of abuse-related sexual difficulties, when combined with items 22 and 23, by way of a new "Sexual Problems" scale. There are currently no psychometric data available for these additional items, however, and thus their inclusion in the TSC (creating a new "TSC-40") should be considered meaningful or helpful only if and when supported by further psychometric research.

The Trauma Symptom Checklist (TSC-33)

How often have you experienced each of the following in the *last two months*?

	Never	Occasionally	Fairly often	Very often
1. Insomnia (trouble getting to sleep)	0	1	2	3
2. Restless sleep	0	1	2	3
3. Nightmares	0	1	2	3
4. Waking up early in the morning and can't get back to sleep	0	1	2	3
5. Weight loss (without dieting)	0	1	2	3
6. Feeling isolated from others	0	1	2	3
7. Loneliness	0	1	2	3
8. Low sex drive	0	1	2	3
9. Sadness	0	1	2	3
10. "Flashbacks" (sudden, vivid, distracting memories)	0	1	2	3
11. "Spacing out" (going away in your mind)	0	1	2	3
12. Headaches	0	1	2	3
13. Stomach problems	0	1	2	3
14. Uncontrollable crying	0	1	2	3
15. Anxiety attacks	0	1	2	3
16. Trouble controlling your temper	0	1	2	3
17. Trouble getting along with others	0	1	2	3
18. Dizziness	0	1	2	3
19. Passing out	0	1	2	3

	0	1	2	3
20. Desire to physically hurt yourself	0	1	2	3
21. Desire to physically hurt others	0	1	2	3
22. Sexual problems	0	1	2	3
23. Sexual overactivity	0	1	2	3
24. Fear of men	0	1	2	3
25. Fear of women	0	1	2	3
26. Unnecessary or over-frequent washing	0	1	2	3
27. Feelings of inferiority	0	1	2	3
28. Feelings of guilt	0	1	2	3
29. Feelings that things are "unreal"	0	1	2	3
30. Memory problems	0	1	2	3
31. Feelings that you are not always in your body	0	1	2	3
32. Feeling tense all the time	0	1	2	3
33. Having trouble breathing	0	1	2	3

Additional, experimental "TSC-40" items (intermix with original TSC-33 items)

For the Sleep Disturbance Scale:
1. Not feeling rested in the morning
2. Waking up in the middle of the night

For a new "Sexual Problems" scale (add to items 22 and 23):
1. Not feeling satisfied with your sex life
2. Having sex that you didn't enjoy
3. Bad thoughts or feelings during sex
4. Being confused about your sexual feelings
5. Sexual feelings when you shouldn't have them

References

Agosta, C., & Loring, H. (1988). Understanding and treating the adult retrospective victim of child sexual abuse. In S. M. Sgroi, *Vulnerable populations* (Vol. 1). Lexington, MA: Lexington Books.

American Psychiatric Association. (1987). *Diagnostic and statistical manual of mental disorders* (3rd ed., rev.). Washington, DC: Author.

Anderson, L., & Shafer, G. (1979). The character disordered family: A community treatment model for family sexual abuse. *American Journal of Orthopsychiatry, 49*, 436–445.

Anderson, S. (1986). The adult incest survivor. *Los Angeles County Protocol for the Treatment of Rape and Other Sexual Assault.* Los Angeles: Los Angeles County Commission for Women.

Armstrong, L. (1983). *The home front.* New York: McGraw-Hill.

Bagley, C. (1984). Mental health and the in-family sexual abuse of children and adolescents. *Canada's Mental Health, June,* 17–23.

Bagley, C., & Ramsay, R. (1986). Disrupted childhood and vulnerability to sexual assault. Long-term sequels with implications for counselling. *Social Work and Human Sexuality, 4,* 33–48.

Bagley, C., & Young, L. (1987). Juvenile prostitution and child sexual abuse: A controlled study. *Canadian Journal of Community Mental Health, 6,* 5–26.

Bass, E., & Davis, L. (1986). *The courage to heal: A guide for women survivors of child sexual abuse.* New York: Perennial Library.

Beck, A. T. (1967). *Depression: Clinical, experimental, and theoretical aspects.* New York: Harper & Row.

Beck, A. T., Emory, G., & Greenberg, R. L. (1985). *Anxiety disorders and phobias: A cognitive perspective.* New York: Basic Books.

Becker, J., Skinner, L., Abel, G., & Treacy, E. (1982). Incidence and types of sexual dysfunctions in rape and incest victims. *Journal of Sex and Marital Therapy, 8*, 65–74.

Bem, S. L., & Lenney, E. (1976). Sex typing and the avoidance of cross-sex behavior. *Journal of Personality and Social Psychology, 33*, 48–54.

Berliner, L. (1987, April). *Response paper*. Presented at the National Symposium on Assessing the Impact of Child Sexual Abuse, Huntsville, AL.

Berliner, L., & Wheeler, J. R. (1987). Treating the effects of sexual abuse on children. *Journal of Interpersonal Violence, 2*, 415–434.

Blake-White, J., & Kline, C. M. (1985). Treating the dissociative process in adult victims of childhood incest. *Social Casework: The Journal of Contemporary Social Work, 66*, 394–402.

Blatt, S. J., Wein, S. J., Chevron, E., & Quinlan, D. M. (1979). Parental representations and depression in normal young adults. *Journal of Abnormal Psychology, 88*, 388–397.

Bliss, E. L. (1984). A symptom profile of patients with multiple personalities including MMPI results. *Journal of Nervous and Mental Disease, 172*, 197–202.

Bowlby, J. (1973). *Attachment and loss: Vol. 2. Separation: Anxiety and anger*. London: Hogarth.

Brickman, J. (1984). Feminist, nonsexist, and traditional models of therapy: Implications for working with incest. *Women and Therapy, 3*, 49–67.

Briere, J. (1984, April). *The effects of childhood sexual abuse on later psychological functioning: Defining a post-sexual-abuse syndrome*. Paper presented at the Third National Conference on Sexual Victimization of Children, Washington, DC.

Briere, J. (1986). *Supervising therapists who work with sexual abuse survivors: Recurrent themes*. Paper presented at the Fourth National Conference on Sexual Victimization of Children, New Orleans.

Briere, J. (1987). Predicting likelihood of battering: Attitudes and childhood experiences. *Journal of Research in Personality, 21*, 61–69.

Briere, J. (1987, April). *Response paper*. Presented at the National Symposium on Assessing the Impact of Child Sexual Abuse, Huntsville, AL.

Briere, J. (1988). The long-term clinical correlates of childhood sexual victimization. In R. A. Prentky & V. Quinsey (Eds.), *Human sexual aggression: Current perspectives* (V. 528). New York: New York Academy of Sciences, 327–334.

Briere, J., Evans, D., Runtz, M., & Wall, T. (1988). Symptomatology in men who were molested as children: A comparison study. *American Journal of Orthopsychiatry, 58*, 457–461.

Briere, J., & Runtz, M. (1986). Suicidal thoughts and behaviors in former sexual abuse victims. *Canadian Journal of Behavioural Sciences,* *18,* 413–423.

Briere, J., & Runtz, M. (1987). Post sexual abuse trauma: Data and implications for clinical practice. *Journal of Interpersonal Violence, 2,* 367–379.

Briere, J., & Runtz, M. (1987, July). *A brief measure of victimization effects: The Trauma Symptom Checklist (TSC-33).* Paper presented at the Third National Family Violence Research Conference, Durham, NH.

Briere, J., & Runtz, M. (1988a). Symptomatology associated with childhood sexual victimization in a non-clinical adult sample. *Child Abuse & Neglect, 12,* 51–59.

Briere, J., & Runtz, M. (1988b). Multivariate correlates of childhood psychological and physical maltreatment among university women. *Child Abuse & Neglect, 12,* 331–341.

Briere, J., & Runtz, M. (1988c). Post sexual abuse trauma. In G. E. Wyatt & G. Powell (Eds.), *The lasting effects of child sexual abuse.* Newbury Park, CA: Sage Publications.

Briere, J., & Runtz, M. (in press,a). University male's sexual interest in children: Predicting potential indices of "pedophilila" in a non-forensic sample. *Child Abuse & Neglect.*

Briere, J., & Runtz, M. (in press,b). The Trauma Symptom Checklist (TSC-33): Early data on a new scale. *Journal of Interpersonal Violence.*

Briere, J., & Zaidi, L. (1988, August). *Sexual abuse histories and sequelae in psychiatric emergency room patients.* Paper presented at the annual meeting of the American Psychological Association, Atlanta, GA.

Browne, A., & Finkelhor, D. (1986a). Impact of child sexual abuse: A review of the research. *Psychological Bulletin, 99,* 66–77.

Browne, A., & Finkelhor, D. (1986b). Initial and long-term effects: A review of the research. In D. Finkelhor, *A sourcebook on child sexual abuse.* Beverly Hills, CA: Sage.

Brownmiller, S. (1975). *Against our will: Men, women, and rape.* New York: Simon & Schuster.

Burgess, A. W., & Grant, C. A. (1988). *Children traumatized in sex rings.* Washington, DC: National Center for Missing and Exploited Children.

Burgess, A. W., & Holmstrom, L. L. (1974). Rape trauma syndrome. *American Journal of Psychiatry, 131,* 981–986.

Burgess, A. W., & Holmstrom, L. L. (1978). Accessory to sex: Pressure, sex, and secrecy. In A. W. Burgess, A. Groth, L. L. Holmstrom,

& S. Sgroi (Eds.), *Sexual assault of children and adolescents.* Lexington, MA: Lexington Books.

Burgess, A. W., & Holmstrom, L. L. (1979). *Rape: Crisis and recovery.* Bowie, MD: Robert J. Brady.

Butler, S. (1978). *Conspiracy of silence: The trauma of incest.* San Francisco: Volcano Press.

Byrne, D. (1961). The repression-sensitization scale: Rationale, reliability, and validity. *Journal of Personality, 29,* 334–339.

Caldwell, A. B., & O'Hara, C. (1975). *A handbook of MMPI personality types.* Santa Monica, CA: Clinical Psychology Services.

Caplan, P. J., & Hall-McCorquodale, I. (1985). Mother-blaming in major clinical journals. *American Journal of Orthopsychiatry, 55,* 345–353.

Coates, D., & Winston, T. (1983). Counteracting the deviance of depression: Peer support groups for victims. *Journal of Social Issues, 39,* 169–194.

Cockreil, M. (1987, December). *Wingspread briefing paper.* Invited paper presentation at the Wingspread Symposium: Child Sexual Abuse—Recommendations for Prevention and Treatment Policy, Racine, WI.

Cole, C. B. (1986, May). *Differential long-term effects of child sexual and physical abuse.* Presented at the Fourth National Conference on Sexual Victimization of Children, New Orleans.

Cole, C. H., & Barney, E. E. (1987). Safeguards and the therapeutic window: A group treatment strategy for adult incest survivors. *American Journal of Orthopsychiatry, 57,* 601–609.

Cole, C. L. (1985). A group design for adult female survivors of childhood incest. *Women and Therapy, 4,* 71–82.

Conte, J. (1987, April). *Response paper.* Presented at the National Symposium on Assessing the Impact of Child Sexual Abuse, Huntsville, AL.

Conte, J., & Berliner, L. (1987). The impact of sexual abuse on children: Empirical findings. In L. Walker (Ed.), *Handbook of sexual abuse of children: Assessment and treatment issues.* New York: Springer.

Conte, J., & Schuerman, J. R. (1987). The effects of sexual abuse on children: A multidimensional view. *Journal of Interpersonal Violence, 2,* 380–390.

Coons, P. M., & Milstein, V. (1986). Psychosexual disturbances in multiple personality: Characteristics, etiology, and treatment. *Journal of Clinical Psychiatry, 47,* 106–110.

Courtois, C. A. (1979a). *Characteristics of a volunteer sample of adult women who experienced incest in childhood or adolescence.* Unpublished doctoral dissertation, University of Maryland.

Courtois, C. A. (1979b). The incest experience and its aftermath. *Victimology: An International Journal, 4,* 337–347.

Courtois, C. A., & Leehan, J. (1982). Group treatment for grown-up abused children. *The Personnel and Guidance Journal, May,* 564–567.

Davidson, H. A., & Loken, G. A. (1987). *Child pornography and prostitution: Background and legal analysis.* Washington, DC: National Center for Missing and Exploited Children.

Davis, G. C., & Akiskal, H. S. (1986). Descriptive, biological, and theoretical aspects of Borderline Personality Disorder. *Hospital and Community Psychiatry, 37,* 685–697.

DeFrancis, V. (1969). *Protecting the child victim of sex crimes committed by adults.* Denver: American Humane Association.

deLange, C. M., & Goodson, B. (1988, April). *A study of the victimization of children of battered women: Intervention, advocacy, and research.* Paper presented at the National Symposium on Child Abuse, Anaheim, CA.

Demaré, D., Briere, J., & Lips, H. M. (1988). Violent pornography and self-reported likelihood of sexual aggression. *Journal of Research in Personality, 22,* 140–153.

Derogatis, L., Lipman, R. S., Rickels, K., Ulenhuth, E. H., & Covi, L. (1974). The Hopkins Symptom Checklist (HSCL): A self-report symptom inventory. *Behavioral Science, 19,* 1–15.

de Young, M. (1982). Self injurious behavior in incest victims: A research note. *Child Welfare, 61,* 577–584.

Donaldson, M. A. (1987, December). *Wingspread briefing paper.* Invited paper presentation at the Wingspread Symposium: Child Sexual Abuse—Recommendations for Prevention and Treatment Policy, Racine, WI.

Donaldson, M. A., & Gardner, R. (1985). Diagnosis and treatment of traumatic stress among women after childhood incest. In C. Figley (Ed.), *Trauma and its wake.* New York: Brunner/Mazel.

Exner, J. E. (1974). *The Rorschach: A comprehensive system* (Vol. 1). New York: Wiley.

Fair, E. (1988, April). *Mixed gender adolescent sexual abuse recovery group.* Paper presented at the National Symposium on Child Abuse, Anaheim, CA.

Finkelhor, D. (1979a). *Sexually victimized children.* New York: Free Press.

Finkelhor, D. (1979b). What's wrong with sex between adults and children? *American Journal of Orthopsychiatry, 49,* 692–697.

Finkelhor, D. (1980). Risk factors in the sexual victimization of children. *Child Abuse & Neglect, 4,* 265–273.

Finkelhor, D. (1984). *Child sexual abuse: New theory and research.* New York: Free Press.

Finkelhor, D. (1987). The trauma of child sexual abuse: Two models. *Journal of Interpersonal Violence, 2,* 348–366.

Finkelhor, D. (1987, April). *Response paper.* Presented at the National Symposium on Assessing the Impact of Child Sexual Abuse, Huntsville, AL.

Finkelhor, D., and associates (Araji, S., Baron, L., Browne, A., Peters, S. D., & Wyatt, G. E.). (1986). *A sourcebook on child sexual abuse.* Newbury Park, CA: Sage.

Finkelhor, D., & Browne, A. (1985). The traumatic impact of child sexual abuse: A conceptualization. *American Journal of Orthopsychiatry, 55,* 530–541.

Freud, S. (1958/1900). The interpretation of dreams. In J. Strachey (Ed. and Trans.), *The complete psychological works of Sigmund Freud, standard edition.* London: Hogarth.

Freud, S. (1959/1920). Beyond the pleasure principle. In J. Strachey (Ed. and Trans.), *The complete psychological works of Sigmund Freud, standard edition.* London: Hogarth.

Freud, S. (1962/1933). The etiology of hysteria. In J. Strachey (Ed. and Trans.), *The complete psychological works of Sigmund Freud, standard edition.* London: Hogarth.

Friedrich, W. N., Beilke, R. L., & Urquiza, A. J. (1987). Children from sexually abusive families: A behavioral comparison. *Journal of Interpersonal Violence, 2,* 391–402.

Fromuth, M. E. (1985). The relationship of child sexual abuse with later psychological and sexual adjustment in a sample of college women. *Child Abuse & Neglect, 10,* 5–15.

Gebhard, P., Gagnon, J., Pomeroy, W., & Christenson, C. (1965). *Sex offenders: An analysis of types.* New York: Harper & Row.

Gelinas, D. J. (1981). Identification and treatment of incest victims. In E. Howell and M. Bayes (Eds.), *Women and mental health.* New York: Basic Books.

Gelinas, D. J. (1983). The persisting negative effects of incest. *Psychiatry, 46,* 312–332.

Gelinas, D. J. (1988a). Family therapy: Characteristic family constellation and basic therapeutic stance. In S. M. Sgroi, *Vulnerable populations* (Vol. 1). Lexington, MA: Lexington Books.

Gelinas, D. J. (1988b). Family therapy: Critical early structuring. In S. M. Sgroi, *Vulnerable populations* (Vol. 1). Lexington, MA: Lexington Books.

Gil, E. (1983). *Outgrowing the pain.* San Francisco: Launch Press.

Gold, E. R. (1986). Long-term effects of sexual victimization in childhood: An attributional approach. *Journal of Consulting and Clinical Psychology, 54,* 471–475.

Goodman, B., & Nowak-Scibelli, D. (1985). Group treatment for women incestuously abused as children. *International Journal of Group Psychotherapy, 54,* 531–544.

Goodwin, J. (1984). Incest victims exhibit Post Traumatic Stress Disorder. *Clinical Psychiatry News, 12,* 13.

Goodwin, J., McCarthy, T., & DiVasto, P. (1981). Prior incest in mothers of abused children. *Child Abuse & Neglect, 5,* 87–95.

Goodwin, J., Simms, M., & Bergman, R. (1979). Hysterical seizures: A sequel to incest. *American Journal of Orthopsychiatry, 49,* 698–703.

Gordy, P. L. (1983). Group work that supports adult victims of childhood incest. *Social Casework, May,* 300–307.

Gross, M. (1979). Incestuous rape: A cause for hysterical seizures in four adolescent girls. *American Journal of Orthopsychiatry, 49,* 704–708.

Gross, R. J., Doerr, H., Caldirola, D., Guzinski, G. M., & Ripley, H. S. (1980–81). Borderline syndrome and incest in chronic pain patients. *International Journal of Psychiatry in Medicine, 10,* 79–98.

Groves, J. E. (1975). Management of the borderline patient on a medical or surgical ward: The psychiatric consultant's role. *International Journal of Psychiatry in Medicine, 6,* 337–348.

Gunderson, J. G., & Singer, M. T. (1975). Defining borderline patients: An overview. *American Journal of Psychiatry, 132,* 1–10.

Haber, J., & Roos, C. (1985). Effects of spouse abuse and/or sexual abuse in the development and maintenance of chronic pain in women. In H. L. Fields et al. (Eds.), *Advances in pain research and therapy* (Vol. 9). New York: Raven Press.

Harrison, P. A., Lumry, A. E., & Claypatch, C. (1984, August). *Female sexual abuse victims: Perspectives on family dysfunction, substance abuse, and psychiatric disorders.* Paper presented at the Second National Conference for Family Violence Researchers, Durham, NH.

Hart, S. N., & Brassard, M. R. (1987). A major threat to children's mental health: Psychological maltreatment. *American Psychologist, 42,* 160–165.

Hartmann, E. (1984). *The nightmare: The psychology and biology of terrifying dreams.* New York: Basic Books.

Henderson, J. (1975). Incest. In A. M. Freedman, H. I. Kaplan, & B. S. Sadock (Eds.), *Comprehensive textbook of psychiatry—II.* Baltimore: Williams and Wilkins.

Henderson, J. (1983). Is incest harmful? *Canadian Journal of Psychiatry, 28*, 34–39.

Herman, J. L. (1981). *Father-daughter incest.* Cambridge: Harvard University Press.

Herman, J. L. (1985). Histories of violence in an outpatient population: An exploratory study. *American Journal of Orthopsychiatry, 55.*

Herman, J. L. (1987, December). *Wingspread briefing paper.* Invited paper, circulated at the Wingspread Symposium: Child Sexual Abuse— Recommendations for Prevention and Treatment Policy, Racine, WI.

Herman, J. L., Russell, D. E. H., & Trocki, K. (1986). Long-term effects of incestuous abuse in childhood. *American Journal of Psychiatry, 143*, 1293–1296.

Herman, J. L., & Schatzow, E. (1984). Time-limited group therapy for women with a history of incest. *International Journal of Group Psychotherapy, 34*, 605–616.

Herman, J. L., & Schatzow, E. (1987). Recovery and verification of memories of childhood sexual trauma. *Psychoanalytic Psychology, 4*, 1–4.

Herman, J. L., & van der Kolk, B. A. (1987). Traumatic antecedents of Borderline Personality Disorder. In B. A. van der Kolk, *Psychological trauma.* Washington, DC: American Psychiatric Press.

Herman, J. L., Perry, J. C., & van der Kolk, B. A. (1988). *Childhood trauma in Borderline Personality Disorder.* Unpublished manuscript.

Hilgard, E. R. (1986). *Divided consciousness: Multiple controls in human thought and action* (Expanded edition). New York: Wiley.

Hinsie, L. E., & Campbell, R. J. (1973). *Psychiatric dictionary* (4th ed.). New York: Oxford University Press.

Holroyd, J. C., & Brodsky, A. M. (1977). Psychologists' attitudes and practices regarding erotic and nonerotic physical contact with patients. *American Psychologist, 32*, 843–849.

Horowitz, M. J. (1976). *Stress response syndromes.* New York: Jason Aronson.

James, J., & Meyerding, J. (1977). Early sexual experience and prostitution. *American Journal of Psychiatry, 134*, 1381–1385.

Janoff-Bulman, R., & Frieze, I. H. (1983). A theoretical perspective for understanding reactions to victimization. *Journal of Social Issues, 39*, 1–17.

Jehu, D., & Gazan, M. (1983). Psychosocial adjustment of women who were sexually victimized in childhood or adolescence. *Canadian Journal of Community Mental Health, 2*, 71–82.

Jehu, D., Gazan, M., & Klassen, C. (1984–85). Common therapeutic targets among women who were sexually abused in childhood. *Journal of Social Work and Human Sexuality, 3*, 25–45.

Jehu, D., Klassen, C., & Gazan, M. (1985–86). Cognitive restructuring of distorted beliefs associated with childhood sexual abuse. *Journal of Social Work and Human Sexuality, 4,* 1–35.

Johanek, M. F. (1988). Treatment of male victims of child sexual abuse in military service. In S. M. Sgroi, *Vulnerable populations* (Vol. 1). Lexington, MA: Lexington Books.

Johnson, M. A. (1985). *What characteristics of adult incest victims suggest that group therapy is an effective treatment modality?* Unpublished manuscript, University of California at Los Angeles, School of Nursing.

Johnson, R. L., & Shrier, D. (1987). Past sexual victimization by females of male patients in an adolescent medicine clinic population. *American Journal of Psychiatry, 144,* 650–652.

Justice, B. & Justice, R. (1979). *The broken taboo.* New York: Human Sciences Press.

Kelly, R. J., MacDonald, V. M., & Waterman, J. M. (1987, January). *Psychological symptomatology in adult male victims of child sexual abuse: A preliminary report.* Paper presented at the joint conference of the American Psychological Association, Division 12, and the Hawaii Psychological Association, Honolulu, Hawaii.

Kernberg, O. F. (1975). *Borderline conditions and pathological narcissism.* New York: Jason Aronson.

Lamb, F. (1986). Treating sexually abused children: Issues of blame and responsibility. *American Journal of Orthopsychiatry, 56,* 303–307.

Langevin, R., Handy, L., Hook, H., Day, D., & Russon, A. (1985). Are incestuous fathers pedophilic and aggressive? In R. Langevin (Ed.), *Erotic preference, gender identity, and aggression.* New York: Erlbaum.

Langmade, C. J. (1983). The impact of pre- and postpubertal onset of incest experiences in adult women as measured by sex anxiety, sex guilt, sexual satisfaction, and sexual behavior. *Dissertation Abstracts International, 44,* 917B.

Lerman, H. (1986). *A mote in Freud's eye: From psychoanalysis to the psychology of women.* New York: Springer.

Lerner, M. J. (1980). *The belief in a just world: A fundamental delusion.* New York: Plenum Press.

Lindberg, F. H., & Distad, L. J. (1985a). Post-traumatic stress disorders in women who experienced childhood incest. *Child Abuse & Neglect, 9,* 329–334.

Lindberg, F. H., & Distad, L. J. (1985b). Survival responses to incest: Adolescents in crisis. *Child Abuse & Neglect, 9,* 521–526.

Lubell, D., & Soong, W. (1982). Group therapy with sexually abused adolescents. *Canadian Journal of Psychiatry, 27,* 311–315.

Lustig, N., Dresser, J. W., Spellman, S., & Murray, T. B. (1966). Incest: A family group survival pattern. *Archives of General Psychiatry, 14,* 31–40.

MacDonald, V. M., Kelly, R. J., & Waterman, J. M. (n.d.). *MMPI profiles of adult male victims of child sexual abuse.* Unpublished manuscript, University of California, Los Angeles.

MacFarlane, K., & Korbin, J. (1983). Confronting the incest secret long after the fact: A family study of multiple victimization with strategies for intervention. *Child Abuse & Neglect, 7,* 225–240.

Maisch, H. (1973). *Incest.* London: Andre Deutsch.

Malamuth, N.M. (1981). Rape proclivity among males. *Journal of Social Issues, 37,* 138–157.

Malamuth, N. M., & Briere, J. (1986). Sexual violence in the media: Indirect effects on aggression against women. *Journal of Social Issues, 42,* 75–92.

Maltz, W. (1988). Identifying and treating the sexual repercussions of incest: A couples therapy approach. *Journal of Sex and Marital Therapy, 14,* 145–163.

Maltz, W., & Holman, B. (1987). *Incest and sexuality: A guide to understanding and healing.* Lexington, MA: Lexington Books.

Masson, J. M. (1984). *The assault on truth: Freud's suppression of the seduction theory.* New York: Farrar, Straus & Giroux.

Masterson, J. F. (1976). *Psychotherapy with the borderline adult.* New York: Brunner/Mazel.

McAnarney, E. (1975). The older abused child. *Pediatrics, 55,* 298–299.

McCann, L., Pearlman, L. A., Sackheim, D. K., & Abramson, D. J. (1985). Assessment and treatment of the adult survivor of childhood sexual abuse within a schema framework. In S. M. Sgroi, *Vulnerable populations* (Vol. 1). Lexington, MA: Lexington Books.

McCord, J. (1985). Long-term adjustment in female survivors of incest: An exploratory study. *Dissertation Abstracts International, 46,* 650B.

McCormack, A., Janus, M. D., & Burgess, A. W. (1986). Runaway youths and sexual victimization: Gender differences in an adolescent runaway population. *Child Abuse & Neglect, 10,* 387–395.

Meiselman, K. C. (1978). *Incest: A psychological study of causes and effects with treatment recommendations.* San Francisco: Jossey-Bass.

Merriam, K. (1988, April). *Treating catastrophic trauma in adult survivors of childhood sexual abuse.* Paper presented at the First Annual Conference for Professionals Working with Adults Molested as Children, Portland, OR.

Miller, A. (1984). *Thou shalt not be aware: Society's betrayal of the child.* New York: Meridian.

Miller, B. A., Downs, W. R., Gondoli, D. M., & Keil, A. (1987). The role of childhood sexual abuse in the development of alcoholism in women. *Violence and Victims, 2,* 157–172.

Miller, D. T., & Porter, C. A. (1983). Self-blame in victims of violence. *Journal of Social Issues, 39,* 139–152.

Miller, J., Moeller, D., Kaufman, A., Divasto, P., Fitzsimmons, P., Pathar, D., & Christy, J. (1978). Recidivism among sex asssault victims. *American Journal of Psychiatry, 135,* 1103–1104.

Murphy, S. M., Kilpatrick, D. G., Amick-McMullan, A., Veronen, L. J., Paduhovich, J., Best, C. L., Villeponteaux, L. A., & Saunders, B. E. (1988). Current psychological functioning of child sexual assault survivors: A community study. *Journal of Interpersonal Violence, 3,* 55–79.

NiCarthy, G., Merriam, K., & Coffman, S. (1984). *Talking it out: A guide to groups for abused women.* Seattle, WA: Seal Press.

Ounce of Prevention Fund (1987). *Child sexual abuse: A hidden factor in adolescent sexual behavior.* Chicago: Author.

Owens, T. H. (1984). Personality traits of female psychotherapy patients with a history of incest: A research note. *Journal of Personality Assessment, 48,* 606–608.

Pearce, T., Cunningham, J., Pearce, P., & Conte, J. (1988, April). *Multivariate analysis of psychosomatic problems in female survivors of sexual victimization.* Paper presented at the National Symposium on Child Abuse, Anaheim, CA.

Perloff, L. S. (1983). Perceptions of vulnerability to victimization. *Journal of Social Issues, 39,* 41–61.

Perry, C. J., & Klerman, C. L. (1978). The borderline patient. *Archives of General Psychiatry, 35,* 141–150.

Peters, J. J. (1976). Children who are victims of sexual assault and the psychology of offenders. *American Journal of Psychotherapy, 30,* 398–421.

Peters, S. D. (1984). *The relationship between childhood sexual victimization and adult depression among Afro-American and white women.* Unpublished doctoral dissertation, University of California at Los Angeles.

Peters, S. D., Wyatt, G. E., & Finkelhor, D. (1986). Prevalence. In D. Finkelhor and associates, *A sourcebook on child sexual abuse.* Beverly Hills: Sage.

Peterson, C., & Seligman, M. E. P. (1983). Learned helplessness and victimization. *Journal of Social Issues, 39,* 103–116.

Piotrowsky, Z. (1957). *Perceptanalysis.* New York: Macmillan.

Pollock, V. E., Briere, J., Mednick, S. A., & Goodwin, D. W. (1988,

August). *Aggression in adults physically abused as children: Data from Denmark.* Paper presented at the annual meeting of the American Psychological Association, Atlanta, GA.

Putnam, F. W., Post, R. M., Guroff, J. J., et al. (1983). *One hundred cases of multiple personality disorder* (New Research Abstract #77). Washington, DC: American Psychiatric Association.

Quinsey, V. L. (1986). Men who have sex with children. In D. N. Weisstub (Ed.), *Law and mental health: International perspectives* (Vol. 2). New York: Pergamon.

Reich, J. W., & Gutierres, S. E. (1979). Escape/aggression incidence in sexually abused juvenile delinquents. *Criminal Justice and Behavior, 6,* 239–243.

Reiker, P. P., & Carmen, E. (1986). The victim-to-patient process: The disconfirmation and transformation of abuse. *American Journal of Orthopsychiatry, 56,* 360–370.

Rinsley, D. B. (1980). *Treatment of the severely disturbed adolescent.* New York, NY: Jason Aronson.

Rokous, F., Carter, D., & Prentky, R. (1988, April). *Sexual and physical abuse in the developmental histories of child molesters.* Paper presented at the National Symposium on Child Abuse, Anaheim, CA.

Rosenberg, M. S. (1987). New directions for research on the psychological maltreatment of children. *American Psychologist, 42,* 166–171.

Rosenfeld, A. (1979). Incidence of a history of incest in 18 female psychiatric patients. *American Journal of Psychiatry, 136,* 791–795.

Rosenthal, R., & Rubin, D. (1982). A simple, general purpose display of magnitude of experimental effects. *Journal of Educational Psychology, 74,* 166–169.

Ross, R. R. (1980). Violence in, violence out. Child abuse and self-mutilation in adolescent offenders. *Canadian Journal of Criminology, 22,* 273–287.

Runtz, M. (1987). *The psychosocial adjustment of women who were sexually and physically abused during childhood and early adulthood: A focus on revictimization.* Unpublished master's thesis, University of Manitoba.

Runtz, M. (1987, June). *The sexual victimization of women: The link between child abuse and revictimization.* Paper presented at the annual meeting of the Canadian Psychological Association, Vancouver, British Columbia.

Runtz, M., & Briere, J. (1986). Adolescent "acting out" and childhood history of sexual abuse. *Journal of Interpersonal Violence, 1,* 326–334.

Runtz, M., & Briere, J. (1988, April). *Childhood sexual abuse, revic-*

timization as an adult, and current symptomatology. Paper presented at the National Symposium on Child Victimization, Anaheim, CA.

Rush, P. (1980). *The best kept secret: Sexual abuse of children.* Englewood Cliffs, NJ: Prentice Hall.

Russell, D. E. H. (1983a). The prevalence and incidence of forcible rape and attempted rape of females. *Victimology: An International Journal, 7,* 1–4.

Russell, D. E. H. (1983b). The incidence and prevalence of intrafamilial and extrafamilial sexual abuse of female children. *Child Abuse & Neglect, 7,* 133–146.

Russell, D. E. H. (1986). *The secret trauma: Incest in the lives of girls and women.* New York: Basic Books.

Scott, R. L., & Stone, D. A. (1986). MMPI profile constellations in incest families. *Journal of Consulting and Clinical Psychology, 54,* 364–368.

Sedney, M. A., & Brooks, B. (1984). Factors associated with a history of childhood sexual experiences in a nonclinical female population. *Journal of the American Academy of Child Psychiatry, 23,* 215, 218.

Seligman, M. E. P. (1975). *Helplessness: On depression, development, and death.* San Francisco: W. H. Freeman.

Sgroi, S. M. (1988). *Vulnerable populations: Evaluation and treatment of sexually abused children and adult survivors* (Vol. 1). Lexington, MA: Lexington Books.

Sgroi, S. M., & Bunk, B. S. (1988). A clinical approach to adult survivors of child sexual abuse. In S. M. Sgroi, *Vulnerable populations* (Vol. 1). Lexington, MA: Lexington Books.

Shapiro, D. (1965). *Neurotic styles.* New York: Basic Books.

Shengold, L. (1963). The parent as sphinx. *Journal of the American Psychoanalytic Association, 11,* 725–751.

Silbert, M. H., & Pines, A. M. (1981). Sexual child abuse as an antecedent to prostitution. *Child Abuse & Neglect, 5,* 407–411.

Silver, R. L., Boon, C., & Stones, M. H. (1983). Searching for meaning in misfortune: Making sense of incest. *Journal of Social Issues, 39,* 81–101.

Simari, C. G., & Baskin, D. (1982). Incestuous experiences within homosexual populations: A preliminary study. *Archives of Sexual Behavior, 11,* 329–343.

Spence, J. T., & Helmreich, R. (1978). *Psychological dimensions of masculinity and femininity: Their correlates and antecedents.* Austin, TX: University of Texas Press.

Steer, M. (1988, April). *A case presentation: An emerging history of abuse via the therapeutic process.* Paper presented at the First Annual Conference for Professionals Working with Adults Molested as Children, Portland, OR.

Strieff, S., & Bitz, M. (1988, April). *Ritualistic abuse: Its victims and the professional's response.* Paper presented at the National Symposium on Child Abuse, Anaheim, CA.

Stukas, C. (1988, April). *Treatment of male survivors.* Paper presented at the First Annual Conference for Professionals Working with Adults Molested as Children, Portland, OR.

Summit, R. (1983). The child sexual abuse accommodation syndrome. *Child Abuse & Neglect, 7,* 177–193.

Summit, R. (1987, December). *Wingspread briefing paper.* Invited paper presented at the Wingspread Symposium: Child Sexual Abuse— Recommendations for Prevention and Treatment Policy, Racine, WI.

Summit, R. (1988). Hidden victims, hidden pain: Societal avoidance of child sexual abuse. In G. E. Wyatt & G. Powell (Eds.), *The lasting effects of child sexual abuse.* Newbury Park, CA: Sage.

Summit, R., & Kryso, J. (1978). Sexual abuse of children: A clinical spectrum. *American Journal of Orthopsychiatry, 48,* 237–251.

Symonds, M. (1975). Victims of violence: Psychological effects and aftereffects. *The American Journal of Psychoanalysis, 35,* 19–26.

Terr, L. C. (1985). Psychic trauma in children and adolescents. *Psychiatric Clinics of North America, 8,* 815–833.

Tsai, M., Feldman-Summers, S., & Edgar, M. (1979). Childhood molestation: Variables related to differential impacts on psychosexual functioning in adult women. *Journal of Abnormal Psychology, 88,* 407–417.

Tsai, M., & Wagner, N. N. (1978). Therapy groups for women sexually molested as children. *Archives of Sexual Behavior, 7,* 417–427.

Tufts' New England Medical Center, Division of Child Psychiatry. (1984). *Sexually exploited children: Service and research project (Final report for the Office of Juvenile Justice and Delinquency Prevention).* Washington, DC: U.S. Department of Justice.

Urquiza, A. J., & Crowley, C. (1986, May). *Sex differences in the survivors of childhood sexual abuse.* Paper presented at the Fourth National Conference on the Sexual Victimization of Children, New Orleans, LA.

van der Kolk, B. (1987). The psychological consequences of overwhelming life experience. In B. van der Kolk, *Psychological trauma.* Washington, DC: American Psychiatric Press.

Wachtel, P. L. (1973). *Psychoanalysis and behavior therapy: Toward an integration.* New York: Basic Books.

Waldinger, R. J. (1987). Intensive psychodynamic therapy with borderline patients: An overview. *American Journal of Psychiatry, 144,* 267–274.

Walker, E., Katon, W., Harrop-Griffiths, J., Holm, L., Russo, J., & Hickok, L. R. (1986). Relationship of chronic pelvic pain to psychiatric diagnoses and childhood sexual abuse. *American Journal of Psychiatry, 145,* 75–80.

Walker, L. E. (1978, March). *Feminist psychotherapy with victims of violence.* Paper presented at the annual meeting of the American Psychological Association, Scottsdale, AZ.

Walker, L. E. (1979). *The battered woman.* New York: Harper & Row.

Williams, T. (1980). *Post traumatic stress disorders in the Vietnam veteran.* Cincinnati, OH: Disabled American Veterans.

Wolfe, F. M. (1986). Meta-analysis: Quantitative methods for research synthesis. In *Sage university series on quantitative applications in the social sciences,* 07-059. Beverly Hills, CA: Sage.

Wortman, C. B. (1976). Causal attributions and personal control. In J. Harvey, W. J. Ickes, & R. F. Kidd (Eds.), *New directions in attribution research.* Hillsdale, NJ: Erlbaum.

Wyatt, G. E. (1985). The sexual abuse of Afro-American and white American women in childhood. *Child Abuse & Neglect, 9,* 231–240.

Wyatt, G. E., & Mickey, M. R. (1987). Ameliorating the effects of child sexual abuse: An exploratory study of support by parents and others. *Journal of Interpersonal Violence, 2,* 403–414.

Yalom, I. (1975). *Theory and practice of group psychotherapy.* New York: Basic Books.

Zingaro, L. (1985, February). [Comments from plenary panel]. Conference on Counselling the Sexual Abuse Survivor, Winnipeg, Manitoba, Canada.

Zivney, O. A., Nash, M. R., & Hulsey, T. L. (1988). Sexual abuse in early versus late childhood: Differing patterns of pathology as revealed on the Rorschach. *Psychotherapy, 25,* 99–106.

Index

Abandonment, 36, 38, 67, 86, 87, 103, 136, 140, 163
Abel, G., 17
Abrahamson, D. J., 11, 15, 42
Abuse:
  and age, 38
  frequency, 83
  statistics, 40
  victim responsibility, 55, 56
"Abuse dichotomy," 88–90
  intervention, 88
Abuse history, therapist's, 74–75
Abuse perspective, 51–52
Abuser:
  bonding with, 41, 89
  stigmatization by, 13, 43
Acting-in, 19, 24–28
Acting-out, 19, 24–28, 58, 59, 86, 87, 123, 129, 132, 135, 155, 157, 164
Adversariality, 22–23
Aggression, 19, 24, 67, 118, 153–155, 159, 160
  sexual, 154, 156
Agosta, C., 49, 141, 158
Alcohol abuse, 1, 24, 25, 26, 27, 28, 37, 103, 105, 132, 144

Ambivalence, 31
Amick-McMullan, A., 16
Amnesia, 9, 10, 30, 49, 53, 118
Anger, 15, 19, 20, 27, 36, 37, 43, 45, 49, 68, 71, 86, 88, 105, 118, 124, 127, 130, 131, 141, 142, 145, 152, 155, 158, 169
Anxiety, 11, 15–18, 29, 49, 62, 100, 104, 109, 112, 124, 133, 145, 150, 152, 163, 169
  free-floating, 133, 169
Anxiety attacks, 16, 133
Anxiety disorders, 16
Armstrong, L., 34, 40, 84
"As if," 87
Attention-getting behavior, 25, 31, 41, 168
Autonomy, 25, 38, 40, 41, 59, 110, 161
Avoidance, 48, 75, 77, 102, 124, 127
Avoidance-intrusion cycle, 102
Awakening, 123

Bagley, C., 14, 16, 17, 24
Barney, E. E., 143, 145, 149
Baskin, D., 154

Bass, E., 83
Beck, A. T., 11, 17, 45, 135
Becker, J., 17
Beilke, R. L., 16
Bem, S. L., 153
Bergman, R., 24, 32
Berliner, L., 16, 18, 49, 85, 183
Best, C. L., 16
Bitz, M., 128
Blake-White, J., 6, 10, 19, 86, 104,
    124, 143, 149, 151, 163
Blatt, S. J., 17
Bliss, E. L., 9
Boon, C., 44
Borderline Personality Disorder
    (BPD), 2, 29, 35–39, 52, 72,
    86, 107, 116, 124, 135
  profile, 37
  symptoms, 36
Boundaries, 41, 42, 72, 77–80
Bowlby, J., 17
Brassard, M. R., 125
Brickman, J., 61, 155
Briere, J., 1, 2, 6, 7, 8, 9, 10, 11,
    14, 15, 16, 17, 18, 20, 21, 22,
    24, 26, 27, 28, 29, 31, 36, 40,
    61, 62, 84, 95, 125, 128, 132,
    152, 153, 156, 183, 184, 185,
    187
Brodsky, A. M., 71
"Broken record syndrome," 87
Brooks, B., 10, 14, 16, 18
Browne, A., 5, 10, 17, 26, 83
Brownmiller, S., 61, 160
Bunk, B. S., 79, 126
Burgess, A. W., 9, 16, 24, 85, 125
Butler, S., 8, 13, 19, 22, 27, 62, 83,
    106
Byrne, D., 48

Catharsis, *see* Emotional
    discharge, catharsis

Caldirola, D., 16, 36
Caldwell, A. B., 180
Campbell, R. J., 15, 30, 31, 32, 33,
    67
Caplan, P. J., 39
Carmen, E., 36, 41, 78
Carter, D., 156
Chevron, E., 17
Christensen, C., 156
Christy, J., 20
Claypatch, C. E., 14
Client-therapist relationship, 57,
    65, 72, 78, 87, 91, 106, 110,
    111, 115, 122, 129, 156, 170
  boundaries, 72, 73, 161, 170
  countertransference, 73–77
  female therapist-female client,
    163–165
  female therapist-male client,
    162–163
  male therapist-female client,
    160–162
  male therapist-male client,
    159–160
  overidentification, 76, 77
  physical contact, 80
  transference, 65–73, 129, 159
  trust, 86
Coates, D., 83, 84
Cockreil, M., 42
Coffman, S., 143, 144
Cognitive effects on victim, 11–15
Cole, C. H., 145, 149
Cole, C. L., 143, 147, 185
Compulsive behavior, 22, 118
  sexual, 21–22, *see also*
    Promiscuity
Concentration problems, 6, 9, 10,
    17
  hyperalertness, 6, 9, 10, 15, 16
Conditional reality, 45–47
Confusion, 2, 53, 70
  identity, 42, 46

Conte, J., 16, 183
Control, loss of, 86, 87, 102, 104
Conversion disorder, 32
Coons, P. M., 9
Coping strategies, 39–49, 56, 85, 103
overdevelopment, 48
Core effects, 39–50
Countertransference, 65, 71, 73–77, 79, 89, 129, 159, 160, 171
definition, 73
Couples therapy, 137
Courtois, C. A., 12, 15, 17, 22, 28, 143, 145, 147, 148, 149
Covi, L., 16
Criminality, 24
Crowley, C., 152
Cultural influences, 61–63, 166, 171
Cunningham, J., 16
Cynicism, 43, 45, 169, 175

Davidson, H. A., 62
Davis, L., 83
Day, D., 156
Decision making, 112, 143
Decompensation, see Deterioration
DeFrancis, V., 13, 16, 24
Dejection, 134
deLang, C. M., 140
Delinquency, 24, 25
Denial, 48–49, 52, 68, 74, 75, 77, 86, 100, 102, 124, 125, 127, 129, 130, 132, 157, 158
Dependency, 31, 117, 162, 170
Depression, 1, 11, 14, 17, 18, 29, 62, 124, 130, 131, 133, 135, 152, 169
symptoms, 17
Derogatis, L., 16

Desensitization, 95–96, 110
role of therapist, 96
systematic, 95, 105
Despair, 86
Destigmatization process, 83
Deterioration, 123, 124–125, 132–134, 136
Devaluation, 129
Developmental stages, 107
freezing, 107, 108
splitting off, 107, 108. See also Dissociation, splitting off
deYoung, M., 13, 22, 24
Disappointment, 19, 20
Disgust, 118
Dissociation, 5, 8, 26, 27, 29, 31, 45, 51, 53, 58, 74, 86, 87, 90, 96, 100, 104, 111, 118, 119, 121, 123, 125, 134, 152, 169
definition, 9
frequency, 9, 112
vs. psychotherapy, 118
splitting off, 108, 110, 118
symptoms, 9
types of, 9
Dissociation intervention, 119–122
process feedback, 119, 121
self-monitoring, 119, 121
Dissociative defenses, 111–122, 124
"as if," 87, 115–116, 118, 120
detachment/numbing, 113–114, 120
disengagement, 112–113, 118, 120
observation, 114, 120
postsession amnesia, 114–115
shutdown, 116–117, 120, 121
total repression, 117–118
Distad, L. J., 6, 7, 9, 24, 25
Distrust, 12, 14–15, 20, 24, 49, 67, 111, 159

Divasto, P., 20, 140
Doerr, H., 16, 36
Donaldson, M. A., 6
Downs, W. R., 24
Drama, 21
Dresser, J. W., 138
Drug abuse, 1, 24, 25, 26, 27, 28,
    37, 86, 105, 131, 132, 144
DSM III-R, 16, 17, 18, 30, 31, 36,
    37, 115, 154
Dysphoria, 27, 31, 74, 106, 125,
    130, 132, 134, 135, 136, 150,
    155, 158, 160, 173, 176
Dysthymic disorder, 17, 18, 92,
    134

Eating disorders, 30, 105
Edgar, M., 17, 179, 180
Egalitarianism, 58–60
Emory, G., 11
Emotional discharge, 85–88, 157
    catharsis, 85, 86, 88, 120, 155,
        157, 173
    closure, 88
    fear of, 86
    intensity, 88
    structure, 88
    surface emotions, 86
Emotional effects, 15–18
Exaggeration, 21, 35
Expected value, 54
Evans, D., 9, 152, 185, 187
Exner, J. E., 181

Fair, E., 147
Family, dysfunctional, 51, 138,
    140
Family therapy, 137
    and abuser, 138, 140
    abuser confrontation, 141, 142
    communication, 140, 141
    familial support, 140, 141

failure, 137
    goal of, 138
    parentectomy, 142
    restructuring, 141
    with nonoffending members,
        139–141
Fantasy, 52, 87, 118, 142. *See also*
    Freud, and fantasy
Fear, 2, 7, 8, 10, 15, 16, 19, 28, 67,
    114, 118, 124, 133, 140, 158,
    160
Feldman-Summers, S., 17, 179,
    180
Finkelhor, D., 1, 5, 6, 10, 13, 14,
    15, 17, 26, 50, 55, 59, 75, 83,
    140, 152, 156, 183
Fitzsimmons, P., 20
Flashbacks, 5, 7, 11, 26, 46, 51,
    53, 66, 96, 100, 102, 103,
    112, 117, 118, 131, 134, 145,
    152
Freud, Sigmund:
    and childhood sexual
        stimulation, 34
    and fantasy, 33, 34
    and hysteria, 31
    and incest, 33
    The Interpretation of Dreams,
        33
    and Oedipus complex, 33, 34
    psychosexual development
        theory, 32, 33–35
    and repression, 49, 134
Friedrich, W. N., 16
Frieze, I. H., 13
Fromuth, M. E., 20

Gagnon, J., 156
Gardner, R., 6
Gazan, M., 11, 12, 13, 17, 18, 21,
    22
Gebhard, P., 156

Gender, therapist, 75–77
  client, 152–166
Gelinas, D. J., 6, 7, 8, 10, 11, 15,
    16, 36, 55, 89, 138, 140
Gil, E., 83, 107
Gondoli, D. M., 24
Goodman, B., 143, 145, 146
Goodson, B., 140
Goodwin, D. W., 156
Goodwin, J., 6, 24, 32, 140, 156
Gordy, P. L., 143, 145, 151
Grant, C. A., 125
Greenberg, R. L., 11
Gross, M., 32
Gross, R. J., 16, 36
Group therapy, 84, 137, 143–151
  advantages of, 143
  exclusion criteria, 144–145
  ground rules, 146–147
  group composition, 147
  identification, 143
  and individual psychotherapy,
    145–146
  interpersonal behavior, 145
  number of sessions, 147
  open *vs.* closed structure, 148
  programmatic *vs.*
    nonprogrammatic, 148–149
  screening interview, 143–144
  session length, 148
  session structure, 150
  and stress, 143, 144, 145
  termination of, 151
Growth, 60–61
Groves, J. E., 38
Guilt, 6, 9, 12, 13, 17, 27, 56, 62,
    76, 88, 126, 127, 139, 141,
    158
Gunderson, J. G., 37
Guroff, J. J., 9
Gutierres, S. E., 24, 25
Guzinski, G. M., 16, 36

Haber, J., 16
Hall-McCorquodale, I., 39
Hallucinations, 7, 97, 102
Handy, L., 156
Harrison, P. A., 14
Harrop-Griffiths, J., 16
Hart, S. N., 125
Hartmann, E., 8
Helmreich, R., 153
Helplessness, 2, 8, 10, 12, 14, 25,
    27, 42, 101, 102, 103, 117,
    133, 169, 175
  learned, 17, 21
Henderson, J., 4, 35, 39, 54
Herman, J. L., 7, 8, 10, 12, 15,
    17, 18, 20, 22, 24, 31, 33,
    34, 36, 37, 49, 60, 75, 76,
    83, 84, 125, 140, 143, 145,
    146, 147, 149, 151, 163,
    165
Hickok, L. R., 16
Hidden observer, 91
Hilgard, E. R., 91
Hinsie, L. E., 15, 30, 31, 32, 33, 67
Histrionic Personality Disorder,
    30, 52, 72, 155
  symptoms, 30–40
Holm, L., 16
Holman, B., 17, 152, 154
Holmstrom, L. L., 9, 16, 85
Holroyd, J. C., 71
Homosexuality, 154
Hook, H., 156
Hopelessness, 12, 14, 27, 134
Horowitz, M. J., 85, 102
Hospitalization, 11, 18, 79, 80,
    86, 135
Hulsey, T. L., 36, 180, 181
Hypermasculine behavior, 159,
    162
Hypersensitivity, 42
Hypervigilance, 40, 69, 78, 111,
    169

Hysteria, 2, 29, 30–35
  profile, 31–32
  seizures, *see* Pseudoepilepsy
  symptoms, 30, 35

Idealization, 19–21, 31, 36, 129
Impulsivity, 36
Incest, 2, 10, 12, 34, 36, 39, 52,
  89, 125, 138, 139
Independence, *see* Autonomy
Individuation, 103
Inner child, 107, 109, 120
  identification phase, 109
  role-playing, 109
Integration, 90–91, 96, 113, 118,
  123, 124, 125
Intellectualization of abuse, 157,
  158
Intensification, PTSD and, 11
Interpersonal problems, 18–28,
  51, 103, 169
Isolation client, 18, 24, 28, 37,
  42, 57, 83, 134, 143
  therapist, 167–169

Janoff-Bulman, R., 13
Janus, M. D., 24
Jehu, D., 11, 13, 17, 18, 21, 22
Johanek, M. F., 154, 155, 156
Johnson, M. A., 143
Johnson, R. L., 154
Justice, B., 16
Justice, R., 16

Katon, W., 16
Kaufman, A., 20
Keil, A., 24
Kelly, R. J., 152, 154, 179
Kernberg, O. F., 37, 39
Kilpatrick, D. G., 16
Klassen, C., 11, 12, 13, 18, 22

Klerman, C. L., 37
Kline, C. M., 6, 10, 19, 86, 104,
  124, 143, 149, 151, 163
Korbin, J., 125
Kryso, J., 16

Lamb, F., 13
Langevin, R., 156
Langmade, C. J., 17
Lanktree, C., 138, 141
Leehan, J., 143, 145, 147, 148, 149
Lenney, E., 153
Lerman, H., 32, 34
Lindberg, F. H., 6, 7, 9, 24, 25
Lipman, S., 16
"Litmus test" for abuse, 53, 187
Loken, G. A., 62
Loneliness, 32, 153
Loring, H., 49, 141, 158
Lubell, D., 143, 145, 147
Lumrey, A. E., 14
Lustig, N., 138
Lying, 46, 54
  profile, 46–47. *See also*
    Exaggeration

MacDonald, V. M., 152, 154, 179
MacFarlane, K., 125
Macro-Interventions, 177
Maisch, H., 138
Malamuth, N. M., 61, 62, 153
Maltz, W., 10, 17, 22, 152, 154
Manipulation, 23–24, 25, 28, 31,
  36, 42, 52, 58, 129, 163, 168
Masculinity, 154, 158
Masochism, 21
Masson, J. M., 32, 33, 34
Masterson, J. F., 37, 39
Maternal failure, 163
Maternalization, 38, 163
McAnarney, E., 32
McCann, L., 11, 15, 42

McCarthy, T., 140
McCord, J., 11, 17, 18, 20
McCormack, A., 24
Medication, 86, 135
Meditation, 104
Mednick, S. A., 156
Meiselman, K. C., 17, 22, 180
Memory, 6, 7, 9, 10–11, 53, 66,
    110, 112, 123, 124, 125, 130,
    132, 142
Men:
    and abuse, 3, 38, 158
    and sex, 153
    and therapy, 155
Merriam, K., 86, 143, 144
Mickey, M. R., 140
Miller, A., 32, 35
Miller, B. A., 24
Miller, D. T., 13
Miller, J., 20
Milstein, V., 9
MMPI profiles, 152, 179–180
    critical items, 180
Moeller, D., 20
Molestation, 83, 126
    child, 2, 4, 51, 52, 91, 101, 138
    disclosure, 53
    statistics, 61
Mood swings, 36
Mothers, adolescent, 1
Multiple personalities, 9, 29, 108,
    118
Murphy, S. M., 16
Murray, T. B., 138

Nash, M. R., 36, 180, 181
Neediness, 24, 42
Negative specialness, 44–45
NiCarthy, G., 143, 144
Normalization, 82–85
Nowak-Scibelli, D., 143, 145, 146
Numbing, 8–9

Object relations, 37–39
Oedipal complex, 33, 34, 55,
    56
O'Hare, C., 180
Other-directedness, 40–42
Owens, T. H., 180

Paduhovich, J., 16
Panic attacks, 104, 124, 133, 134,
    154
Paralysis, 16, 30
Parenting, 51
Passivity, 14, 21, 43, 154, 159
Pathar, D., 20
Pearce, P., 16
Pearce, T., 16
Pearlman, L. A., 11, 15, 42
Perception of danger, chronic,
    42–43
Perloff, L. S., 15
Perpetrators, 138, 153–157
Perry, J. C., 36, 37
Peters, J. J., 15
Peters, S. D., 1, 17
Peterson, C., 14
Phenomenology, 56–58
Phobias, 16
Piotrowsky, Z., 15
Pollock, V. E., 156
Pomeroy, W., 156
Porter, C. A., 13
Post, R. M., 9
Posttraumatic Stress Disorder
    (PTSD), 1, 2, 5–11, 16, 31,
    46, 66, 74, 83, 85, 95, 100,
    113, 114, 133
    by proxy, 169
    criteria, 5
    gender of victim, 152
    intensification, 11
    symptoms, 16, 102, 134, 152
    and therapy, 50

Power, 41, 45, 67, 159
  dynamics, 159–165
Powerlessness, 13, 14, 15, 16, 17,
  58, 158
Prentky, R., 156
Preoccupation, fearful, 133
Prison, 157
Promiscuity, 22, 24, 32
Prostitution, 22, 23, 24, 42, 113
  child, 47
  teenage, 1, 22, 23, 44
Pseudoepilepsy, 32
Pseudofemininity, 155
Pseudoparticipation, victim, 126
Pseudosexuality, 118, 155
Psychological abuse, 125–126,
  163, 164
Psychological testing, 179–181
Psychopathology, theories of, 29,
  37–39
Psychosis, 7
  atypical, 135
Psychotic behavior, 144
Putnam, F. W., 9

Quinlan, D. M., 17
Quinsey, V. L., 138

Rage, 4, 19, 20, 22, 24, 27, 28, 56,
  58, 59, 67, 68, 69, 71, 86, 87,
  101, 104, 114, 123, 129, 139,
  140, 142, 158, 159, 169
Ramsay, R., 14, 16, 17
Rape, statistics, 77
Reality, contact with, 52, 90
Reexperiencing, PTSD and, 7–8
Reframing symptoms, 101–103
Regressive behavior, 11, 100, 109,
  123, 162, 170
Reich, J. W., 24, 25
Reiker, P. P., 36, 41, 78
Rejection, 24, 87, 103, 127, 129

Relatedness, disturbed, 19–24
Relationship:
  abuser-victim, 58, 70, 139
  abuse-symptom, 52
  client-therapist, *see* Client-
    therapist relationship
  family, 100
  mother-child, 39, 164
  sexual, 21, 52
Repression, 11, 31, 33, 49, 68, 75,
  86, 100, 102, 117–118, 121,
  125, 126, 127, 129, 130, 132
  definition, 49
Responsibility for abuse, 54–56
Restimulation, 100, 125, 134,
  145, 152
Revictimization, 20, 21, 76, 86,
  139
Rickels, K., 16
Rinsley, D. B., 38
Ripley, H. S., 16, 36
Ritualistic abuse, 128
Rokous, F., 156
Role-playing, 90–94, 142
  adult-child dialogue, 92, 93
  goals of, 90
Role-playing exercises
  abuser-victim confrontation,
    94
  externalizing the anger, 94
  "Good Person, Bad Person," 93
  "The Observer," 91–93
  perpetrator role-taking, 94
  timing of, 91
Roos, C., 16
Rorschach test, 36, 179, 180–181
  ideographic responses to, 181
Rosenberg, M. S., 125
Rosenfeld, A., 31
Rosenthal, R., 185
Ross, R. R., 24
Rubin, D., 185
Runaways, 32

Runtz, M., 1, 2, 6, 7, 8, 9, 10, 14, 15, 16, 17, 18, 20, 21, 22, 24, 26, 27, 28, 31, 36, 40, 62, 84, 95, 125, 132, 152, 156, 184, 185, 187
Rush, P., 32, 34, 83
Russell, D. E. H., 1, 6, 7, 13, 15, 20, 34, 77, 140
Russo, J., 16
Russon, A., 156

Sackheim, D. K., 11, 15, 42
Sadistic abuse, 127–128
Sadness, 86, 114, 158, 160
Sadomasochism, 12
Saunders, B. E., 16
Schatzow, E., 10, 49, 125, 143, 145, 146, 147, 149, 151
Schizophrenia, 135
Shrier, D., 154
Schuerman, J. R., 16
Scott, R. L., 179
Sedney, M. A., 10, 14, 16, 18
Seductiveness, 42, 44, 45, 55, 70, 72
Self-acceptance, 90, 91, 93, 119
Self-blame, 13, 17, 44, 62, 91, 126, 130, 138
Self-control techniques, 87, 101, 103–107, 131
  distraction, 104
  grounding, 104, 120
  journaling, 106
  leaving the scene/time out, 105–106
  portable therapist, 106–107
  relaxation, 104–105
  self-talk, 105
Self-destructive behavior, 14, 24, 29, 36, 52, 103, 104, 105, 107, 118, 130–132, 135, 169.

  See also Acting-in; Acting-out; Self-mutilation
Self-disgust, 12, 43, 126, 134, 154
Self-esteem:
  impaired or negative, 1, 12–13, 21, 23, 26, 32, 41, 43, 90
Self-evaluation, 92
  negative, 12, 17, 21
Self-hatred, 4, 12, 14, 26, 28, 43, 44, 45, 86, 92, 93, 124, 130
Self-help groups, 84
Self-knowledge, 119
Self-mutilation, 24, 25, 26, 27, 36, 37, 43, 51, 104, 105, 130, 131, 132
Self-observation, 92
Self-punishment, 26, 43, 104, 105. *See also* Self-mutilation
Self-statements, 93, 105
Self-sufficiency, 103
Self-understanding, 92
Seligman, M. E. P., 14, 17
Separation-individuation period, 37, 38, 41
Sexual abuse:
  definition, 2, 6
  characteristics of, 125
Sexual adversariality, 22, 67, 70
Sexual dysfunction, 17, 21, 22, 31, 51, 52
  statistics, 17
Sexuality, male *vs.* female, 153
Sexualization by client, 67, 68, 69, 70, 72, 73, 76, 129, 153, 163
  by therapist, 71, 75, 76
Sgroi, S. M., 79, 126, 138
Shafer, G., 138
Shame, 13, 76, 83, 126, 127, 143, 158
Shapiro, D., 21
Shengold, L., 34
Silver, R. L., 44

Simari, C. G., 154
Simms, M., 24, 32
Singer, M. T., 37
Skinner, L., 17
Sleep disturbances, 5-6, 9, 10, 17, 152
  nightmares, 7-8, 102, 118, 134
  sleepwalking, 30
  types of, 10
Soong, W., 143, 145, 147
Spellman, S., 138
Spence, J. T., 153
Steer, M., 122
Stigmatization, 13, 43-44
Stone, D. A., 179
Stones, M. H., 44
Strieff, S., 128
Stukas, C., 154, 157, 158
Suicidal behavior, 14, 24, 25, 26, 27, 32, 36, 37, 59, 86, 130, 131, 132, 144, 168
Suicidal ideation, 17, 18, 124
Suicide-abuse statistics, 27
Summit, R., 16, 19, 28, 43, 54, 71, 124, 167
Symonds, M., 12

Tape recognition, 96-99
  disattention, 97, 99
  identification, 97, 99
  recognition, 97, 98
Terr, L. C., 14, 15
Therapist:
  as authoritarian, 59
  behavior of, 69, 72, 87, 95, 101, 110, 119, 121, 159
  burnout, 167, 175, 176
  case load, 174
  as client, 171-172
  consultation session, 173, 175
  co-panic, 135
  and co-workers, 168
  debriefing, 172-173, 175
  as egalitarian, 59, 159
  and empathy, 169, 170
  feedback, 85, 168
  gender of, 15, 69, 75, 76, 78, 147, 159, 172
  incompetence, 136
  isolation, 167
  mismanagement, 168
  networking, 173, 174, 175
  nonparticipation, 72
  orientation, 51, 64, 79
  overinvesting, 170
  and posttraummatic stress disorder, 169
  projection by, 74
  reframing, 72, 73
  social circle, 175, 176
  social intervention, 177
  and stress, 169, 171, 176
  as victim statistics, 74
Therapy:
  abuse-oriented, 15, 20, 32, 35, 47, 51, 52, 53, 55, 59, 65, 90, 103
  boundaries of, 72, 79
  client strengths, 60
  cognitive, 84
  crisis of faith, 134
  and growth model, 60
  intensity of, 57, 115
  pace of, 57, 115, 124, 134, 135
  patient disclosure, 53
  patient feedback, 58
  patient resistance, 57, 58, 78, 89
  phenomenological analysis, 56
  remission during, 134
  termination of, 58, 80
  transference, *see* Transference

Transference, 59, 65–73, 81, 129, 161
  angry, 71
  definition, 65
  negative, 81
  and sex-role training, 66
  sexual, 71
  types of, 66–67
Trauma Symptom Checklist (TSC-33, TSC-40), 152, 183–191
Traumatic "freezing," 107, 108
Treacy, E., 17
Trocki, K., 7
Trust, 143, 159
Truthfulness of abuse reports, 52–54
Tsai, M., 15, 17, 143, 144, 147, 148, 149, 179, 180

Ulenhuth, E. H., 16
Urquiza, A. J., 16, 152

van der Kolk, B. A., 6, 36, 37, 135
Veronen, L. J., 16
Villeponteaux, L. A., 16

Wachtel, P. L., 49
Wagner, N. N., 15, 143, 144, 147, 148, 149

Waldinger, R. J., 71
Walker, E., 16
Walker, L. E., 61
Wall, T., 9, 152, 185, 187
Waterman, J. M., 152, 154, 179
Wein, S. J., 17
Wheeler, J. R., 18, 49, 85
Williams, T., 85
Winston, T., 83, 84
Withdrawal, 5, 8, 11, 28, 47, 112, 117
Wolfe, F. M., 185
Women:
  and abuse, 3
  abused vs. nonabused, 20, 36
  and anxiety, 16
  and Borderline Personality Disorder, 36, 39
  and depression, 17
  and revictimization, 153
  and Rorschach test responses, 36
  and sex, 153
Wortman, C. B., 13
Wyatt, G. E., 1, 140

Yalom, I., 143

Zaidi, L., 1, 14, 24, 36
Zingaro, L., 11, 22
Zivney, O. A., 36, 180, 181

or Nantucket or Block Island, their valuables left behind, easy pickings for a weasel, or any reasonably resourceful burglar.

But I didn't have a clue which apartments they were, or an easy way to find out. What I had managed to learn, by calling a slew of realtors from the Lehrman apartment that afternoon, was that there were at least three Boccaccio apartments currently offered for sale. One of them was occupied at present by its owners. A second was sublet for a handsome monthly fee, and would be available to its purchaser when the sublease expired the end of August.

The third, 5-D, was vacant.

The woman who told me about 5-D was a Ms. Farrante, from the Corcoran Group. As Bill Thompson, I'd made an appointment to see it with her on Wednesday afternoon, but I'd decided I couldn't wait that long. So here I was now.

Once I'd locked up I took a quick tour of the premises, using my pocket flashlight to supplement what light came in from the windows. The apartment fronted on Park Avenue, and there were no drapes or shades or venetian blinds, nothing to bedim the view of anyone outside who happened to look in my direction. I could have switched the lights on anyway—there's nothing terribly suspicious about a man pacing around in a completely empty apartment—but you never know what will prompt some busybody to dial 911, or walk across the street and say something to the concierge.

It was as empty as an apartment could be, with nothing on the floors, nothing on the walls, nothing in the closets or the kitchen cupboards. The walls smelled very faintly of paint, and the parquet floors of wax. The apartment, Ms. Ferrante had assured me, was in move-in condition, the owners had relocated to Scottsdale, Arizona, and the price was negotiable, but not *very* negotiable. "They've turned down offers," she said.

They wouldn't get a chance to turn down mine. I didn't

want their apartment. I didn't even want to burgle it. My entry had been illegal, sure enough, so I had probably crossed the line into felonious territory, but my intentions were pure enough.

I just wanted a place to sack out for the next seven or eight hours.

But what an unwelcoming abode I'd picked! It would have been nice to sit down in a comfortable chair, but there were no chairs, comfortable or otherwise. It would have been nice to stretch out in a canopied four-poster, or a big brass bed, or a sagging couch, but there was nothing of the sort, not even an old mattress on the floor.

It would have been nice to soak in a tub. There were two well-appointed bathrooms, one with a gleaming modern stall shower, the other with a massive old claw-footed tub. I started drawing myself a bath—the water came out rusty for the first twenty seconds, but then ran nice and clear. Then I realized there weren't any towels. Somehow I couldn't see myself having a nice hot bath and then standing around waiting to evaporate to dryness. I had some useful things in the flight bag, clean clothes for the morning, a razor and toothbrush and comb, but I sure didn't have a towel.

I pulled the plug and looked around some more. They'd left toilet paper, thank God, but as far as I could tell that was the only thing that hadn't made the trip to Scottsdale with them.

I didn't feel very sleepy. I might have, given more comfortable surroundings, because Lord knows I'd had a tiring day. But the way I felt I'd be awake for hours.

At least I had something to read. I'd tucked a P. G. Wodehouse paperback into my bag when I'd originally packed it, and neither I nor Carolyn had had occasion to remove it, so it was still there. I could take it to the bathroom and perch on the throne, and with the door closed I'd be safe in turning on the lights.

I did all that, and when I worked the light switch nothing

happened. I tried the other john and got the same result. Well, it figured. Why pay the light bill when nobody was living there? Fortunately I had my pocket flash. It wasn't the world's best reading light, any more than the toilet seat was an ideal library chair, but it would do.

And it did, too, until I was somewhere in the middle of Chapter Six, at which point the beam of my flashlight gradually faded down to a soft yellow glow, a fit illumination for lovemaking, say, but nowhere near bright enough to read by. If I'd been genuinely well prepared I'd have had a couple of replacement batteries in my bag, but I wasn't and I didn't, and that was all the reading I was going to do that night.

So much for that. I went out into another room—the living room, one of the bedrooms, who knew, who cared—and stretched out on the floor. I understand that some floors are harder than others, and that I was lucky to be on wood rather than, say, concrete. That must be true, but you couldn't prove it by me. I can't imagine how I'd have been any less comfortable on a bed of nails.

There were no hangers in the closets—they really did take everything, the bastards—so I hung my slacks and jacket over the rail that would have supported a shower curtain, but for their having taken that along, too. I took off my shoes and slept in the rest of my clothes, using my flight bag as a pillow. It was about as useful in that capacity as the floor was as a bed.

I couldn't afford to oversleep, and of course I hadn't brought an alarm clock with me. But somehow I didn't think that was likely to be a problem.

Did I really have to do this? Couldn't I pay a visit to some other apartment? It was a holiday weekend, so it stood to reason that a substantial number of Boccaccio residents were out of town until Monday night at the earliest.

Suppose I just picked a likely door and opened it. If nobody was home, I was in business. And even if someone was on the premises, was that necessarily a disaster? I have burgled apartments while the tenants slept, even on occasion creeping around in the very room where they were snoring away. No one would call it relaxing work, but there's this to be said for it: you know where they are. You don't have to worry about them coming home and surprising you.

This would be different, but couldn't I sleep on the living-room couch, say, while they were sleeping in the bedroom? I'd make sure I woke up before they did. And if something went wrong, if they found me dozing in front of the fireplace, wasn't it the sort of thing I could talk my way out of? Drunk, I'd say, shrugging sheepishly. Got the wrong apartment by mistake, just dumb luck my key fit in the lock. Terribly sorry, never happen again. I'll go home now.

Was that so utterly out of the question? I could pull that off, couldn't I?

No, I told myself sternly. I couldn't.

I squirmed around, trying to find the most comfortable position, until I realized with dismay that I'd found it early on and it wasn't going to get any better. I heaved a sigh and closed my eyes. I was as snug as a bug on a bare floor, and there's a reason that metaphor has not become part of the language.

It was going to be a long night.

It was a long night.

Every hour or so I would wake up, if you want to call it that, and look at my watch. Then I would close my eyes and go back to sleep, if you want to call it that, until I woke up again.

And so on.

At six-thirty I gave up and got up. I splashed water on my face, dried my hands with toilet paper, and put on the slacks and shoes I'd taken off. I had a clean shirt and socks and underwear in my bag, but I was saving them until I had a clean body to put them on.

It was light out, so I could read again. I went back to Bertie

Wooster, and everything he did and said made perfect sense to me. I took this for a Bad Sign.

At seven-thirty I checked the hall, and there were two people in it, waiting for the elevator. I eased the door silently shut. Two minutes later I tried again, and they were gone but someone else had taken their place. It seemed like a lot of traffic for a luxury building early on a holiday morning, but evidently the residents of the Boccaccio were an enterprising lot, not given to lazy mornings in bed. Or maybe they'd spent the night on the floor, too, and were as eager as I to be up and doing.

When I cracked the door a third time there was yet another person in the hall, but she looked to be a cleaning woman who'd just emerged from the elevator and was headed for an apartment at the far end of the hallway. I stepped out and drew the door shut, unwilling to lock up after myself as I usually do, not with so much traffic all around me. The empty apartment would have to spend the next little while guarded only by the spring locks, which meant anybody with a credit card could steal inside and make off with the toilet paper.

So be it. I walked to the stairwell, setting a brisk pace, and its fire door closed behind me without my attracting any attention.

So far so good.

I climbed seven flights of stairs, telling myself that people paid good money to do essentially the same thing on a machine at the gym. I'll admit I paused a couple of times en route, but I got there.

At the twelfth-floor landing, I waited until I'd caught my breath, which took longer than I'd prefer to admit. Then I opened the door about an inch and a half and looked out. I'd picked the right stairwell, and from where I was I had a good if narrow view of his door.

I hunkered down, which for years I thought was something people only did in westerns. It turns out you can do it anywhere, even in a ritzy building on Park Avenue. It was less tiring than holding a fixed upright position for a long period of time, and I was less likely to be seen; people do most of their looking at eye level, and my own eyes, lurking behind a slightly ajar door all the way at the end of the hall, wouldn't be as noticeable if I kept them half their usual distance from the floor.

I checked my watch. It was seventeen minutes to eight. It seemed to me that should give me plenty of leeway, but I hadn't been there five minutes before I started to worry that I'd missed him.

According to him, he was a creature of habit, leaving the house at the same time and taking the same walk every morning. The previous morning I'd been loitering in a doorway across the street, drinking bad coffee from a Styrofoam cup and waiting for him to make his appearance. He'd done so at ten minutes after eight, and if he stayed on schedule today he'd leave his apartment sometime between a quarter to eight and eight-thirty.

Unless he didn't.

If he was later today than yesterday, I could just wait him out. It's not as though I had a train to catch, or a longstanding appointment at the periodontist. But if he was earlier, more than twenty-seven minutes earlier, say, then I'd get to see him return while I was still waiting for him to leave.

Not good.

If you ever start thinking you're a long ways from being neurotic, just spend a little time squinting at a closed door waiting for it to open. I couldn't get my mind to shut up. I'd made a big mistake, I told myself, staying as long as I had in the empty apartment. Suppose I'd missed him. Suppose the apartment was magnificently empty right now, while I squatted there like a constipated savage. I should have been in place by seven-thirty at the latest. Seven o'clock would have been better, and six-thirty would have been better still.

On the other hand, how long could I perch at the stair landing without someone turning up to ask me what the hell I thought I was doing there? It did not seem unlikely that the stairs would see a certain amount of casual traffic, whether of tenants or building staff. I didn't expect a whole lot of coming and going, but all it would take was one mildly curious individual and the best I could hope for was a summary exit from the premises.

The time crawled. I asked myself what Bogart would do, and right away I knew one thing he'd have done. He'd have smoked. By ten minutes after eight (his departure time yesterday, so where the hell *was* he?) the floor would have been littered with butts and cigarette ash. He'd have tapped cigarettes out philosophically, ground them out savagely, flicked them unthinkingly down the stairs. He'd have smoked like crazy, the son of a gun, but when it came time to take action, by God he'd have taken it.

What if I just went over there and rang his goddam bell? Now, without waiting for any more time to pass. If he'd left early, I'd be able to get in there now instead of wasting the whole day. And if he was still home, if he hadn't left yet, and he answered the bell, well, I would just think of something.

Like what?

I was trying to think of it when his door opened, and I'd been staring at it so hard for so long that it barely registered. Then he emerged, looking quite dapper in flannel trousers and a houndstooth jacket, and wearing the hat he'd been wearing that first night, when he opened the door for Captain Hoberman and blinked in surprise to see me there as well.

He had what seemed like a long wait for the elevator, but he waited patiently, and I tried to follow his example. A young couple emerged from the E or F apartment just as the elevator door opened, and the man called for them to hold the door while the woman locked up. Then they joined Weeks in the elevator and away they all went.

I let out my breath, looked at my watch. It was fourteen minutes after eight.

Three minutes later I was inside his apartment.

TWENTY

I figured I had an hour before he was likely to return. If I wanted to play it safe, all I had to do was be out of there by nine o'clock.

As it turned out, it didn't take me anywhere near that long to do what I wanted to do. I was out of his apartment by twenty to nine, out of the building shortly thereafter.

I probably would have had time for a shower.

You know, I thought about it. I could have shucked my clothes, treated myself to a minute and a half under a spray of hot water, then rubbed myself speedily dry with one of his fluffy mint-green towels. I could have stuffed the towel in my flight bag, carrying the evidence away with me. He'd never have missed it.

But I didn't. Nor did I sneak a cup of the leftover coffee. He probably wouldn't have missed that, either, and God knows I could have used it, but I was a good little burglar and left it untouched.

I got in, I got out. When I hit the street I looked around, and he was nowhere to be seen. I caught a cab, gave the ethnically indeterminate driver my address, and sat back with my Braniff bag cradled on my lap. I felt grimy and grubby and I couldn't stop yawning.

I didn't see the suspect car in front of my building, and I wasn't worried I'd find Ray Kirschmann in the lobby, but it seemed a bad time to leave anything to chance. I got the driver to circle the block and let me off around the corner in front of the service entrance. I'd just finished paying the tab when a fellow in a glen plaid suit and a horrible tie came out of the very door I was planning on opening. "Hold it!" I sang out, and he did, and I was inside my building without having to pick any locks.

Now isn't that a hell of a thing? I'd never seen this clown before, so it was odds-on he'd never laid eyes on me, and here he was letting me through a door that was supposed to be kept locked.

I very nearly had a word with him about it. I've been known to do that. After all, I live in the building; the last thing I want is unauthorized persons roaming its halls and imperiling its tenants, one of them myself. I've bluffed and smiled and sweet-talked my way into any number of buildings. I know how it works, and I'd just as soon nobody worked it on the place where I live.

But I held my tongue. I'd talk to the fellow another time. For now, I had other things to do.

First a shower and a shave, neither of which could possibly have been called premature. Then, clad in fresh clothes, I took the subway downtown and ate a big breakfast at a Union Square coffee shop. It was another beautiful day, the latest in a string of them and a fitting finale for Memorial Day weekend. I treated myself to a second cup of coffee, and I was whistling as I walked to my store.

I got a royal welcome from Raffles, who was trying to see how much static electricity he could generate by rubbing against my ankles. I fed him right away, more to keep him from getting underfoot than because I felt he was in great danger of starvation.

Then I dragged my bargain table outside—I've thought of putting wheels on it, but I just know if I did some moron would roll it away and I'd never see it again. I wanted the bargain table out there not for the trade it would bring but because I needed the space it otherwise occupied. If all went according to plan, I was going to have a full house this afternoon.

The first person through the door was Mowgli. "Whoa!" he said. "You trying to get rich, Bernie? Man, it's a holiday. Why aren't you at the beach?"

"I'm afraid of sharks."

"Then what are you doing in the book business? I'm surprised to find you here, is all. First Carolyn was here to keep the place open yesterday and the day before, and now you're here in person. You get a chance to look at those books I left for you?"

I hadn't, of course, and didn't really have time to look at them now, but I found the sack of them behind the counter and gave its contents a fast look-through. It was good stuff, including a couple of early Oz books with the color frontispiece illustrations intact. We agreed on a price of seventy-five dollars, less the ten bucks Carolyn had advanced him, and I found four twenties in the cash drawer and held them out to him.

"Haven't got change," he said. "You want to give me sixty and owe me five, or can I owe you the fifteen? That's what I'd rather do, but maybe you don't want to do it that way."

"I'll tell you what," I said. "Help me move some furniture and you won't owe me a dime."

"Move some furniture? Like move it where, man?"

"Around," I said. "I want to create a little space here, set up some folding chairs."

"Expecting a crowd, Bernie?"

"I wouldn't call it a crowd. Six, eight people. Something like that."

"Be a crowd in here. I guess that's why you want to move some stuff around. What's on the program, a poetry reading?"

"Not exactly."

"Because I didn't know you were into that. I read some of my own stuff a while back at a little place on Ludlow Street. Café Villanelle?"

"Black walls and ceiling," I said. "Black candles set in cat-food cans."

"Hey, you know it! Not many people even heard of the place."

"It may take a while to find its audience," I said, trying not to shudder at the memory of an evening of Emily Dickinson sung to the tune of "The Yellow Rose of Texas" and a lifetime supply of in-your-face haiku. This wouldn't be a poetry reading this afternoon, though, I added. It was more of a private sale.

"Like an auction?"

"In a way," I said. "With dramatic elements."

He thought that sounded interesting, and I told him he could hang around and sit in if he wanted. He helped me bring some chairs up front from the back room, and about that time Carolyn turned up. She had a couple of folding chairs at the Poodle Factory, and Mowgli went with her to fetch them.

Right after they left I got a phone call, and when they came back I made a phone call, and then I actually got a couple of customers, one of whom asked about an eight-volume set of Defoe and actually pulled out his wallet when I agreed to knock fifteen dollars off the price. He paid cash, too, and left me to wonder if I'd been making a mistake all these years, closing up on Sundays and holidays.

At twelve-thirty Carolyn went around the corner to the Freedom Fighter Deli and brought back lunch for all three of us. We each got a Felix Dzerzhinsky sandwich on a seeded roll and a bottle of cream soda, and we sat on three of the chairs I'd set up and pushed two of the others together to make a table. Afterward I repositioned the chairs and stood back to survey the result.

Carolyn said it looked good.

"That's the easy part," I said. "But do you figure anybody will show up?"

Mowgli put his hands together and made a little bow. "If you build it," he announced, his voice unnaturally deep and resonant, "they will come."

And, starting an hour later, they did just that.

The first arrivals were two men I'd never laid eyes on before, but even so I knew them right away. One was tall and hugely fat, with a big nose and chin and impressive eyebrows. He was wearing a white suit and a white-on-white shirt with French cuffs, the links made from a pair of U.S. five-dollar gold pieces. A black beret looked perfectly appropriate on top of his mane of steel-gray hair.

His companion was rain-thin, with a weak chin and not nearly enough space between his shifty little eyes. He had the kind of pallor you could only acquire by sleeping in a coffin. A lit cigarette burned unattended in one corner of his sullen mouth.

The fat man looked us over. He acknowledged Carolyn with a polite nod, checked out Mowgli and me, and guessed correctly. "Mr. Rhodenbarr," he said to me. "Gregory Tsarnoff."

"Mr. Tsarnoff," I said, and shook his hand. "It's good of you to come."

"We seem to be early," he said. "Punctuality is a fault of mine, sir, and the lot of the punctual man is perennial disappointment."

"I hope you won't be disappointed today," I said. "I haven't met your uh friend, but I believe we spoke on the telephone."

"Indeed. Wilfred, this is Mr. Rhodenbarr."

Wilfred nodded. He didn't extend his hand, nor did I offer mine. "A pleasure," I said, as sincerely as I could. "Uh, Wilfred, I'm afraid I'll have to ask you to put out the cigarette."

He gave me a look.

"The smoke gets in the books," I said. And in the air, I might have added. Wilfred glanced at Tsarnoff, who nodded shortly. Wilfred then took the cigarette from his lips. I thought he was going to drop it on my floor, but no, he opened the door and flicked it expertly out into the street.

"A deplorable habit," Tsarnoff said, "but the young man has other qualities which render him indispensable to me. I should find it as hard to forgo his services as he to abjure Dame Nicotine. But are we not all slaves to something, sir?"

I couldn't argue with that. I steered him to my desk chair, saying I thought he'd find it the most comfortable of the lot, and he eased his bulk into it. The chair bore the load well. Wilfred, not a whit less sullen without the cigarette, took a folding chair over to the side.

"I wonder," Tsarnoff said. "Might we make lemonade of the sour fruit of punctuality? I am here, sir, and you are here. What do you say we do a deal and leave the latecomers out in the cold?"

"Ah, I wish I could."

"But you can, sir. You have only to act on the wish."

I shook my head. "It wouldn't be fair to the others," I said, "and it would leave some important points unaddressed. Besides, people will be arriving any minute now."

"I daresay you're right," he said, and nodded at the door, where a woman with her arms full of packages was trying to get a hand free to reach for the knob.

It was the flower matron, Maggie Mason, breathless with anticipation. "I never thought you'd be open today," she said. "How's Raffles? Is he working too, or did you give him the day off?"

"He's always on the job," I said. "But as a matter of fact I'm not. The store's closed."

"It is?" She looked around. "That's curious. It *looks* as though you're open. You have people in the store."

"I know."

"Yes, of course, you would have to know that, wouldn't you? But your Special Value table is outside."

"That's because there's no room for it in the store this afternoon," I said. I reached for the CLOSED sign and hung it in the window. "We're having a private sale this afternoon. We'll be open regular hours tomorrow."

"A private sale! May I come?"

"I'm sorry, but—"

"I'm a wonderful impulse buyer, really I am. Remember the last time I was here? I just came in to talk to Raffles, and look at all the books I went home with."

I remembered it well, as who in my business would not? A two-hundred-dollar sale, completely out of the blue.

"Please, Mr. Rhodenbarr? Pretty please?"

I was tempted, I have to tell you. For all I knew she'd sit there starry-eyed, ready to outbid everybody, and when the dust had settled she'd own a dozen more art books and that leather-bound set of Balzac.

"I'm sorry," I said reluctantly. "It really is by invitation only. But next time I'll put you on the invitation list. How's that?"

It was good enough to send her on her way. I turned back to my guests and had started to say something when Mowgli caught my eye and gave me the high sign. I went to the door and opened it to admit Tiglath Rasmoulian.

This time he was wearing a belted trench coat, and the shirt under it was either persimmon or pumpkin blush, depending which mail-order catalog you prefer. He had the same straw panama, but I could swear he'd changed the feather in its band to one that matched his shirt. "Mr. Rhodenbarr," he said, smiling as he crossed the threshold. Then he caught sight of the man in the white suit and the spots of color on his cheeks looked on the point of spontaneous combustion.

"Tsarnoff," he cried. "You Slavic blot! You foul corpulence!"

Tsarnoff raised his eyebrows, no mean task given the bulk of them. "Rasmoulian," he purred, investing the name with a full measure of malice. "You Assyrian guttersnipe. You misbegotten Levantine dwarf."

"Why are you here, Tsarnoff?" He turned to me. "Why is he here?"

"Everybody's got to be someplace," I said.

This left him unmollified. "I was not told he would be here," he said. "I am not happy about this."

"While I on the contrary am delighted to see you, Tiglath. I find your feculent presence enormously reassuring. How good to know you're not somewhere else, causing unimaginable trouble."

They looked daggers at each other, or possibly scimitars, even yataghans. Rasmoulian's hand slipped into his trench-coat pocket, and across the way young Wilfred matched this escalation by sliding a hand inside his Milwaukee Brewers warm-up jacket.

"Gentlemen," I said inaccurately. "Please."

Across the way, Carolyn seemed to be looking around for a place to hide when the shooting started. Mowgli, standing beside her, showed less alarm. Maybe he was just blasé, considering what he had to be used to in the abandoned buildings he called home. Or maybe he thought these were a couple of book collectors about to lose their heads over something from the Kelmscott Press, and that Wilfred had been reaching for a cigarette, and Rasmoulian for a handkerchief.

For a moment nobody moved, and the two of them kept their agate eyes fastened on one another. Then, in unison, as if in response to some high-pitched tone no human ear could detect, they brought their empty hands into view.

I'll admit it, I breathed easier. I didn't want them shooting each other, not in my store. Not this early in the game, certainly.

The next to arrive was Weeks.

He stood at the door, eyeballed the CLOSED sign, turned the knob, and came on in. He was wearing the same outfit I'd seen him leave the apartment in that morning, houndstooth jacket, flannel slacks, brown-and-white spectator wing tips, and that cocoa hat of his. It was quite a crowd for headwear, with Tsarnoff's beret, Rasmoulian's panama, and Weeks and his natty homburg. I hadn't seen this many hats all at once outside of the Musette Theater, where on some evenings the screen was dark with them.

Tsarnoff and Rasmoulian still had their hats on, but Weeks took his off when he caught sight of Carolyn. His ever-watchful eyes scanned the room, and a smile spread on his face.

"Gregorius," he said. "How nice to see you again. And Tiglath. Always a pleasure. I'd no idea you two gentlemen would be here." As if we hadn't discussed the two of them at great length. He smiled happily at Wilfred, who stared hard at him in return. "I don't believe I've had the pleasure," he said. "Gregorius, won't you introduce me to your young friend?"

Tsarnoff said, "Charles, this is Wilfred. Wilfred, this is Charles Weeks. Mark him well."

Weeks did a double take. " 'Mark him well,' eh? Whatever could you mean by that, Gregorius?" To Wilfred he said, "My pleasure, son," and extended his hand. Wilfred just looked at the hand and made no move to take it.

"For Christ's sake," Weeks said, disgusted. "Shake hands like a man, you wretched toad-sucking little maggot. That's better." He wiped his hand on his pants leg and turned to me. "Weasel," he said warmly. "Introduce me to these nice people."

I made the introductions. Weeks bowed over Carolyn's hand, brushing it with his lips, then shook hands with Mowgli and asked him if he'd really been raised by wolves. First raised, then lowered, Mowgli told him.

I said, "Have a seat, Charlie."

"Why, thank you," he said. "Yes, I think I will." He took a moment to make his choice, finally selecting the chair two to the left of Tsarnoff, placing his hat on the chair that separated them. "Mowgli's from Kipling's *Jungle Book*, but of course you would know that, wouldn't you, Gregorius?" Tsarnoff rolled his eyes at the question. "Were your parents great Kipling fans, son? Or did you choose the name yourself?"

We weren't to find out, because the door opened before Mowgli could answer. I knew who it was, I'd caught a glimpse of her as she'd crossed the sidewalk in front of the store, and I didn't want to watch her come in. I wanted to watch them watching her, but I couldn't help myself. When she was in a room, that's where my eyes went.

And she did it again.

So I said it again, and out loud for a change. "Of all the bookstores in all the towns in all the world," I said, "she walks into mine."

TWENTY-ONE

Of course she remembered the line. Her eyes brightened with recognition, and she smiled that smile of hers, the one that made her look like the Mona Lisa who swallowed the canary. "Bernard," she said, except of course that wasn't how she said it. "Bear-naard"—*that's* how she said it.

I said, "It's good to see you, Ilona. I've missed you."

"Bear-naard."

"Are you alone? I thought you'd be in company."

"I wanted to come in alone first," she said. "To make sure that . . . that the right people are here."

"Look at these people," I said. "Don't they look right to you?"

Now I managed a look at the rest of them, and they were a sight to see. Charlie Weeks, already bareheaded, sprang to his feet and smiled his little smile. Tsarnoff didn't stand, but snatched off the black beret and held it with both hands in his lap. He looked at Ilona as if trying to decide the best way to prepare her for the table. Rasmoulian took his hat off, held it for a moment, then put it back on his head. His eyes were full of hopeless longing, and I knew just how he felt.

235

I couldn't read Wilfred's look. His hard little eyes took her in, sized her up, and didn't show a thing.

God knows what Ilona thought looking at that crew, but she evidently found nothing to put her off stride. "I will be right back," she said, and ducked out the door, returning moments later with Michael Todd in tow. He was wearing a gray shark-skin suit and, while he was bareheaded, his tie sported a dozen or more colorful hats floating on a red background.

"Michael," she said (it came out as a sort of cross between Michael and Mikhail), "this is Bernard. Bernard, I would like you to meet—"

"But we have met," Michael cut in. "Only the name was not Bernard. It was—" He searched his memory. "Bill! Bill Thomas!"

"Thompson," I said, "but that's still pretty impressive. I didn't think you were paying any attention."

"He came to the door," he told her. "The other morning. He was collecting for a charity." His eyes narrowed. "He *said* he was collecting for a charity."

"The American Hip Dysplasia Association," I said, "and that's where your money went, so don't worry about it. It's a hell of a worthy cause, and if you'd like I'm sure Miss Kaiser would be happy to tell you more than you could possibly want to know about it."

"But you are not Mr. Thompson? You are Mr. Bernard?"

"Mr. Rhodenbarr," I said, "but you can call me Bernie. Why don't you have a seat, Your—" I stopped myself. "And you too, Ilona. I thought a third person would be coming along with the two of you. Actually he was supposed to pick the two of you up, and I'm a little surprised that you happened to get here without him. I hate to start before he gets here, so perhaps we can—"

"Perhaps we can," Ray Kirschmann said from the doorway. He shouldered his way into the store, cast a cold eye on the assembled company, and propped an elbow on a convenient bookshelf. He was wearing another costly if ill-fitting suit, and damned if he didn't have a hat on, and a fedora at that. I happen to think all plainclothes policemen should wear hats, just like in the movies, but they mostly don't in real life, and I couldn't recall ever seeing Ray in a hat before. It looked good on him.

"What I am," he said, "is I'm touched, Bernie. The idea you'd wait for me. You want to innerduce me to these folks?"

I went around the circle, naming names, and then I got to Ray. "And this is Raymond Kirschmann," I said, "of the New York Police Department."

There were some interesting reactions. Charlie Weeks's eyes brightened and his smile took up a little more of his face. Tsarnoff looked unhappy. Rasmoulian had an air of resignation; the introduction couldn't have come as a surprise to him, since he'd already met Ray twice before, and even Ray's presence was probably something less than a shock, given Ray's propensity for turning up whenever Tiggy paid a visit to Barnegat Books.

Wilfred didn't seem surprised, either, and I figured it was because he'd made Ray the minute he walked in. Wilfred struck me as the sort of fellow who could spot a cop a block away. On the other hand, I don't suppose his face would have changed expression if I'd introduced Ray as a first vice president at Chase Manhattan, in charge of repairing broken automatic teller machines. Wilfred wasn't much on changing expressions, or of showing one in the first place.

Anyway, the big reaction came from Ilona and Mike, who mumbled and stammered something to the effect that they'd thought Ray was affiliated not with the police at all but with the Immigration and Naturalization Service.

"Now that's innarestin'," he allowed, "an' I can see where you would get the impression, an' maybe I even went an' made a slip of the tongue, sayin' INS when I meant NYPD. It's one batch of initials or another, an' it coulda come out AFL-CIO just as easy. But Bernie here is right, what I am is a cop, an' just for form I prob'ly oughta read you all this here." He held up a little wallet-size card and read, " 'You have the right to remain silent,' " and went all the way to the end, Mirandizing the hell out of everybody.

"I don't understand," Tsarnoff said. "Am I to take it, sir, that we have been placed under arrest?"

"Naw," Ray said. "Why'd I wanna go an' arrest anybody? I don't see nobody breakin' no laws. An' even if I did, I ain't in no hurry to make an arrest. You arrest somebody nowadays, you're lookin' at twelve, fifteen hours of paperwork by the time you're done. Why, on my way in here I saw a young fellow take a book off of Bernie's outside table, an' do you think I was gonna arrest him for that?"

"Probably not," I said.

"Of course not. So if anybody in this room should happen to be carryin' a concealed weapon, with or without you got a permit for it, as long as it don't see the light of day you got nothin' to worry about. Or if there's a person here with outstandin' warrants, well, put your mind at rest. That ain't what I'm here for."

"And yet you read us our rights," Tsarnoff persisted.

"That's just a contingency procedure," Charlie Weeks said. "Figure it out, Gregorius. From this point on, anything anybody says is admissible as evidence. At least that's the supposition. I don't know what a lawyer would make of it, or a judge."

"A lawyer would make a buck," Ray said, "bein' as they generally do. An' nobody ever knows what a judge'll make of anything. An' the real reason I read the Miranda card is so we'll all take this seriously, even though it ain't official an' I'm just here to see what my old friend Bernie's gonna pull out of his hat. He's done this before, an' I got to admit he generally comes up with a rabbit."

That was my cue, and I hopped to it. The line that came to me was *I suppose you're wondering why I summoned you all here,* and I'll admit it's one I've used to good effect in the past, but it didn't really apply this time. They weren't wondering. They knew, or at least thought they did.

"I want to thank you all for coming," I said. "I know you're all busy people, and I don't want to take up too much of your time. So I'll get right to it."

I would have, too, but some clown picked that moment to stick his head in the door. "The sign says you're closed," he said, sounding peeved.

"We are," I said. "There's a private sale going on. We'll be keeping our usual hours tomorrow."

"But you got a table outside," he said, "plus your door's not locked."

"I'll fix that," I said, and closed it in his face, and thumbed the catch to lock it. He gave me a look and turned away, and I turned back to my guests.

"Sorry," I said. "Mowgli, if anybody else tries to come in—"

"I'll take care of it," he said.

"Thanks. Where was I?"

"You were getting right to it," Charlie Weeks said.

"So I was," I said, and found a bookcase to lean against. "I want to tell you a story, and I may have to jump around a little, because this story starts in a few different places at a few different times. It has its roots deep in the nineteenth century, when nationalist sentiments began to stir throughout the lands administered by the Austro-Hungarian and the Ottoman empires. One of those Balkan nationalisms precipitated the outbreak of the First World War, when a young Serb shot the Austrian archduke. By the time that war ended, self-determination of nations was a catchphrase throughout the western world. Independence movements flowered across Europe. Among the presumptive nations to declare their independence was the sovereign nation of Anatruria. It was designated as a kingdom, and its monarch was to be King Vlados the First."

This couldn't have been news to any of them, except for Ray

and Mowgli, and possibly Wilfred. But they all paid close attention.

"The Anatrurians did what they could to add substance to their proclamation of sovereignty," I went on. "An extensive series of stamps was printed at Budapest, and some were actually used postally within the borders of Anatruria. Some pattern coins were struck and distributed to friends of the new nation, although a general issue was never produced for circulation. There were a few medals issued as well, bearing the new king's likeness and presented to some men who had been the mainstay of the independence movement."

"Scarce as hen's teeth, all of them," Tsarnoff declared. "And about as eagerly sought in the collector market."

"Anatrurian hopes were dashed at Versailles," I went on, "when Wilson and Clemenceau remade the map of Europe. What would have been Anatruria was parceled up among Romania, Bulgaria, and Yugoslavia. King Vlados and Queen Liliana lived out the remainder of their lives in exile, still serving as a rallying point for those who continued to believe in the Anatrurian cause. But the movement died down."

"The flame flickered," Ilona murmured. "But it was never extinguished."

"Maybe not," I said, "but there was a time when it would have taken it a long time to bring a kettle to the boil. Then, during World War Two, the Anatrurian partisans had an active role."

"They were opportunists," Tsarnoff put in, "switching allegiance as it served their interests. One day they'd be fighting side by side with Ante Pavelič's Croatian Ustachi, murdering Serbs, and the next thing you knew they'd be on the Serbian side, sacking Croat villages. Were they for Hitler or against him? It depended when you asked the question."

"They were for Anatruria," Ilona said. "Every day, every week, every month of the year."

"They were for themselves," Tiglath Rasmoulian said. "As who is not?"

"When the war ended," I went on, "national borders in that

part of the world remained essentially unchanged, but governments were in upheaval. The Soviet Union's span of influence quickly took in all of Eastern Europe, and Truman had to draw a line in the sand to keep Greece and Turkey this side of the Iron Curtain. Several American intelligence agencies, at least one of them an outgrowth of the wartime OSS, sought to even the balance in that strategically vital area of the world." I frowned, annoyed at the tone I was taking. In spite of all the films I'd seen lately, I was managing to sound like an Edward R. Murrow voice-over for a documentary.

"Among the clandestine missions dispatched to the region"—damn, I was still doing it—"was a group of five American agents."

I hesitated for an instant, and Charlie Weeks read my mind. "Oh, they were all Americans, all right. Hundred percent red-blooded nephews of their Uncle Sam. No wretched refuse of your teeming shores in the Bob and Charlie Show, not on your life."

"Five Americans," I said quickly. "Robert Bateman and Robert Rennick. Charles Hoberman and Charles Wood. And Charles Weeks."

"Charles Weeks?" Ray said. "This fellow here?"

"This fellow here," said Charlie Weeks.

I told how, for convenience' sake, the Roberts had become Bob and Rob respectively, the Charleses Cappy, Chuck, and Charlie. "And," I said, "they all had animal names."

Mowgli said, "Animal names? I'm sorry, Bernie, I didn't mean to interrupt, but I want to make sure I heard you right."

"Animal names," I said. "You heard me right. Code names, really. Bateman was the cat and Rennick was the rabbit."

"Actually," Weeks put in, "it was the other way around. Not that it matters much, at this late date."

"I stand corrected. Cap Hoberman was the ram. Charlie Weeks was the mouse."

"Squeak squeak," said Charlie Weeks.

"And Chuck Wood's totem, perhaps inevitably, was the

woodchuck. His was the only one which was a play on words rather than a reference to some perceived personal characteristic, and I mention that because it's relevant. I'm guessing now, but I'd say that Wood selected the name for himself."

"Ha!" said Weeks. He looked up and to the left, reaching for the memory. "You know," he said, "I think you're right, weasel."

Carolyn said, "Weasel?"

I let it pass. "Five Americans," I said, "each with an animal for a code name, undercover in the Balkans. Working together and with partisans and dissidents of every description, all with the aim of destabilizing . . . Yugoslavia? Romania? Bulgaria?"

"Any one would do," Weeks said dreamily. "Or all three. Be nice, wouldn't it? Real feather in the collective cap for Hannibal's Animals." He winked at me. "Another name we had for ourselves. I didn't tell you about that one, did I? After the old man in Adams-Morgan who was running us. *His* code name was Hannibal, don't ask me why, and the name we made up for him was the elephant." He put his fingertips together. "But don't get me started, weasel. It's your party, yours to tell the tale."

I said, "One possible lever they found was the movement for Anatrurian independence. Causes don't die out in that part of the world, they just go dormant for a generation or two. King Vlados was well up in his seventies, a widower living on the Costa de Nada with a succession of housekeepers, his social life the same endless round of drinks and cardplaying with other once-crowned heads that had been sustaining him for the past forty years. He was a valuable symbol of Anatrurian greatness, but you couldn't expect him to march in the van of a renewed patriotic movement. The last thing he was going to do was give up the Spanish sun for some back-room rallies in the Anatrurian hills."

"Mountains," Ilona said.

"But Vlados and Liliana had a son. *L'aiglon*, the French would say. The eaglet, the crown prince, the heir apparent."

"The colt," Weeks put in. "We called the old man the stallion, you see. Just among ourselves, mind you. He had that mouthful of horse teeth, and then he had retired to stud, hadn't he? So that made his son the colt."

"Todor was his name. Todor Vladov, because that's how Anatrurian names work, with a Christian name and a patronym. His father was Vlados, so his last name was Vladov. Even as your name"—I nodded at Ilona—"is Ilona Markova. You father's name would have been Marko."

"Except for what?" Tiglath Rasmoulian demanded. "You say the man's name *would* have been Marko. What prevented it from being Marko? And what was it in fact?"

"It is still Marko," she said indignantly. "Marko Stoichkov. He has never changed it. He would never do such a thing."

We got that straightened out, though you don't want to know how, believe me.

"Todor Vladov was a toddler when his father accepted the Anatrurian crown. He was in his early thirties when the Bob and Charlie Show took up the cause of Anatrurian independence."

"Time and tide, sir," Tsarnoff said. "They wait for no man, and the bell tolls for us all."

"What does he mean by that?" Rasmoulian snapped. "Why does he not speak that he may be understood?"

"If your cognitive ability had not been arrested along with your physical development," the fat man said, "perhaps you might be able to follow a simple sentence."

"You glutton," Rasmoulian said. "You gross Circassian swine."

"You rug-peddling justification for the Turkish genocide."

"It is on such a rug that your mother lay with a camel when she got you."

"Yours rolled in the dirt with a boar hog, sir, for her husband ran off with the rug to sell it."

Then they both said several things I couldn't make out. It sounded as though each was speaking a different language, and I don't know that either could entirely understand what the other was saying. But they must have gotten the gist of it, because Rasmoulian's hand went into his trench-coat pocket even as Tsarnoff's gunsel was reaching inside his baseball jacket.

"Let's hold it right there," Ray said, and damned if he didn't have a revolver in his hand, a big old Police Special. I couldn't guess how long it had been since he'd heard a shot fired in anger, or even for practice, and the gun he was holding might very well blow up in his hand if he ever pulled the trigger, but they didn't know that. Tiggy tossed his head and sank deeper into his trench coat, but withdrew his hand from its pocket. Wilfred also showed an empty hand, but otherwise stayed his endearingly expressionless self.

"Back to Anatruria," I said quickly. "Old King Vlados may have given up dreams of a Balkan kingdom, but his son Todor found the idea intoxicating. Contacted by the American agents, he entered Anatruria surreptitiously and had a series of meetings with potential supporters. The stage was set for a popular uprising."

"Never would have stood a chance," Charlie Weeks mused. "Look what the Ivans did in Budapest and Prague, for Christ's sake. But look what a black eye they got for their troubles in the world press." He sighed. "That was all we were after. We were getting the Anatrurians to rise up just so the Russkies could cut them down." He flashed a rueful smile at Ilona, who looked horrified by what he'd just said. "Sorry, Miss Markova, but that was the job they handed us. Stir something up, make some mischief, embarrass the comrades. Like Werner von Braun with his rockets. His job was to get them off the ground. Where they came down was somebody else's department. He wrote an autobiography, *I Aim for the Stars*." He winked. "Maybe so, Werner, but you sure hit London a lot."

"The Anatrurian rising never did get off the ground," I went on. "There was a betrayal."

"The woodchuck's doing," Weeks said. "At least that was what we always thought."

"The Americans scattered," I said, "and left the country separately. Government authorities swooped down on the Anatrurians and took the heart of the movement into custody. There were some long prison sentences, a few summary executions. According to rumor, Todor Vladov got a bullet in the back of the neck and a secret burial in an unmarked grave. In point of fact he slipped through a border checkpoint just in time and never again returned to Anatruria."

Ray wanted to know how old he'd be now.

"He'd be close to eighty," I said, "but he died last fall."

"And the treasury," Tsarnoff said. "What becomes of the treasury upon Todor's death?"

"The treasury?"

"The war chest," Rasmoulian said, impatient. "The Anatrurian royal treasury."

"Old Vlados's backers were grabbing with both hands when the Austrian and Ottoman empires were falling apart," Tsarnoff explained. "When they found themselves disappointed at Versailles, they packed their bags and hied themselves to Zurich, where they established a Swiss corporation and shunted everything they had into it. The corporation's liquid assets went into a numbered account, everything else into a safe-deposit box."

"Much must be worthless," Rasmoulian said, from deep within the shelter of his trench coat. "Czarist bonds, deeds to property expropriated by dictatorships of the left and right. Shares of stock in defunct corporations."

"The Assyrian is correct, sir. Much would indeed be worthless, but that which is not worthless could very well be priceless. Valid deeds, shares in firms which have thrived. And, while the bonds and currencies of fallen regimes would be of value only as curiosities, instruments of title to business and real property seized by the communists are worth another look now that communism has itself gone obsolete."

"There is no telling what it's all worth," Rasmoulian said, his spots of color glowing.

"Indeed, sir. There is no telling what money remains in that numbered account, or what assets the corporation retains. What could old Vlados have drained off? And what about his son, of blessed memory? No one goes through capital like a pretender trying to maintain a pretense."

"Vlados had an income," Weeks said. "Remember, the people who chose him for the throne didn't pick him off a dunghill. He was a shirttail cousin of the king of Sweden and claimed descent on his mother's side from Maria Theresa of Austria. Queen Liliana was some kind of grandniece of Queen Victoria. They weren't rich enough to buy the Congo from Leopold of Belgium, but Liliana never had to shop at Kmart either. They had an income and they lived within it."

"And Todor?"

"Same story for the colt. We didn't get him back to Anatruria by dangling some dough in front of him. He worked for a living, fronting an investment syndicate based in Luxembourg, but he was comfortable." He grinned. "We hooked him by the ego. He figured he'd look good with a crown on his head."

"He was a patriot," Ilona said. "That is not ego, to go to the aid of your people. It is self-sacrifice."

"How would you know so much about it, little lady? He was long gone from Anatruria before you were born."

He didn't sound as though he expected an answer, and she didn't give him one. I said, "Let's flash-forward to the present, okay? I'd like to tell you about a man named Hugo Candlemas. That's an unusual name, and he was an unusual man, erudite and personable. Earlier this year he came to New York and took an apartment on the Upper East Side. And a matter of days ago he came into this store and introduced himself to me. He persuaded me to break into an apartment a few blocks away from his and steal a leather portfolio."

"You, Bernie?" The question came from Mowgli, who may

have been the only person in the room who didn't know what I did when I wasn't selling books. "Why would he think you'd be up for something like that?"

"At the time," I said, "I thought he'd heard my name years ago from a man he mentioned as a mutual acquaintance, a gentleman named Abel Crowe." Both Rasmoulian and Tsarnoff started at the name, which didn't much surprise me. "Until he died, Abel Crowe was at the very top of his profession, which happened to be the receiving of stolen goods."

"He was a fence, all right," Ray Kirschmann agreed. "An' you gotta hand it to him, he was the best wide receiver in the business."

"And I was a burglar," I said. Mowgli, wide-eyed at this news, remained silent, probably because of the elbow Carolyn dug into his ribs. "But I've changed my mind about that. I don't think Abel would have bandied my name about."

"Abel was discreet," Tsarnoff said.

"He was," I agreed, "and even if my name did come up, how would Candlemas remember it years later when he happened to need a burglar? I don't think that's how it happened."

"He must have looked in the Yellow Pages," Charlie Weeks suggested.

"I don't think so," I said. "I think he followed Ilona."

"A couple of weeks ago," I said to her, "you walked into my store. I tried to figure out how you got here, because I couldn't believe it was coincidence. But at the time there was nothing for it to coincide with, was there? I'd never met Candlemas or heard of any of the people in this room. I didn't know Anatruria from God's Little Acre.

"And you were just looking for something to read. You picked out a book, and we got talking and found out we shared a passion for Humphrey Bogart. There was a Humphrey Bogart film festival just getting underway, and you knew about it, and we arranged to meet at the theater that night. Before we knew it we were going every night, watching two movies together, eating popcorn from the same container, then going our separate ways."

I looked into her eyes, and I thought of Bogart and tried to borrow a little nobility from him. "You're a beautiful woman," I said, "and I could have gone for you in a big way if you'd ever given me the slightest encouragement, but you never did. It was clear from the start that you had someone else. And that was okay. I liked your company, and I guess you liked mine, but what we both liked was up there on the screen."

There was gratitude in her eyes now, and a touch of relief, and something else as well. Wistfulness, maybe.

"I don't know if Candlemas was on your tail when you came into the bookstore," I said. "Probably not. But if he followed you at all he could hardly help running into me, because we were spending seven nights a week at the movies. He'd want to know who I was, and it wouldn't have been hard for him to find out. The kind of people he'd have asked would have known about my sideline as a burglar."

"It's the booksellin' that's a sideline," Ray put in.

I ignored that. "Candlemas needed a burglar," I said, "and he probably did know Abel Crowe, who spent the war in a concentration camp and knocked around Europe for a few years before he came over here. He would have learned I was a good burglar—"

"The best," Ray said.

"—and he had a name to drop to establish his bona fides. He sounded me out, and when the address he wanted me to burgle didn't ring a bell, he knew Ilona hadn't told me about the man who lived there."

"And who was that?" Ray wanted to know.

"The man in her life," I said. "The man, too, whom Candlemas had pursued to New York. He's right here. Mr. Michael Todd."

"*Around the World in Eighty Days*," Mowgli said. "Great flick. But didn't his plane go down?"

"Michael Todd," I said. "You speak good unaccented English, Mike, so why shouldn't your name be just as American as your speech? But you anglicized it along the way, didn't you? Why don't you tell them what it was before you changed it?"

"I'm sure you'll tell them," he said.

"Mikhail Todorov," I said. "The only son of Todor Vladov, the only grandson of Vlados the First. And, if there is such a thing, the rightful heir to the Anatrurian throne."

TWENTY-TWO

I guess we're all suckers for royalty. Half the house must have known or suspected Mike's place in the scheme of things, but all the same a hush fell over the room, and it hung there until Carolyn broke it. "A king," she said. "I can't believe it. In my store."

"Your store?"

"Well, it's almost my store, Bern. Who kept it open over the weekend? Uh, speaking of my store, Your Majesty, I don't suppose you have a dog that needs washing, but if you ever do—"

"I'll most certainly think of you," he said, whereupon Carolyn looked almost glassy-eyed enough to drop a curtsy. "Mr. Rhodenbarr, I haven't said anything until now, but perhaps I should. This business of an Anatrurian throne makes me quite uncomfortable. My grandfather's moment of glory occurred ages ago, and my father's little adventure took place before I was born, and very nearly cost him his life. That my family had a tentative claim on a putative crown was interesting, even amusing, something to impress a girl or enliven a social gathering. I have my own life, with a small amount of capital and a career in international finance and economic development. I don't spend time nostalgic for a royal past or dreaming of a royal future."

"And yet you came to New York," I said gently.

"To get away from Europe and its talk of thrones and crowns."

"And you brought a gold-stamped leather portfolio."

He sighed heavily. "When my father lay dying," he said, "he called me to his side and turned over to me the portfolio of which you speak. Until then I did not know of its existence."

"And?"

"He had scarcely spoken to me of Anatruria. You must understand that none of our family had ever lived there. My grandfather was chosen to be king of the Anatrurians, but he was not previously Anatrurian himself. Now, on his deathbed, my father spoke of his deep love for this small mountainous nation, of the loyalty our family commanded there and the responsibility which consequently devolved upon us. I thought he was raving, affected by the drugs his doctors had given him. And perhaps he was."

"He was a great man," Ilona said.

"I would say so, but then he was my father. Middle-aged when I was born, often absent while I was growing up, but surely a great man in my eyes. With his dying breath he told me of my duty to Anatruria, and passed on the royal portfolio."

"What did it hold?"

"Papers, documents, souvenirs. Shares of stock in a Swiss corporation."

"Bearer shares," I said.

"Yes, I believe so."

"Like bearer bonds," Charlie Weeks said. "The Swiss are nuts about that sort of thing. When they change hands, there's no need to go through any paperwork to record the transfer. They're like cash, they belong to whoever is in possession of them."

"And with them in your hands," I said, "you could take possession of all the assets of the corporation."

Todd—Mikhail? The king?—shook his royal head. "No," he said.

"No?"

"You need the account number *and* the shares," he said. "Believe me, I went to Zurich, I consulted bankers and attorneys there. This corporation was set up in an unusual fashion, and one must be in possession of the bearer shares and know the number of the account in order to lay hands on any of the corporation's assets. My father passed on the shares, which he had received from his father, but neither he nor his father had been entrusted with the account number."

"Out with it, man," said Tsarnoff. "Who has it?"

"Probably no one," Todd said.

"Ridiculous! Someone must know."

"Someone must have known once, some leader of the Anatrurian movement. Perhaps several people knew. You have already said that my father was lucky to get out of Anatruria with his life. Others were not so lucky. So many were taken from their families, only to receive a bullet in the back of the neck and burial without ceremony in an unmarked grave. I would guess that many secrets were buried along with those men, and that the number of the Swiss account was one of those secrets."

He sighed again. "I remember sitting at a café after my last meeting with a lawyer and a banker, sitting with a glass of wine and wishing my father had taken the portfolio to the grave with him as some Anatrurian had taken the account number. But instead he'd entrusted it to me. In a sense, he'd pressed a crown on my head, and it was not so easy to lay it aside. I told you how I had never thought of Anatruria. Now I could scarcely think of anything else."

"Who could even say how much the wealth might be?" This from Rasmoulian, his eyes wide at the possibilities. "It could be nothing. It could be millions."

"The money is the least of it," the king said. "What am I to do? That is the only question of any importance."

Ray didn't understand, and said so.

"For decades," the king said, "the world's few reigning kings have been anachronisms, while uncrowned royals have been little more than a joke. But all of a sudden this is not so. There are monarchist movements throughout all of the old Eastern Bloc. Portions of portions of nations are all at once reaching out and achieving sovereignty. If Slovenia and Slovakia can join the United Nations, is an independent Anatruria such an impossibility? If Juan Carlos can be king of Spain, and if men can seriously urge a Romanov restoration in Russia—the Romanovs! in Russia!—"

"Not entirely out of the question," Tsarnoff allowed.

"—then who is to say Anatruria cannot have a king? And who am I to deny my people if indeed they want me?" He smiled suddenly, and now the resemblance was unmistakable—to Ilona's photograph of Vlados, to Mikhail's own photo of his father resplendent in uniform. "And so I came to New York," he said, "to get away from Europe, and to decide what I shall do next."

"It looks as though Hugo Candlemas followed you here," I said. "As I said, he picked me to steal the portfolio from you, although I didn't know what I was stealing or whose apartment I was taking it from."

"Not like you, Bernie," Ray said.

"I know," I said. "It wasn't. I don't know why I went for it, and all I can come up with is a combination of his charm and all those Bogart movies I was watching. He made the proposition one afternoon, and the following night I was with a man named Hoberman, on my way to . . . excuse me, but what do I call you? Your Highness? Your Majesty?"

" 'Michael' will be fine."

"I was on my way to Michael's apartment."

"Hoberman," Ray said. "That's a name you mentioned before, Bernie."

I nodded. "Cappy Hoberman was the ram, one of the five agents in Anatruria. Candlemas paired me with him because Hoberman could escort me into the high-security building where Michael lives. He could go there on the pretext of visiting another tenant in the building."

"Which is where I come in," Charlie Weeks said.

"Interesting," Tsarnoff said. "Of all the buildings in all the cities in America, the young king moves into yours."

The line had a familiar ring to it. I had an answer, but Weeks got there first. "No coincidence at all," he said. "Michael gave me a call as soon as he got to New York. He'd never met me, of course, but I'd kept in touch with Todor ever since I helped him get out of Anatruria two steps ahead of the KGB. Michael needed a place to stay, and I knew there was an owner in the building looking to sublet, and he liked the place and moved in right away."

"As it turned out," I said, "I didn't steal the portfolio. I'll admit I tried, Michael, but I couldn't find it."

"There was one night last week when I took it from the apartment," he said. "Ilona thought a friend of hers should see one of the documents."

"I must have just missed it. Meanwhile, Cappy Hoberman went back to Candlemas's apartment, where somebody stabbed him to death."

"Wait a minute," Ray said. "That's the guy? Hoberman?"

"Right."

"Cap Hob," he said, staring hard at me. "Cap Hob. Captain Hoberman."

"Right."

"But why in the hell would he—"

I held up a hand. "It's complicated," I said, "and it's probably easier all around if I just tell it straight through. Cappy Hoberman was stabbed to death in the Candlemas apartment. But he lived long enough to leave a message. He printed C-A-P-H-O-B in block capitals on the side of a handy attaché case."

"Which happened to belong to a certain burglar we all know," Ray said.

"Didn't it," I said sourly. "He died, and left a dying message that didn't make sense to anyone. Meanwhile, Hugo Candlemas disappeared."

"So this Candlemas killed him," Ilona said.

"It seems obvious, doesn't it? But who was Candlemas? Well, he was someone who knew Hoberman and Weeks, someone who was familiar with Anatrurian history and had come over from Europe to keep tabs on Michael here. And he was someone with a lot of fake ID, because in addition to forged identification in the name of Hugo Candlemas, he also had high-quality counterfeit passports in the names Jean-Claude Marmotte and Vassily Souslik. That gives it away. I should have known before, but—"

"The last name you mentioned," Tsarnoff said. "Say it again, sir, if you please."

"Vassily Souslik."

"Souslik," he said, and chuckled. "Very good, sir. Very good indeed."

"What is so good?" Rasmoulian demanded. "It is good because he has a Russian name? I do not understand."

"Now that you mention it," Ray said, "neither do I. I'm the one told you about those names, Bernie, and they didn't mean a thing to me, an' if they meant anything to you I never heard a peep out of you about it. What in hell's a sousnik, anyway?"

"A souslik," I said. "Not a sousnik. And it's a Russian word, which is why Mr. Tsarnoff understood it and why the rest of us didn't, although you'll find it in some English dictionaries and encyclopedias. And it means a large ground squirrel indigenous to Eastern Europe and Asia."

"Well, for Christ's sake," Ray said, "that explains everything, don't it? A big fat squirrel. That cracks the case wide open, all right."

"What it does," I said, "is identify Candlemas for us. So does his French alias, because a marmot is pretty much the same thing as a souslik. But I should have known earlier on if I'd been paying attention to what he called himself this time around. Candlemas is a church festival commemorating the purification of the Virgin Mary and the presentation of the infant Christ in the temple. But it's celebrated on the same date every year like Christmas, not tied to the lunar calendar like Easter."

Someone asked the date.

"February second," I said.

They met this with mystified silence and shared the silence like Quakers through whom God had, for the moment, nothing to say. Then Wilfred, silent skulking Wilfred, said, "My favorite holiday."

Everybody looked at him.

"Groundhog's Day," he said. "Second of February. Most useful holiday of the year. He pops out, he don't see his shadow, you got yourself an early spring. Bright sunny day, he sees his shadow, forget about it. Six more weeks of winter."

I said, "The groundhog, the souslik, the marmot. All names for—"

"The woodchuck," said Charlie Weeks, smiling his tight little smile. "Alias Chuck Wood, alias Charles Brigham Wood. Disappeared into Europe after the balloon went up in Anatruria. Some people thought he was killed. The rest of us figured he was the one who sold us out."

I let that last pass. "Candlemas was the woodchuck," I agreed. "I guess he kept tabs on people from afar. He knew where Michael was living, and he knew that his old friend the mouse was in the same building. But he couldn't approach the mouse himself."

"I'd had enough of him in Anatruria," Weeks said.

"So he used Hoberman as his cat's-paw," I said, and frowned at the metaphor, an inappropriate one among all these rodents.

"And when Cappy had served his purpose," Weeks said, "the woodchuck killed him."

"In his own apartment?"

"Why not?"

"And on his own rug? Candlemas might sacrifice an old friend, but why throw in a valuable rug?"

"How valuable?" Ray wanted to know. I couldn't tell him, and Tsarnoff suggested dryly that we consult the rug peddler in our midst for an evaluation.

"Stop that!" Rasmoulian said. "Why does he do that? I am not an Armenian. I know nothing about carpets. Why does he say these things about me?"

"The same reason you call me a Russian," Tsarnoff said smoothly. "Willful ignorance, my little adversary. Willful ignorance founded on malice and propelled by avarice."

"I shall never call you a Russian again. You are a Circassian."

"And you an Assyrian."

"The Circassians are legendary. The women are exquisite whores, and the males are castrated young and make great gross eunuchs."

"The Assyrians at their height were noted chiefly for their savagery. They have dwindled and died out to the point where the few in existence are wizened dwarves, the genetically warped spawn of two millennia of incestuous unions."

We were making progress, I was pleased to note. For all the verbal escalation, neither Rasmoulian's hand nor Wilfred's had moved so much as an inch toward a concealed weapon.

"Candlemas didn't kill Hoberman," I said. "Even if he didn't care about the rug, even if he had some dark reason to want Hoberman out of the picture, the timing was all wrong. Would he risk having a corpse on the floor when I got back with the royal portfolio?"

"He'd kill you, too," Weeks said.

"And write off another rug? No, it doesn't make sense that way. It's a shame, too, because Candlemas makes a very convenient killer."

"That's the truth," Ray said. "Tell 'em why, Bernie."

"Because he's dead himself," I said, "and can't argue the point. He died within hours of Hoberman, but he took longer to turn up. The cops found him in an abandoned building at Pitt and Madison."

"That's the place to find one," said Mowgli, as one who knew. "A corpse or an abandoned building. Or both."

"How was he killed?" Tsarnoff wanted to know.

"He was shot," Ray said. "Small-caliber gun fired at close range."

"Two different killers," Tiglath Rasmoulian suggested. "This woodchuck stabbed the ram, and was shot by someone else."

"If this happened in Anatruria," Ilona said, "you would know that the woodchuck was shot by a son of his victim, or perhaps a brother. Even a nephew." She shrugged. "But you would not inquire too closely, because this would not be a police matter. It is merely blood avenging blood, and honor requires it."

"There's no honor here," I said. "And a good thing, too. There was only one killer. He followed Hoberman when he left the Boccaccio, tagged him to the woodchuck's apartment a few blocks away, and stabbed him right off. Then he abducted Candlemas, took him down to Pitt Street—"

"Pitt Street," Mowgli said. "You're down there, you might as well be dead."

"—and killed him when he'd learned all he could from him. Or maybe he took him somewhere else, killed him after interrogating him, and took the dead body to Pitt Street."

"Coals to Newcastle," Mowgli said.

"Then someone was watching my building," Michael said.

"No."

"You mean this Hoberman was under surveillance all along?"

I shook my head. "The ram was visiting his old friend, the mouse. They hadn't seen each other in years. And when the mouse told me about that visit, he made a real point of saying how the ram was in a hurry to get out of there."

"Ah," Charlie Weeks said. "You mean he was going to meet somebody on his way back to the woodchuck's place."

"No," I said. "That's not what I mean."

"It's not?"

"It's not," I said. "What I mean is that you wanted me to know that Hoberman was hardly in your apartment for any time at all. That way it wouldn't occur to me that you had plenty of time to get him settled in with a cup of coffee and excuse yourself long enough to make a quick phone call."

"Why would I do that?"

"Because you knew something was up. You didn't know what, but you were the mouse and you smelled a rat. You couldn't tag along with Hoberman. He'd be on guard. But you could call a confederate and stall Hoberman long enough for the man you called to post himself within line of sight of the Boccaccio's front entrance. Whether or not he knew Hoberman by sight, you could supply a description that would make identification an easy matter."

"Oh, weasel," Charlie Weeks said. "I'm disappointed in you, coming up with a wild theory like that."

"You deny it, then."

"Of course I deny it. But I can't deny the possibility that somebody followed Cappy home. It seems a little farfetched to me, but anything's possible. Thing is, I don't see how you're going to guess who it was."

"And if you had called someone, I'd just be guessing as to his identity, wouldn't I?"

"Since I didn't call anyone," he said, "the question's moot. But we can say that you'd just be taking a shot in the dark."

"Wait a minute," Carolyn said. "What about the dying message?"

"Ah, yes," I said. "The dying message. Could Hoberman have left a clue to his killer? We know what his message was." I walked over to my counter and reached behind it for the portable chalkboard I'd stowed there earlier. I propped it up where everybody could see it and chalked CAPHOB on it in nice big block caps. I let them take a good long look at it.

Then I said, "Cap hob. That's what it looks like. That's because we're in America. If we were in Anatruria it would look entirely different."

"Why's that, Bernie?" Ray asked. "Have they got their heads screwed on upside down over there?"

"I could show you in the stamp catalog," I said. "The Anatrurians, like the Serbs and the Bulgarians, use the Cyrillic alphabet. This is an important matter of national identity over there, incidentally. The Croats and Romanians use the same alphabet we do, while the Greeks use the Greek alphabet."

"It figures," Mowgli said.

"The Cyrillic alphabet was named for St. Cyril, who spread its use throughout Eastern Europe, although he probably didn't invent it. He did missionary work in the region with his brother St. Methodius, but they didn't name an alphabet after St. Methodius."

"They named an acting technique," Carolyn said. "After him and St. Stanislavski."

"The Cyrillic alphabet is a lot like the Greek," I said, "except that it's got more letters. I think there's something like forty of them, and some are identical in form to English letters while some look pretty weird to western eyes. There's a backward N and an upside-down V and one or two that look like hen's tracks. And some of the ones that look exactly like our own have different values."

Carolyn said, "Values? What do you mean, Bern? Is that like how many points they're worth in Scrabble?"

"It's the sound they make." I pointed to the blackboard. "It took me forever to think Cappy's dying message might be in Cyrillic," I said, "and for two reasons. For one, he was an American. Early on I didn't know the case had an Anatrurian connection, or that he'd ever been east of Long Island. Besides, all six of the letters he wrote were good foursquare red-blooded American letters. But it so happens they're all letters of the Cyrillic alphabet as well."

"I do not know this alphabet," Rasmoulian said carefully. "What do they spell in this alphabet?"

"The A and the O are the same in both alphabets," I said. "The Cyrillic C has the value of our own S. The P is equivalent to our R, just like the rho in the Greek alphabet. The H looks like the Greek eta, but in Cyrillic it's the equivalent of our N. And the Cyrillic B is the same as our V."

In a proper chalk talk, I'd have printed a transliteration of the Cyrillic on the slate. Instead I gave them a few seconds to work it out for themselves.

Then I said, "Mr. Tsarnoff, I don't know which alphabet Circassians favor, but certainly you've spent enough time in the former Soviet Union to be more familiar than the rest of us with Cyrillic. Perhaps you can tell us what message the gallant Hoberman left us."

Tsarnoff stayed in his chair, but just barely. His face was florid and his eyes bulged; if Charlie Weeks wanted an animal name for him, you'd almost have to go with bullfrog.

"It is a lie," he said.

"But what does it say?"

"S-A-R-N-O-V," he said, pronouncing each letter separately and distinctly, as if pounding nails into a coffin. "That is what it says, and it is a lie. It is not even my name. My name is Tsarnoff, sir, T-S-A-R-N-O-F-F, and that is not at all what you have written there, in Cyrillic or any other alphabet known to me."

"And yet," I said, "it strikes one as an extraordinary coincidence. I suppose you would pronounce it Sarnov, and—"

"That is not my name!"

"Tsue me," I said. "It's not that far off."

"I never met your Captain Hoberman! Until this moment I never heard of him!"

"I'm not sure that last is true," I said, "but we'll let it go. The point you're trying to make is that you didn't kill Hoberman, and you can give it a rest, because I already know that."

"You do?"

"Of course."

"Then why did Hoberman write his name?" Ray asked.

"He didn't," I said. "He didn't write a damn thing. That's a dying message, whether you pronounce it Caphob or Sarnov, and Hoberman was doing the dying, and it was his blood that formed the letters and his forefinger that traced them. I don't know if Hoberman even knew Cyrillic after so many years away from the region, but it certainly wasn't second nature to him, and what he'd automatically turn to in his haste to name his killer before his life drained out of him."

"Then who left the message?" Carolyn wanted to know. "Not what's-his-name, the groundhog—"

"The woodchuck. No, of course not. The killer left the message as a diversionary tactic. He probably chose Cyrillic because he knew little about his victim beyond the fact that he was somehow connected to Balkan politics. He wrote what he did because he wanted to implicate you, Mr. Tsarnoff, and he misspelled your name because his familiarity with Cyrillic was tenuous. So what do we know about our killer? He is not Anatrurian, he did not know his victims from the days of the Bob and Charlie Show, and he has a murderous antipathy toward Mr. Tsarnoff."

"Piece of cake," said Ray Kirschmann. "Gotta be Tigbert Rotarian, don't it? Only thing, if he's in the rug business, why's he want to ruin a good carpet like that?"

Rasmoulian was on his feet, his face whiter than ever, his patches of color livid now. He was protesting everything at once, insisting he was not in the rug trade, he had killed no one, and his name was not whatever Ray had just said it was.

"Whatever," Ray said agreeably. "I'll make sure I got the name right when we get down to Central Booking. Main thing's did he do it or not, an' I think you still got your touch, Bernie. Tigrid, you got the right to remain silent, but I already told you that, remember?"

Rasmoulian's mouth was working but no sound was coming out of it. I thought he might go for a gun, but his hands stayed in sight, knotted up in little fists. He looked like a kid again, and you got the sense that he might burst into tears, or stamp his foot.

The whole room was silent, waiting to see what he'd do. Then Carolyn said, "For God's sake, Tiggy, tell 'em it was an accident."

Jesus, I thought. What could have induced her to come out with a harebrained thing like that?

"It was an accident," Tiglath Rasmoulian said.

TWENTY-THREE

It was unquestionably an accident, he explained. He had never meant to harm anyone. He was not a killer.

Yes, admittedly, he had been armed. He had outfitted himself that evening with a pistol and dagger as well, although it was never his intention to use either of them. But this was New York, after all, not Baghdad or Cairo, not Istanbul, not Casablanca. This was a dangerous city, and who would dream of walking its streets unarmed? And was this not even more to be expected if one was of diminished stature and slightly built? He was a small person, if not the dwarf that a certain hideously obese individual was wont to label him, and he could only feel safe if he carried something to offset the disadvantage at which his size placed him.

And yes, it was true, he had received a telephone call from Mr. Weeks, with whom he had had occasional business dealings over the years. At Mr. Weeks's bequest, he'd driven to the Boccaccio and parked across the street with the motor running. When Hoberman emerged from the building he watched him flag a cab and tailed him a short distance to what would be the murder scene. He entered the brownstone's vestibule just as Hoberman was being buzzed in and caught the door before it closed, following his quarry upstairs to the fourth-floor apartment. But evidently his activities had not gone unnoticed; he was standing in the hallway, trying to hear what was going on inside and deliberating his next move, when the door opened suddenly and Hoberman grabbed him by the arm and yanked him inside.

He had no time to consider the matter. His response was automatic and unthinking; in an instant the dagger was free of its sheath and in his hand, and in another instant it was in Hoberman's body. He did not know who the man was, nor had he any knowledge of the identity of the other man, the slender white-haired fellow in the suit and checkered vest. He did not know anything of the pursuit in which the two were engaged. All he knew was that he had just killed a man. Reflexively, of course, and in self-defense, to be sure, but the man was dead and Tiglath Rasmoulian was in trouble.

The white-haired man, the one they now seemed to be calling the woodchuck, was far too slow to react. He just stood there, staring in shock, and before he could do anything Rasmoulian was holding a gun on him. He put him against a wall with his hands in the air while he went through the pockets of the man he'd killed until he came up with a wallet. He stuffed it in his own pocket to examine at leisure.

And, while he was kneeling by the unfortunate man's body, yes, something came over him, some hostility to an old foe. He took hold of the poor man's hand, dipped the forefinger in the blood, and wrote that foe's name on a convenient surface, which happened to be the side panel of an attaché case. And if his Cyrillic was imperfect, well, he'd come close enough. It was a barbaric alphabet anyway.

Then came the tricky part. Down the stairs and all the way to where he'd parked the car, he covered Candlemas with one hand in his pocket gripping the pistol; he was ready to fire through his own coat if he had to, and it was a good coat, the very one he was wearing today. It was late and the streets were empty; he waited for an opportune moment, then forced Candlemas to climb into the trunk. He locked the trunk, got behind the wheel, and drove downtown.

And yes, he knew the streets of the Lower East Side, and knew he and his prisoner would be undisturbed in one of the abandoned buildings to be found down there. He had asked Candlemas many questions, and had obtained some answers, but by no means managed to get the whole story. He knew that a bookstore proprietor had been engaged to steal some very valuable documents from an apartment in the building Hoberman had emerged from, and he got my name from Candlemas, and the name of the store. He knew there was an Anatrurian connection, and that was about all he knew.

He might have learned more, but there was another accident. Candlemas tricked him, pretending to cooperate fully, lulling him into inattention, then making a bid to escape. Once again Rasmoulian's reflexes sprang unbidden into action, and Candlemas, trying to get away, was shot dead. A single bullet had snuffed out the man's life.

Accidents, two of them. What else could you call what had occurred? It was tragic, he regretted it deeply, he was a man who had always deplored violence. Surely he could not be held accountable for the violence that had taken place in spite of all he had done to prevent it?

"Yeah, well, accidents'll happen," Ray said. "Guy who got stabbed, I looked at him lyin' there and I knew I was lookin' at one hell of an accident. You see a guy with four stab wounds in him, you know right off he's been in a real bad accident."

"My reflexes are good," Rasmoulian said.

"I guess they are. Candlemas, now, down there on Pitt Street, was tryin' to escape when he got hisself cut down. I got to say, though, he wasn't very good at it, because there were powder burns on his ear, so he couldn't have escaped more than a foot or so from the gun that killed him. Guy like that, he better not set up shop givin' people escape lessons."

There was a stretch of silence, broken by Charlie Weeks,

who leaned back in his chair and crossed his legs first. "There are accidents and accidents," he said.

"Can't argue with that," Ray allowed.

"It was an accident, for instance, that I myself played an unwitting part in Cappy Hoberman's death. I'm less inclined to regret Chuck Wood, considering the little stunt he pulled in Anatruria."

I'd let that pass once, but enough was enough. "I don't think so," I said.

"I beg your pardon, weasel?"

"Let's ease up on the 'weasel' routine," I said. "You can call me Bernie. What I don't think is that the woodchuck sold out the good guys in Anatruria."

"Really? That's what we all thought."

"I think it was the mouse," I said. "I think you must be proud of it, too, or you probably wouldn't hang on to that letter of commendation from Dean Acheson."

"Now how could you possibly know about that?" Weeks said. "If I had a letter like that I'd certainly keep it in a locked drawer, wouldn't I? And you've never been in my apartment that I wasn't constantly in the same room with you."

"It's puzzling, all right," I said.

He seemed to shrink under the combined gaze of Ilona and Michael, melting away like the water-soaked Wicked Witch of the West. "It was a strategic decision made at a high level," he said. "I had no part in the decision and no choice but to implement it."

"And the good sense to see that it was the woodchuck who got blamed for it, and not the mouse."

"It happened over forty years ago. I won't apologize for it now, or explain the justification. I was a young man then. I'm an old man now. It's done."

"And the two men Rasmoulian killed?"

"I never thought that would happen," he said. "I wanted to know what the hell was going on. Cappy Hoberman called up, came to see me on the flimsiest of pretexts, and was eager to be on his way almost immediately. It never occurred to me he was running interference for a burglar. I thought he wanted something, or was setting me up somehow. For all I knew he'd tumbled to the way it all went kerblooey in Anatruria, and he had some curious notion of revenge." He shrugged. "The whole point is I didn't know. I needed to call someone who could tag him and report back. And the redoubtable Assyrian tagged him a little more forcefully than any of us would have preferred."

"It is unfair," Ilona said.

"Life's unfair, honey," Charlie Weeks said. "Better get used to it."

"It is unfair that you get away with this, while Tiglath Rasmoulian pays the penalty."

"There should be no penalty," Rasmoulian said. "An accident, an act of self-defense—"

"I got to tell you," Ray Kirschmann said. "We got us a problem here."

Another silence. Ray let it stretch for a bit, then broke it himself.

"Way I see it," he said, "I got enough to arrest Mr. Ras—" He broke off, made a face. "What I'm gonna do is call you TR," he told Rasmoulian, "which is your initials, and also stands for Teddy Roosevelt, who it just so happens was police commissioner of this fair city before he got to be president of the United States."

"Thank you very much," Rasmoulian said.

"I got enough to arrest TR," Ray said, "an' I wouldn't be surprised if there's enough to indict him. He confessed to a double homicide after bein' Mirandized one or two times, dependin' how you calculate it. So his confession ain't admissible, since nobody wrote it down an' got him to sign it, or had the presence of mind to tape it. But anybody here could testify that he confessed, same as a cellmate can rat out a defendant, sayin' he confessed, except in this case it happens to be the truth. TR here did confess, an' we all heard him."

"So?"

He glared at me. "So I can arrest him, an' as far as the trial's concerned, well, who knows what'll happen, because you never know. What I can promise you, though, is he'll get bail. Was a time nobody made bail on a murder charge, but now they do, an' my guess is TR here'll have to post something like a quarter mil max and he's on the street. And once he's on the street, citizen of the world that he is, all he's gotta do is bail out, if you follow me."

"Bail out?"

"Skip the country, forfeit the bond, and go about his business. And what's even more of a shame is me and my fellow officers'll be makin' life hard for all the rest of you, even with TR here off the hook and out of the country. Takin' testimony from Mr. Weeks, inquirin' into the source of Mr. Sarnoff's income—"

"Tsarnoff, officer."

"Whatever. Makin' sure everybody's papers are legit. An' of course there'll be reporters crawlin' up everybody's ass, poppin' flash bulbs at the king an' queen of Anna Banana—"

"Anatruria."

"Whatever. Be more important for you people to remember the name of the country, bein' as they'll probably wind up sendin' you back to it. Not Mr. Weeks, though, on account of he's an American citizen, an' they'll most likely want to keep him around so Congress can ask him some questions."

He went on in this vein, probably longer than he had to. After all, these people were professionals. They'd played the game before, in the Balkans and the Middle East.

Weeks said, "Officer . . . Kirschmann, is it?" He picked up his homburg, balanced it on his knee. "You know, I got a speeding ticket a couple of years ago in the state of Montana. They had to pass a speed limit there, and in order to qualify for federal highway funds it had to be a max of sixty-five on the interstates and fifty-five everywhere else."

"That a fact," Ray said.

"It is," Charlie Weeks said. "Now, Montana's too large and too sparsely settled for those limits to make any sense. And the federal government could make them pass that law, but they couldn't regulate how they enforced it. So Montana assigned only four state troopers to speed limit enforcement, and you know how large the state is."

"Prolly as big as Brooklyn and Manhattan put together."

Weeks's smile spread across his face. "Very nearly," he said. "The federal government couldn't establish penalties for violating the speeding laws, either, so Montana set the fine at five dollars per violation. If one of the state's four traffic cops nails you for doing a hundred and twenty-five miles an hour in a fifty-five zone, it costs you five bucks."

"Reasonable," Ray said.

"Very reasonable, but here's the point I'm trying to make. Just so no one's grossly inconvenienced, neither the motorist nor the arresting officer, the fine may be collected on the spot. You pull me over, I give you five dollars, and I go on my way."

"An' everybody's happy," Ray said.

"Exactly. And the state's best interests are served. Admirable, wouldn't you say?"

"In a manner of speakin', yeah."

"Officer," Gregory Tsarnoff said, "if the Assyrian is only going to forfeit bond, perhaps he could post it directly, without going through the usual channels."

"I'll tell you this," Ray said. "It's irregular."

"But expedient, surely."

"I don't know about that," he said, "but it'd get the job done."

"Tiglath," Charlie Weeks said, "how much dough have you got on you?"

"You mean money?"

"No, I'm thinking about starting a bakery. Yes, I mean money. You came here thinking you'd have a chance to bid on those bearer shares. How much did you bring?"

"Not so much. I am not a rich man, Charlie. Surely you know that."

"Don't dick around, Tiggy, it's late in the game for that. What are you carrying?"

"Ten thousand."

"That's U.S. dollars, I hope. Not Anatrurian tschirin."

"Dollars, of course."

"What about you, Gregorius?"

"A little more than that," Tsarnoff said. "But can you possibly be suggesting that I help raise bail money for the Assyrian? He wrote my name in blood!"

"Yeah, but credit where it's due, Gregorius. He spelled it wrong. Do I think you should kick in? Yes, I do." He frowned. "You know what else I think? I think there's too many people in the room. We need a private conference, Gregorius. You and me and Tiggy and Officer Kirschmann here."

"And Wilfred."

"If you prefer, Gregorius."

"An' Bernie," Ray said.

"And the weasel, to be sure."

I steered everybody else to my office in the back. That didn't seem fair to Ilona and Michael, but they didn't seem to mind, Ilona smiling her ironic smile while the king looked as though he'd suffered a light concussion. Between them they were less irritated than Carolyn and Mowgli, who were unhappy to be missing the next act.

I left them admiring the portrait of St. John of God, the patron saint of booksellers, and got back in time to hear Weeks explaining that he had the bearer shares. "Michael's a nice fellow," he was saying, "but that family was never loaded with smarts. After I heard about the burglary attempt, I told him I wanted to check the portfolio. I haven't given it back to him yet, and when I do the shares won't be in it."

Tsarnoff stroked his big chin. "Without the account number—"

"Without the number the shares are just paper, but who's to

say there's no one alive who knows the number? For that matter, who's to say you can't create a hairline fissure in the rock-solid walls of the Swiss banking system? If the three of us threw in together . . ."

"You and I, sir? And the Assyrian?"

Weeks was smiling furiously. "Be like old times," he said. "Wouldn't it, now?"

"Well, now," Ray said, and there was a knock on the door. I looked up, and the knock was repeated, louder. I gave a dismissing wave, but the large young man at the door refused to be dismissed. He knocked again.

I went to the door, cracked it a few inches. "We're closed," I said. "Private meeting, not open for business today. Come back tomorrow."

He held up a book. "I just want to buy this," he said. "It's off that table there, fifty cents, three for a buck. Here's a buck."

I pushed the money back at him. "Please," I said.

"But I want the book."

"Take the book."

"But—"

"It's a special," I said. "Today only. Take it, it's free. Please. Goodbye."

I closed the door, turned the lock. I turned back to the five of them and found they'd made their deal. Rasmoulian had taken off his trench coat and was hunting under his clothes for a money belt. Wilfred handed a manila envelope to his employer, who opened it and began counting hundred-dollar bills. Weeks drew a similar stack of bills from his pocket, removed a rubber band, licked his thumb, and began counting.

"I wish I knew why the hell I was doing this," Weeks said. "I've got all the money I need. What the hell do you think it is, Gregorius?"

"You miss the action, sir."

"I'm an old man. What do I need with action?" No one had an answer, and I don't think he wanted one. He finished counting his bundle, collected bundles from the other two, weighed all three in his cupped hands. I gave him a shopping bag from behind the counter and he dropped all the money into it. A few hours ago that bag had contained books, the ones I'd bought from Mowgli for seventy-five dollars. Now it was full of hundred-dollar bills.

Four hundred of them, according to Weeks, who held it out toward Ray.

"I don't know," Ray said, and shot a quick glance my way. I moved my head about an inch to the left and an inch to the right. Ray registered this, widened his eyes. I met his eyes, then raised mine a few degrees toward the ceiling.

"Thing is," he said, "there's a lot's gotta be done, a bunch of police personnel gotta be brought in on this. Seems to me forty grand's gonna spread too thin to cover it all."

"Well, I'll be a son of a bitch," Charlie Weeks said. "I thought we had a deal."

"Make it fifty an' we got a deal."

"That's an outrage. We'd already agreed on a figure, for Christ's sake."

"Put it this way," Ray said. "You got yourself a real good deal when that trooper stopped you out in Montana. But you ain't in the Wild West this time around. This here's New York."

TWENTY-FOUR

"It doesn't seem right," Carolyn said. "Tiggy murdered both of those men. And he winds up getting away with it."

It was around four-thirty and we were around the corner at the Bum Rap. Carolyn was staying in shape with a glass of Scotch on the rocks; I was getting back into shape gradually, nursing a beer.

"Mrs. Kirschmann needs a new fur coat," I said.

"And she gets it, and Tiggy gets away clean. But when does justice get served?"

"Justice gets served last," I said, "and usually winds up with leftovers. The fact of the matter is there would never have been enough evidence to convict Rasmoulian, even if he didn't skip the country in advance of trial. He'd never wind up in prison, and this way at least he winds up out of the country, and so do the rest of them."

"Tsarnoff and who else?"

"Wilfred, of course. Getting Wilfred and Rasmoulian out of the country means a saving of untold lives. They're a pair of stone killers if I ever saw one."

"And now they'll be working together."

"God help Europe," I said. "But there's always the chance

that they'll kill each other. Charlie Weeks is on his way out of the country, too. He'll be catching the Concorde as soon as he makes arrangements to close his apartment at the Boccaccio. Between the three of them, they think they've got a chance of coming up with the Swiss account number and looting the long lost treasury of Anatruria."

"You figure they'll get hold of the number?"

"They might."

"And do you think there's an Anatrurian treasury left for them to loot?"

"If they ever get that account number," I said, "I think they're in for the greatest disappointment since Geraldo broke into Al Capone's vault. But what do I know? Maybe the cash is gone, depleted by banking fees over the past seventy years. Maybe the stuff in the safe-deposit box is nothing but czarist bonds and worthless certificates. On the other hand, maybe whoever gets in there will be sitting on a controlling interest in Royal Dutch Petroleum."

She thought about it. "I think the important thing for those three is to be in the game," she said. "It doesn't really matter who wins the hand, or how much is in the pot."

"I think you're right," I said. "Weeks even said as much. He wants to play."

She picked up her drink, shook it so that the ice cubes clinked pleasantly. "Bern," she said, "I was really glad I could be around for most of it at the end there. I never met a king before."

"I'm not sure you met one today."

"Well, that's as close as I expect to come. Mowgli was impressed, incidentally. He said he was seeing a whole new side of the book business today." She sipped her drink. "Bern," she said, "there's a few things I'm not too clear on."

"Oh?"

"How'd you know it was Tiggy?"

"I knew it was somebody," I said. "When Rasmoulian turned up at the bookstore, I assumed Candlemas had told him about me. When it turned out Candlemas was dead all along, I figured he must have done some talking before he died, probably to the man who killed him. Rasmoulian knew me by name, not by sight, so he hadn't followed Candlemas or Ilona to my store, or spotted me with Hoberman and followed me home."

"And you knew Charlie Weeks had called him. How did you know that?"

"When I called Weeks and went over to his apartment," I said, "he didn't know what the hell I wanted. He really did think I was some guy named Bill Thompson who'd come up on the elevator with Cappy Hoberman. When I said I wanted to talk to him, he probably thought I'd heard something about Hoberman's death, but not that I had anything to do with the burglary."

"But if Tiggy told him . . ."

"Tiggy told him Candlemas had admitted hiring a burglar to break into the king's apartment. But Weeks didn't know that burglar was the guy who'd said two words to him in the hallway. Then, once we started talking, he put two and two together."

"And?"

"And he tried to keep what he knew to himself, but he made a slip. When I said how Rasmoulian had known my middle name, he said, 'Grimes.' Now where did that come from?"

"Maybe you told him."

I shook my head. "When it was time to leave," I said, "he was still calling me Bill Thompson, pretending he didn't have a clue that wasn't my real name. If he knew the Grimes part, he'd know about the Bernie and the Rhodenbarr, too. So he knew more than he should, and for all his talk about joining forces he was keeping what he knew to himself. I played along, but I knew then and there that he was more than an old friend of Hoberman's and a ticket into the building. He was involved clear up to his hat."

"And when did you know Candlemas was the woodchuck?"

"Not as soon as I might have. The names on the passports did it for me. Not Souslik, I had to check some reference books before I found out what a souslik was, but I recognized the word 'marmot' even if Candlemas did give it a French-style ending on his fake Belgian passport. Then I looked up 'Candlemas' and found out it was just Groundhog's Day with hymns and incense."

"Wilfred's favorite holiday."

"Yes, and wasn't that a revelation?" I transferred some beer from my bottle to my glass, then from the glass to me. "I should have guessed earlier. On my first visit to Candlemas's apartment, one of the knickknacks I noticed was what I took for a netsuke."

"What kind of a rodent is that, Bern?"

"You know, those little ivory carvings the Japanese collect. They originally functioned something like buttons for securing the sash on a kimono, but for a long time now they've made them as objets d'art. I didn't look close at the one Candlemas had, but I figured it was ivory, and that it was supposed to be a beaver but the tail was broken off."

"And actually it was a woodchuck?"

"It was still there yesterday," I said, and took a little velvet drawstring bag from my pocket, and drew Letchkov's bone woodchuck from it. "If I'd been paying attention I would have known it wasn't a beaver. It's a perfect match for Charlie Weeks's mouse—the bone's yellowed in just the same way. You know, when Charlie showed me the mouse, I got a little *frisson.*"

"*That's* a rodent, right?"

I gave her a look. "It's a feeling," I said. "I knew there was something familiar about the mouse, but I couldn't think what it was. Anyway, Candlemas was the woodchuck, and he kept his carved totem all those years. I guess he had the mouse, too, and gave it to Hoberman to pass on to Weeks."

"Why did he need Hoberman? If he was the woodchuck, he

knew Weeks as well as Hoberman did. Why couldn't he sneak you into the Boccaccio himself?"

"I'm not positive," I said. "He may have been afraid of the reception he'd get from Weeks. Remember, Weeks had spread the story that Candlemas had sold out the Anatrurians. Candlemas knew he hadn't, but he couldn't afford to find out if Weeks really believed it. Either way, he might not get a warm reception from the mouse."

"So he figured he'd be safer using Hoberman."

"But not safe enough," I said.

She had more questions and I had most of the answers. Then she started to order another round and I caught her hand on the way up. "No more for me," I told her.

"Aw, come on, Bern," she said. "It's been weeks since we had drinks together after work, and on top of that it's a holiday. Get in the spirit of it, why don't you?"

"We're supposed to remember the war dead," I said, "not join them. Anyway, I've got somewhere to go."

"Where's that?"

"Guess," I said.

In *The Big Shot*, Humphrey Bogart plays Duke Berne, a career criminal who's trying to go straight because a fourth felony conviction will put him in prison for life. But he can't stay away from it, and goes in on the planning of an armored-car heist. The head of the gang is a crooked lawyer, and the lawyer's wife is Bogart's old sweetheart. *She* won't let Bogie risk his life, and keeps him from participating in the robbery by holding him in his room at gunpoint. A witness picks him out of a mug book anyway, which strikes me as questionable police work, but that's my professional point of view showing.

The lawyer's jealous, and screws up Bogie's alibi, and he winds up going down for the count. There's a prison break, and Bogie gets away, but one thing after another goes wrong, until finally Bogie hunts down the rat lawyer and kills him. He's shot, though, and dies in the hospital.

That was the first picture, and I'd never seen it before. I got caught up in it, too, and maybe that was why I didn't eat much of the popcorn, or it may have been because I'd been munching peanuts at the Bum Rap. Either way, I had more than half a barrel left at intermission. I had to use the john—beer's like that—but I went and came back without hitting the refreshment counter.

I didn't feel like seeing the guy with the goatee, or any of the other regulars I'd gotten to know by sight. I just felt like sitting alone in the dark and watching movies.

The second picture was *The Big Sleep,* and whoever put the program together had been having fun, combining two pictures with near-identical titles. But of course this was the classic, based on the Chandler novel with a screenplay by William Faulkner, starring Bogie and Bacall and featuring any number of good people, including Dorothy Malone and Elisha Cook, Jr. I won't summarize it for you, partly because the plot's impossible to keep straight, and partly because you must have seen it. If not, well, you will.

Ten minutes into the picture, at a moment when I was really immersed in what was happening on the screen, I heard the rustle of cloth and got a whiff of perfume, and then someone was settling into the seat beside me. A hand joined mine in the popcorn barrel, but it wasn't groping for popcorn. It found my hand, and closed around it, and didn't let go.

We both watched the screen, and neither of us said a word.

When the movie ended we were the last ones to leave the theater, still in our seats when the credits ended and the house lights came up. I guess neither of us wanted it to be over.

On the street she said, "I bought a ticket. And then the man told me to get my money back. He said you left a ticket for me."

"He's a nice man. He wouldn't lie to you."

"How did you know I would come?"

"I didn't think you would," I said. "I didn't know if I would ever see you again, sweetheart. But I thought it was worth a chance." I shrugged. "It was just a movie ticket, after all. It wasn't an emerald."

She squeezed my hand. "I would take you to my apartment, but it is not mine anymore."

"I know. I was there."

"So you will take me to yours."

We walked, and neither of us spoke on the way. Inside, I offered to make drinks. She didn't want one. I said I'd make coffee. She told me not to bother.

"This afternoon," she said. "You said we went to the movies together, but that we were no more than friends."

"Good friends," I said.

"We went to bed together."

"What are friends for?"

"Yet you did not let anyone know we went to bed together."

"It must have slipped my mind."

"It did not slip your mind," she said with cool certainty, "nor will it ever slip from mine. I will never forget it, Bear-naard."

"It made such an impression on you," I said, "that you emptied out your apartment and moved right out of my life."

"You know why."

"Yes, I guess I do."

"He is the hope of my people, Bear-naard. And he is my destiny, even as Anatrurian independence is my life. I came here to be with him, and to . . . to strengthen his commitment to our cause. To be a king, to have a throne, all that is nothing to him. But to lead his people, to fulfill the dreams of an entire nation, that stirs his blood."

Play the song, I thought. Where the hell was Dooley Wilson when you needed him?

"And then you came along," she said, and reached out a

hand to touch my face, and smiled that smile that was sad and wise and rueful. "And I fell in love with you, Bear-naard."

"And once we were together . . ."

"Once we were together we had to be apart. I could be with you once and keep you as a memory to warm me all my life, Bear-naard. But if I had been with you a second time I would have wanted to stay forever."

"And yet you came here tonight."

"Yes."

"Where do you go from here, Ilona?"

"To Anatruria. We leave tomorrow. There's a night flight from JFK."

"And the two of you will be on it."

"Yes."

"I'll miss you, sweetheart."

"Oh, Bear-naard . . ."

A man could drown in those eyes. I said, "At least you won't have Tsarnoff and Rasmoulian and Weeks getting in your way. They'll be off playing hopscotch with the gnomes of Zurich, trying to find a way into a treasure your guy already gave up on."

"The real treasure is the spirit of the Anatrurian people."

"You took the words right out of my mouth," I said. "But it's a shame you don't have much in the way of working capital."

"It is true," she said. "Mikhail says the same thing. He would like to raise funds first so we will have money on which to operate. But the time is now. We cannot afford to wait."

"Hang on a minute," I said. "Just wait here, okay?"

I left her on the couch in the living room and paid a quick visit to my bedroom closet. I came back with a cardboard file folder.

"Weeks had these," I said. "He slipped them out of the portfolio along with the bearer shares, and I scooped them up this morning when I was in his apartment. I figured it was safe to take these because I don't think he paid much attention to them. His whole orientation is politics and intrigue. As far as he's concerned, these were just a propaganda device."

She opened the folder, then nodded in recognition. "The Anatrurian postage stamps," she said. "Of course. King Vlados received a complete set and passed them on to his son, and they have come down to Mikhail. They are pretty, aren't they?"

"They're gorgeous," I said. "And this isn't a set, it's a set of full sheets."

"Is that good?"

"They're a questionable issue from a philatelic standpoint," I said, "or else they'd be damn near priceless, considering their rarity. As it is, they're still valuable. They're unpriced in Scott, but Dolbeck prices provisional and fantasy issues, and the latest Dolbeck catalog has the full set at twenty-five hundred dollars."

"So these stamps are worth over two thousand dollars? That is good."

"If you're selling," I said, "you generally figure on netting two-thirds to three-fourths the Dolbeck value."

"Two thousand, then. A little less."

"Per set."

"Yes," she agreed. "That is very nice."

"It's nicer than you realize," I said. "The stamps are printed fifty to a sheet, so you're holding fifty sets. That's somewhere around a hundred thousand dollars."

She stared. "But . . ."

"Take it before I change my mind," I said. "There's a man at Kildorran and Partners who specializes in this kind of material. He'll either buy it from you or arrange to sell it for you. He's in London, on Great Portland Street, and his name and the firm's address are written down on the inside of that folder you're holding. I don't know if you'll get a hundred grand. It may be more, it may be less. But you'll get a fair price." I extended a forefinger, chucked her under the chin. "I don't know how your flight's routed tomorrow night, but if I were you I'd

change things and take a day or two in London. You don't
want to wait too long with those things. You might make a mistake and use one to mail a letter."

"Bear-naard, you could have kept these."

"You think so?"

"But of course. No one knew you had them. No one even
knew they were valuable."

I shook my head. "It wouldn't work, sweetheart. The hopes
and dreams of a couple of little people like you and me don't
add up to a hill of beans next to the cause you and Michael are
fighting for. Sure, I could use the money, but I don't really
need it. And if I ever do I'll go out and steal it, because that's
the kind of man I am."

"Oh, Bear-naard."

"So pack them up and take them home with you," I said.
"And I think you'd better go now, Ilona."

"But I thought . . ."

"I know what you thought, and I thought so too. But I went
to bed with you once and lost you, and I don't want to go
through that again. One time is a good memory. Twice is
heartbreak."

"Bear-naard, I have tears in my eyes."

"I'd kiss them away," I said, "but I wouldn't be able to stop.
So long, sweetheart. I'll miss you."

"I'll never forget you," she said. "I'll never forget Twenty-
fifth Street."

"Neither will I." I took her arm, eased her out the door.
"And why should you? We'll always have Twenty-fifth Street."

TWENTY-FIVE

It was a full week before I got around to telling Carolyn about that final evening in Ilona's company. I don't think I ever made a conscious decision to keep it from her. But it turned out to be a busy time for both of us. I kept my usual hours in the bookstore, and put in some overtime as well, riding the Long Island Rail Road to Massapequa one evening to appraise a library (for a fee; they didn't want to sell anything), and spending another evening at a book auction, bidding on behalf of a customer who was shy about attending those things himself.

Carolyn had a busy schedule herself, with a kennel club show coming up that meant a lot of dogs for her to pretty up. And there were a lot of phone calls and visits back and forth when Djinn and Tracey got back together again, and Djinn accused Tracey of having an affair with Carolyn, which was what Djinn had done after a previous breakup. "Pure dyke-o-drama," Carolyn called it, and eventually it blew over, but while it lasted there were lots of middle-of-the-night phone calls and phones slammed down and loud confrontations on street corners. When it finally cleared up, she plunged with relief into the new Sue Grafton novel she'd been saving.

So we had lunch five days a week and drinks after work, and then on Tuesday, a week and a day after Memorial Day, we were at the Bum Rap after work and Carolyn was telling a long and not terribly interesting story about a Bedlington terrier. "From the way he acted," she said, "you'd have sworn he thought he was an Airedale."

"No kidding," I said.

She looked at me. "You don't think that's funny?"

"Yeah, it's funny."

"I can see you think it's a scream. *I* thought it was funny."

"Then why aren't you laughing?" I said. "Never mind. Carolyn, there's something I've been meaning to tell you." And then I signaled Maxine for another round of drinks, because this was going to be thirsty work.

I told her the whole story and she listened all the way through without interrupting me, and when I was done she sat and stared at me with her mouth open.

"That's amazing," she said. "And you didn't say a word about it for a week and a day. That's even more amazing."

"I just kept forgetting to bring it up," I said. "You know what I think it was? I must have wanted a little time to digest it."

"Makes sense. Bern, I'm amazed. I don't want to work the word to death, but I am. I'll tell you this, kiddo. It's the most romantic story I ever heard in my life."

"I guess it's romantic."

"What else could it be?"

"Stupid," I said. "Real stupid."

"You gave away a hundred thousand dollars."

"Something like that."

"To a woman you'll probably never see again."

"I might see her on a stamp," I said. "If Anatruria makes the cut. But no, I'll probably never see her again."

"She didn't even know about the stamps, did she? That you had them, or that they were worth anything?"

"Tsarnoff or Rasmoulian would have known what they were worth, or at least known they were worth plenty. Candlemas might have known—he had a collector's orientation. The others didn't think in those terms. And no, nobody knew I had them, least of all Ilona."

"And you gave them to her."

"Uh-huh."

"And you got to make the famous hill-of-beans speech."

"Don't remind me."

"Why'd you do it, Bern?"

"They needed the money," I said. "I can always use money, but I can't pretend I had a genuine need for a hundred thousand dollars. They needed it."

"Hell, Bern, the hip dysplasia people need it, too, and it was all I could do to get twenty bucks out of you."

"The stamps came from Anatruria," I said.

"I thought they came from Hungary."

"You know what I mean. They were issued in the cause of Anatrurian freedom, and if they were worth all that money after all those years, then the money belonged to the cause. If there is such a cause, or if there even is such a country." That was confusing, and I stopped and took a sip of my drink and started over. "If she hadn't shown up at the Musette," I said, "I don't know what I would have done. I meant to call the king and give him the stamps, and maybe I would have done it, but maybe not. I just don't know.

"But the point is she *did* show up. I bought that extra seat, and I swear I wasn't all that surprised when she wound up sitting in it."

"And once she did . . ."

"I held her hand, fed her popcorn, took her home, gave her a fortune in rare stamps, and sent her on her way."

"With the hill-of-beans speech echoing in her cute little ears."

"Forget the hill-of-beans speech, will you?"

"Schweetheart, the hopes and dreams of a couple of little

shitkickers like you and me don't amount to a hill of beans when you pile 'em up next to the Anatrurian Alps, and—"

"Dammit, Carolyn."

"I'm sorry. You know what happened to you, don't you?"

"I think so."

"All those movies."

"That's what I was going to say."

"You watched Bogart do the noble self-sacrificing thing one time too many, and when the opportunity came your way, you didn't have a prayer. Poor Bernie. Everybody made something out of this business but you. Ray was the big winner. What did he wind up with, forty-eight grand?"

"He had to spread that around a little. The official story now is that Candlemas killed Hoberman, then went down to the Lower East Side to cop some dope."

"Right, he was your typical junkie."

"And got shot when the deal went sour. I would guess somewhere between twenty-five and thirty-five thousand dollars'll wind up in Ray's pocket."

"And of course he insisted you take some of the money."

"It must have slipped his mind."

"Not fair, Bern. After all, you solved the whole case. He just stood there."

"He doesn't just stand. He looms."

"Good for him. He gets the money, Ilona and the king get the stamps, and the three mouseketeers get the bearer shares and go chasing after the lost treasure of Anatruria. And what about you? You didn't even get laid."

"Maybe that was dumb, too," I said. "But all she's going to be for me is a memory, and I didn't have to repeat the experience to be sure I'd remember it. I'm in no danger of forgetting."

"No."

I picked up my drink, held it to the light. "Anyway," I said, "it's not as though I wind up empty-handed."

"How do you figure that, Bern?"

"I got the bone woodchuck from Candlemas's apartment, remember?"

"Wow, Bern."

"And when I stopped by Charlie Weeks's place, the stamps weren't all I swiped. I got the mouse carving Hoberman gave him."

"Gee, you can just about retire when you sell those two little beauties, can't you?"

"No, I think I'll hang on to them as souvenirs. My real profit comes tomorrow night."

"What happens tomorrow night?"

"A man named Sung-Yun Lee goes to see *The Chink in the Armoire.*"

"Is that a show?"

"On Broadway, at the Helen Hayes. Very hot ticket. I got a pair from a scalper and it cost me perilously close to two hundred bucks."

"All in the interests of getting him out of the house," she guessed. "But who the hell is he, and what house do you want to get him out of? Oh, *wait* a minute. The people downstairs from Candlemas, but I forget their names."

"The Lehrmans."

"And he's in their place on an exchange program. Right?"

I nodded. "And they'll be gone for another month, and their place is absolutely overflowing with good stuff, and you couldn't ask for a better setup. The security is nothing, the locks are child's play, and the guy who's living there won't have a clue that anything's missing, because it's not his stuff. He'll go on being careful not to look in their closets or poke around in their drawers, and everything I take will be converted into cash long before they're even back in the country."

I went on, telling her about some of the items I'd noticed on my brief passage through the Lehrman apartment. When I stopped she said, "I'll tell you something, Bern. I'm relieved."

"What do you mean?"

"You're your old self again. Bogart's great on the screen, but all that Noble Loser stuff is no way to go through life. I'm glad you're getting ready to steal something. It's tough on the Lehrmans—"

"Oh, I'm sure they're insured."

"Even if they're not, I'm happy for you." She frowned. "That's tomorrow, right? Not tonight?"

"No, why? Oh." I brandished my glass. "No, it's tomorrow. You know I don't drink when I'm working."

"That's what I was wondering."

"Anyway," I said, "I've got something else planned for tonight. In fact, you might want to come along, but we'll have to go straight from here."

"I don't know," she said. "I'm about halfway into the new Sue Grafton and I'm kind of anxious to get back to it. It's really something."

"Well, you always like her work."

"One of the things I like is she never repeats herself, and this one's kind of shocking."

"Really?"

She nodded. "Sadism and perversion," she said. "Roman orgies, incest. Toga parties. I've got to tell you, it's a whole lot kinkier than what Kinsey usually gets herself mixed up in."

"Gee, maybe you were right about Kinsey."

"I know I'm right, but she doesn't do anything wild herself. Everybody else does, though."

"What's it called, anyway?"

" 'I' Is for Claudius."

"Catchy," I said. "But you can stay home and read anytime. Come on and keep me company."

"Where, Bern?"

"A movie."

"The Bogart festival's over, Bernie. Isn't it?"

"Over and done with. But down at the Sardonique in Tribeca they're starting an Ida Lupino film festival."

"Bern, I got a question. Who cares?"

"What have you got against Ida Lupino?"

"Nothing, but I never knew you were such a big fan. What's the big deal about Ida Lupino?"

"I always liked her," I said. "But tonight's movies are kind of special. *They Drive by Night* and *High Sierra*."

"I'm sure they're both terrific, but . . . wait a minute, Bern. I know *High Sierra*. It's not an Ida Lupino movie."

"It most certainly is."

"She may be in it, but that doesn't make it her movie. It's a Humphrey Bogart movie. He's trapped on a mountain peak with a rifle, and they kill him."

"Why'd you have to ruin the ending for me?"

"Come on, Bern, you know the ending. You've seen the movie."

"Not recently."

"What's the other one? *They Drive by Night*? Who's in that, if you don't mind my asking? Besides Ida Lupino."

"George Raft," I said. "And I think Ann Sheridan."

"And?"

"And Bogart. He plays a one-armed truck driver. They showed *High Sierra* at the Musette, but on a night I couldn't go. I was stuck at that auction. And *They Drive by Night* never played the Musette."

"Maybe for a good reason."

"Don't be silly," I said. "I'm sure it's great. What do you say? Do you want to go? I'll buy the popcorn."

"Oh, what the hell," she said. "But one thing, Bern. Can we get one thing straight?"

"What's that?"

"This is entertainment," she said. "These are not training films. Is that understood?"

"Of course."

"Good," she said. "Don't forget, sweetheart."